Americans on
the Road

Americans on the Road

From Autocamp to Motel, 1910–1945

Warren James Belasco

The MIT Press
Cambridge, Massachusetts, and
London, England

First MIT Press paperback edition, 1981
Copyright © 1979 by Warren James Belasco

This book was set in VIP Bookman by Grafacon, Inc., and printed and bound by Halliday Lithograph Corp. in the United States of America

Library of Congress Cataloging in Publication Data

Belasco, Warren James.
   Americans on the road.

   Bibliography: p.
   Includes index.
   1. Automobiles—Touring—History. 2. Tourist camps, hotels, etc.—United States—History. 3. Motels—United States—History. I. Title.
GV1021.B37   796.7'0973   79-15304
ISBN 0-262-02123-4 (hard)
      0-262-52071-0 (paper)

Contents

Preface

Writing this book has been a bit like the early motoring it describes: sudden breakdowns and forced detours, fresh encounters and chance discoveries. I set out to explore the roots of our automotive love affair. Why did Americans first welcome cars? How did this reception relate to other trends of the early twentieth century? How did the romance change over forty years? This destination remained constant throughout my journey, but the route I eventually took was quite unanticipated. Indeed, starting out as a casual Sunday drive through neighboring countryside, my trip lengthened into a cross-country jaunt through unfamiliar territory.

At first I planned to examine the car's effects on New York, my home city. By concentrating on just one city, I hoped to assess the car's meaning within a particular geographical context. Such a work would have fit well into a growing body of environmental impact literature, and following the lead of several urban historians, I began to look at trolleys, horses, streets, commuting patterns, suburbs, urban planning, accident rates, and road building. After six months of research, however, I decided that I had not gotten very far. Influenced by the anti-automobile arguments of the 1970s, I found myself concentrating on negatives such as pollution, traffic, and central-city deterioration. Moreover, from personal experience, I could not help feeling that New York had been ill served by cars, and I projected this attitude back into the early years of this century. Yet, as a historian, I felt a responsibility to step back and take up the view of the earlier period. That is, *I* may not like what cars have done, but people back then did. Why?

A thought suddenly occurred—one of those conceptual flashes that seems obvious enough in restrospect but is jarring at the time: Why not look at what Americans actually did *with* their cars rather than try to judge what cars did *to* Americans? In other words, perhaps the car's appeal might be better revealed by looking at motorist behavior rather than looking at effects, which are unanticipated and hard to measure. Since car use was primarily recreational before World War II, I decided to focus on motor touring. Why did people like to take car trips? What did they do on these trips? At this point I stumbled on the Library of Congress's large collection of touring literature. I was off on my own cross-country tour.

It was fascinating to read what motorists had to say about early touring, for they experienced a sense of novelty and adventure that has long since been lost. This material also led me to new research avenues. Writers commonly contrasted motoring with previous train experiences. The many tourists who carried camp equipment claimed liberation from bad hotels. Complaints against these established travel institutions revealed a broad critique of early twentieth-century America, while the case for cars reflected new trends in family organization, health maintenance, leisure patterns, and class structure. Since this case revealed why Americans welcomed cars at a particular time in history, I decided to devote considerable space to the rail and hotel context.

Back on the road, I moved into the 1920s, when touring began to engender a variety of services catering specifically to tourist needs—tourist camps, food stands, tea rooms, and filling stations. Reasoning that no one knew more about tourist behavior than those trying to profit from it, I began to look at roadside trade literature. This material contained a wealth of social data, for in a highly competitive, ever-changing new industry, entrepreneurs had to pay close attention to what motorists wanted and did.

I became particularly interested in autocamping, which changed remarkably quickly from romantic retreat to public institution to private business—the tourist camp or motel. For several reasons, I decided to spend the rest of my time retracing this evolution. For one thing, the motel was *there,* relatively untouched by scholarly hands, ready for serious treatment. In part, the historian in me delighted in detailing *process*—the fascinating way that one year's novelty becomes next year's out-of-date. This process of rapid obsolescence was particularly speedy in leisure-related industries, of which the motel was an excellent example. Also, the motel offered an opportunity to study the transformation of myth into commodity. More than a building, the motel sold a package of car-related images and experiences, a package that emerged around 1930 as literary touring accounts lost their sense of novelty and relinquished their barometric role to specialized trade journals. Sharing recent fears that cultural history may have relied too heavily on purely literary and intellectual concerns, I saw the motel as a revealing interface between business and culture, a material embodiment of tourist dreams of community, independence, equality, and spontaneity.

Yet the replication was not complete. Seeing the gap between vision and reality was perhaps the strongest reason for studying the motel. As a product of the automobile, the motel shared the inequities and disappointments of the motor experience, particularly the tensions between democracy and status, liberty and order, public welfare and private profit. Like the car, the motel did not fulfill the dreams that created it. Thus my journey ended with a feeling of frustration, a sense that for all this movement, basic needs remained unsatisfied. Maybe motorists took the wrong path. Instead of escaping to the road, perhaps they should have looked for answers closer to home.

Acknowledgments

Like touring, writing is a cooperative venture. I may have been behind the wheel, but I had lots of help en route. For giving directions, lubricating the chassis, and peering under the hood, I am particularly grateful to Milton J. Belasco, Blaine A. Brownell, James J. Flink, Mark Foster, William W. Freehling, David L. Lewis, Gerald F. Linderman, Robert H. Mattoon, Jr., John B. Rae, Michael A. Rockland, Mark Rose, and Robert Sklar. That marvelous public campground for itinerant intellectuals, the Library of Congress, allowed me to pitch my tent free of charge for more seasons than I care to admit. In addition to appreciating the Library's easy-going hospitality, I was privileged to share facilities with a splendid band of fellow tourist-scholars; their warm company helped me through more than one rainy day. Finally, I must thank my partner, Amy Fried Belasco, whose constant support and interest made the trip possible.

Americans on
the Road

Itinerary

Touring has been a major element in the American infatuation with cars. It has also spawned new industries. Using touring literature and trade journals, this study shows how autocamping, an inexpensive, individualistic sport with antimodernist implications, gave birth to the motel, a nationally standardized, up-to-date roadside business. Since highway businessmen were acutely sensitive to shifting middle-class tourist expectations and behavior, this examination of the evolving roadside reveals trends in what these motorists wanted on the road. As a history of one automobile-related recreation industry, it also shows how, in an emerging mass-consumption society, hunger for escape was directed into conservative commercial channels.

The evolution took thirty-five years. In the first stage, 1910–1920, several hundred thousand middle-class families toured the countryside, camping each night in a different spot along the road, sleeping in cars or in tents, cooking meals over smoky campfires. Autocampers called this squatter-anarchist stage "gypsying." Likening the car to the stagecoach and the roadside camp to the homestead, enthusiasts declared their independence from the monopolistic rail-hotel complex. Behind their delight in traveling off the beaten track was a profound desire to discover new perspectives, to experience unconventional intimacies with fellow Americans, and to break away from the hectic work routines and bureaucratic institutions of an urban-industrial civilization. Slow, arduous, and close to nature, autocamping revived what tourists imagined to be the more leisurely pace, personal independence, simplicity, and family solidarity of pre-industrial times. Yet autocampers were essentially recreationists, not rebels. Their protest was temporary; after several weeks on the road, tourists generally returned to home and job.

This escapist orientation led to major health and environmental problems. Determined to be as free as possible during their brief vacations, tourists littered the countryside, tangled with roadside property owners, and drank dirty water. These problems worsened as car ownership broadened and millions of Americans went a-gypsying. The need for social control became obvious. Meanwhile, this growing vacation market attracted the attention of merchants who wanted to lure tourist trade to downtown stores. Beginning around 1920, public regulatory authority and private economic interest combined to produce free municipal campgrounds centrally located in towns along major touring routes. Finding roadside camping too difficult and too time consuming, many autocampers welcomed the convenience of established campsites; comparing camps became an integral part of the touring routine. Anxious to establish a good local reputation through the tourist grapevine, each town tried to outdo the others with such additional facilities as electric lights, hot showers, and central kitchens.

This intertown competition strained municipal park budgets, and as free camps began to attract impoverished travelers who drove good spenders away, local enthusiasm began to wane. In 1923, some towns began to charge a small fee to finance rising maintenance costs and to screen out migrants, itinerants, and other low-budget tourists viewed as "undesirables." The fee system opened the camp field to private entrepreneurs who had not been able to compete with subsidized free camps. These operators often provided better service and greater selectivity. In 1925, some private camps built cabins for tourists desiring more comfort and privacy.

Thus the motel industry was born. In the late 1920s, as more tourists tired of carrying equipment, cabin operators added good beds, linen, stoves, and indoor plumbing. During the depression, when many former hotel patrons turned to these low-cost "cottage camps," proprietors further upgraded facilities to suit the tastes of these fastidious travelers. By 1945, the "motor court" was sufficiently well established to interest large-scale developers.

Although all classes shared the road, the motel evolved through systematic discrimination. Early autocamping promoters heralded open-road democracy but appealed to affluent vacationists fleeing increasingly pluralistic resort hotels. Boosters praised the free municipal camp "melting pot," but dismissed nonspenders as "riff-raff." Competing with expensive hotels, cabin operators considered themselves anti-establishment, but they relentlessly pursued the "better-class" tourist. The 1945 motel was far more expensive, luxurious, and exclusive than the 1925 cabin. Indeed, its hard-won respectability made it ready for national mass production and hotel-style management. In part, this evolution testified to the skill and ambition of roadside entrepreneurs. But the main responsibility lay with the middle-class market they pursued. As antimodernist gypsies, these tourists wanted simplicity, self-sufficiency, and comradeship; as modern consumers, however, they valued comfort, service, and security. Ultimately, the gypsy gave way to the consumer, not because the urge to stray off the beaten path was insincere or unimportant but because the bourgeois route was safer and easier.

Gypsying
1910–1920

Autocamping began as a vacation alternative for the relatively comfortable middle classes. Although no longer just a rich man's toy, an automobile was the prerogative of fewer than 500,000 owners in 1910. Even in 1920, with over eight million passenger cars registered, most Americans still relied on rail transportation when leaving home. The era of mass motoring serviced by an elaborate commercial infrastructure lay just ahead, but autocamping originally appealed to affluent individualists for whom the very lack of an established infrastructure was its major attraction.

By carrying equipment in their cars, these pioneers avoided fixed rails and crowded hotels. At first they parked by the side of the road and set up camp for the night. In remote areas their "roadside hotel" might be an alluring clearing, perhaps with a good view and a nearby stream for bathing, drinking, and fishing. It might be a pasture or an orchard, perhaps with the farmer's permission gained in advance. Some small towns allowed autocampers to stop overnight in public schoolyards. Or the site might be the narrow shoulder between the road and someone's fence. No space seemed too remote or too difficult, as long as there was room to pull off, pitch a tent, and build a fire. Since even rough trails were considered roads in these early years, hardy tourists found their way up the highest mountains and set up home there with that exquisite joy of hard-won possession.

Inevitably, their discoveries spawned a host of pamphlets, manuals, travel diaries, and sporting magazine columns, all promoting motor camping. Enthusiastic tourists kept journals and then published them privately for friends and families. Freelance journalists with a keen eye for a potential fad wrote accounts of transcontinental journeys for newspapers and magazines, while more serious essayists probed the long-run implications for society as a whole. Highway associations, camping goods manufacturers, automobile clubs, and other special-interest groups sponsored some of this literature.[1] Yet motive was largely irrelevant to message; whether personal reminiscence or commercial advertisement, early touring literature sounded a common theme in experience, advice, and metaphorical imagination. Written by and for the upper middle class, its ebullient vocabulary reflected a shared eagerness to impart wider significance to "automobility."[2]

The key words in travel literature were *will* and *anywhere*. Autocamping seemed to unharness will and to erase property boundaries. The tourist could camp "where fancy dictates." "You are limited only by the quality of the roads and in no other way." Everything was up to *you*; everything was open, like the road itself. "You are your own master, the road is ahead; you eat as you please, cooking your own meals over an open fire; sleeping when you will under the stars, waking with the dawn; swim in a mountain lake when you will, and always the road ahead. Thoreau at 29 cents a gallon." "Time and space are at your beck and call; your freedom is complete."[3] The self-sufficient autocamper could be frivolous, even fickle, and flaunt it. "Now, any fertile farming country will afford a good camping place and the best of fare. If one doesn't like a neighborhood, a day's run will change the state and scenery; the auto contains everything wanted—bed, board, and shelter."[4]

To one journalist, this wonderful self-reliance suggested the life of a sea captain on the high seas, free to determine his ports of call and move on should spirit or circumstance require. "A touring automobile is like a little yacht on wheels. You have your provisions and equipment, your maps and compass, your eager consultations with other mariners, your dangerous Cape Horns, your snug, cozy harbors. . . . You sail up to a hotel, and if you do not like its looks, you sail away again, with no more concern as to where you will finally lay your head than a tramp."[5]

To *Outing* editor Frank Brimmer, a feudal analogy seemed more apt.

The car or trailer is M'Lord autocamper's castle. . . . And the whole wide world is his manor! The autocamper, properly equipped, is a petty feudal monarch in a horizon that is all his own. On his rubber-shod castle grounds, with all the *lares et penates* of his home hearth carried with him, he may set up roadside housekeeping anywhere on God's green footstool, free and independent of the whole wide world.[6]

Most writers likened autocampers not to mariners or feudal lords but to gypsies and vagabonds. Scores of articles and books boosted "motor gypsying," "motor hoboing," "nomadic motor-

Pioneer motorist in Toledo
car surveys his private
realm—the Grand Canyon,
Arizona, 1902. "You can get
anywhere and everywhere."
(Library of Congress)

"Happy Romanies," 1902.
This carefully staged portrait
expressed the gypsy ideal so
attractive to early motor campers: idyllic setting, colorful
costumes, traditional family
ties, leisurely ambience.
(Library of Congress)

ing," "gypsying deluxe," "autotramping," and "motor vagabonding."

To some extent the name *gypsy* merely carried over from the horse-drawn camping popular in Britain, New England, and California. Since the late nineteenth century, wealthy camping parties had loaded up their wagons with household goods and had gone a-gypsying along rural lanes, in farmers' fields, and on national park trails. By 1910 some "gentleman gypsies" were switching to cars. The car was cleaner, more powerful, and more compact, and one could still tow a caravan—or trailer—or sleep in the car itself. Given the camper's inveterate utilitarianism, the switch seemed eminently sensible. "The cumbersome, uncomfortable features [of horse gypsying] have been eliminated, while all the fun has been retained," wrote one modernizer. And one could range far wider.[7]

Actually, horse gypsying was a minor, obscure sport that few motor gypsies even knew about. But there was more to the phrase than simple anachronism: *gypsying* seemed especially appropriate to this new, automobile-age experience.

At the most general level, gypsying stood for the unconventional. In legend gypsies came from Bohemia, and since the 1820s bohemianism had come to embrace an ill-defined rejection of bourgeois values. Reaching the United States first in the 1850s, it enjoyed a brief upsurge in the 1890s before the Greenwich Village vogue of 1913–1925. Purists might have abhorred the postwar invasion of Greenwich Village by the "slumming bourgeoisie" and the profitable appropriation of such bohemian symbols as bobbed hair, flannel shirts, and orange and black tea rooms. Similarly, real gypsies might have doubted the unconventionality of white-collar "gypsies à la Edison." But to veterans of the Victorian summer resort, autocamping was really different and daring. To go sliding around in the mud, careening around mountains, wearing old clothes, getting good and dirty, and living off the land, was to defy the hotel veranda, with its fancy dress parade and genteel idleness.

Although both the Greenwich Village bohemian and the autocamper scorned such self-satisfied Victorianism, their rebellions took quite different directions. Rejecting everything old-fashioned, bohemians flaunted avant garde values. Autocampers, on the other hand, identified with the traditional gypsy images of spiritual campfire, medieval caravansary, and tight patriarchal family. Unlike ultramodernist bohemians, gypsies seemed reassuringly premodern in their stubborn attachment to tribal values. Gypsy women dressed traditionally, and male leaders forbade bobbed hair and faddish style books. Gypsies thus appealed to the middle-class autocamper fearful of moral decay and family disintegration. Moreover, unlike bohemians, gypsies and motorists preferred the country road to the city cafe. Their escape was mobile, not aesthetic, their haven the roadside, not the salon.[8]

This connection to the road was one reason why autocampers could not fully identify with the woodsman model of earlier campers. The wilderness camper was more sedentary; he either settled in one camp or traveled laboriously over a small area by foot or canoe. The gypsy, on the other hand, covered a lot more ground. Gypsies were also more picturesque than backwoods pioneers. Wearing bright costumes, they presented "a veritable pagaentry of color." Furthermore, their manners seemed more appropriate to the emerging leisure ethic. While woodsmen worked hard and long to achieve a bare subsistence, gypsies seemed carefree and easygoing. Like Parisians they seemed to know how to live graciously and deliberately, without hurry. "Among the tents and on the sand the gypsy people loll at ease. They have eaten; they rest." To one writer a roadside gypsy encampment suggested a mellow reverie, "the essence mingled of violin notes, of fluttering rags, pipes smoking, embers charring."[9] Gypsies and vagabonds, with their outcast, timeless, quasi-tragic, romantically international associations, appealed to urbane tourists who desired vacation models more sophisticated than the hunter or trapper.

To the motor camper "gypsying" was interchangeable with "hoboing." The tramp had a related unconventionality. He, too, inhabited the open road. Although essentially a loner, he lived in encampments, had his tribal loyalties, and spoke his own road language. According to popular legend, he did not like to work and, moreover, did not feel guilty about it. In everyday life few championed the cause of the supposedly lazy tramp; yet even the most sarcastic tramp jokes contained a hidden ambivalence, a secondary sense—half dread, half envy—that despite his alleged immorality, the tramp might know something worthwhile. The same period that produced numerous studies of hobo pathology also hailed Charlie Chaplin's heroic tramp. Living by his wits, the tramp seemed to get away with things, to succeed without trying. Thus, one 1913 tramp joke titled "Modernized" only slightly exaggerated contemporary wonder at the tramp's brash ability to get along:

Hubby: What does that dirty tramp want at the gate?
Wifey: He just arrived in a rickety last year model automobile and asked me to get him a set of old tires.[10]

For businessmen in need of rest but unable to unwind on conventional resort vacations, the tramp's free and easy style could seem worth emulating. "The tramp is in reality a survival," wrote Stephen Leacock in explaining why tramps seemed to be on perpetual vacation, while businessmen officially on vacation found it so hard to relax. A relic of some pre-industrial paradise where men "existed on the bounty of nature or died for want of it, but never worked," the tramp seemed the "supreme example of the vacation man."[11] The upper class had been playing tramp since the late nineteenth century—wearing loose clothes and getting along with a minimum of servants at well-equipped Adirondacks camps—but only with the car could vacationists capture the tramp's easy mobility. The tramp did not sit around on his front porch or veranda; such a person might better be called a bum. Rather, he wandered.

The gypsy-tramp ideal blurred over into a generalized hunger for a slower, less obsessive, more attentive life-style than that possible in a hectic business civilization. Tired of endlessly deferring gratification, the professional-managerial class longed for the here and now. The dream was expressed in "Gypsying," published in one tourist magazine:

All horizons open outward,
All tomorrows wait ahead.
Life is yours while you are living,
You are life's when you are dead.

Every day a new adventure,
Every road a golden chance.
Why remain a captive longer,
Spirit slave to circumstance?[12]

The aim was to shift gears, to vacation in a carefree style, living just for the moment, leisurely taking in the passing show. Thus one motor camper set out in a Liberty touring car with the sole desire "to laze along the road like gypsies and see everything and do everything just as our fancies dictated, not to hurry, but to really enjoy every minute of the trip." Aching to break loose of everyday ruts, the tired office worker hoped to re-establish more transcendent priorities.[13]

Yet the gypsy analogy must not be taken too literally. These motorists were not real vagabonds. Indeed, tourists generally avoided contact with these traditional outcasts. Small towns who welcomed motor vagabonds continued to exclude real gypsies and tramps, who gained little from their new symbolic status. As with other discoveries of the period—the Lower East Side, Greenwich Village, Harlem, Paris—the admired virtues were to be shared selectively. How then did touring literature explain this affinity for aimless wandering shared by good citizens and feared vagrants alike?

The most common explanation was a shared "instinct." Instinct had long been cited as justification for camping out. "It is

Roadside campsite, Colorado, 1917. "On his rubber-shod castle grounds," the motor camper was "free and independent of the whole wide world." Note the banner and the way this proud auto-camper has chopped down a tree for use as a temporary awning. (U.S. Forest Service, National Archives)

an elemental instinct," went one turn-of-the-century vacation article, "and it thrills into active life at Nature's vernal call." Gypsying, like sedentary camping, seemed to appeal to a basic opposition between human nature and city life. The ways of civilization were just a "veneer upon the primal man." The city dweller was actually a "gypsy under the skin" for whom every opportunity to sleep out under canvas was a refreshing return to "the primeval days of man's long infancy, when he lay upon the green breast of the earth." A vacation in the woods meant renewed contact with "more primitive and stronger currents of being."[14]

To this conceptual foundation autocamping proponents added a new element, a nomadic instinct or "primal wanderlust" that made one want to travel as well as to live outdoors. Man was naturally migratory, yet modern life made him stay in one place. "Hemmed in by the restrictions of modern business life, people no longer . . . move by tribes or companies into new homelands. But the restlessness remains." The urge to wander was "an inherent primitive quality," an "inherent yearning laying dormant in us all."[15]

Only with the car could this subconscious need be fulfilled. "In many a Gentile breast there beats a Gypsy beat. Happily for those of us with urgent nomadic tendencies, the motor car enables us to release long-suppressed desires for vagabondage."

There is the vestige of the nomad still remaining in most of us. Not that we want to spend our time trading horses or living on stew cooked over a smoking fire. We passed that state some time ago, and thought we were settling down to civilized living, when along came the automobile and made it so easy for us to get from one place to another that our wanderlust reared its head and would not down.[16]

The migratory motorist could rejoin the "ancient human heritage" of the open road and camp. Cars ended the frustration of not being able to escape for a vacation without "a sense of being thwarted." Even the "weekend wild man"—the overnight autocamper—could touch base with primal roots by driving out of the city for just a Saturday night stay along the road.[17]

This sense of free-wheeling mobility and its subconscious roots was nicely caught in a *Touring Topics* poem, "Nomad Blood":

Breezes tugging at the topbows,
  Motor singing glad refrain,
Far from the clamor of the city
  In the open—born again!

Nomad blood in pulses leaping,
  Nothing cools it but the rain,
Cracking heavens, pouring, slashing,
  Then bright sun as hillsides drain.

Magic land of savage freedom,
  Forests spread like mighty lawns,
Lure us into vagabondage,
  Counting not the speeding dawns.[18]

For minds disciplined to follow fixed routines, the opportunity to go anywhere and to see everything could not help but seem a savage self-indulgence.

To be sure, answering one's inherent yearning was strictly a summer affair. As historian Peter Schmitt amply demonstrates in *Back to Nature: The Arcadian Myth in America,* turn-of-the-century nature enthusiasts did not necessarily hate city life. Rather, they hoped to mitigate its harsh effects through periodic, ritualistic contact with a somewhat tamed wilderness. Advocates of scouting, the suburban homestead, and city and national parks all aimed not to replace the city but to enrich it. They were moderate reformers, not primitivist rebels.[19]

Autocamping literature made this clear in the "virus" analogy. For example, Philadelphia newsman Melville Ferguson found himself susceptible to an attack of "Wanderlust." His body was physically—instinctively—disposed to wander, and failure to do so had resulted in a sort of malnutrition. "His impoverished blood was incapable of throwing it off." The source of the attack was city life, which failed to provide for organic requirements. "He had been looking at brick walls, the asphalt pavement, the hard, narrow cañons of cut stone for forty-eight years." All furnishings of civilization aggravated him. "He hated the alarm clocks, the cellar heater, and faces of the conductors who twice daily punched his ticket on the suburban train." Finally, when frustration threatened serious illness, the gypsy impulse— encouraged by an article on motor camping—broke into action. He had to go.[20]

Other writers agreed that the virus found easy acceptance in malnourished civilized blood and that the only cure was to indulge in wandering. "Once the fever gets a grip on its victim, there is nothing to do but start." But the virus could be cured, much like spring sickness resulting from an inadequate winter supply of greens. This is an essential point, for the ideal result of the trip was to return renewed, rededicated, glad to be back at home and job. The worst thing was to become permanently infected with *Bacillus wanderlusticus* and become a dangerous migrant.[21] It was fine to be bitten by the bug, but disastrous to fall victim to a more chronic hobodom. Even in its most libertarian stage, autocamping was always dedicated to reviving everyday commitments.

Still, despite considerable limitations on acceptable vagabondage, vacationists claimed extraordinary freedom. Like another recent innovation, the motion picture, the automobile offered unprecedented experiences of time, space, and movement. There was a childlike quality to motorists' choice of absolutes— anywhere, everywhere—and to the unabashed willfulness of tone—"wherever suits your fancy." It was as if they had been set free in a candy shop with no adult around to tell them what to choose or how much to spend. "You can be just as long, or just as short a time about it as you wish."[22]

The autocamper's liberty had a precise context. When motor gypsies exulted in their revolt, it was defined by specific experiences with railroads and hotels. If the tourist was the playing child, the restraining parental authority was the rail-hotel complex that channeled movement along collective, monopolized lines.

Cars versus Trains
Back to Stagecoach Days

Aside from being profitable in its own right, nostalgia has other uses. In a provocative analysis of sightseeing, sociologist Dean MacCannell suggests that modern industrial society solidifies its triumph over the premodern by turning the latter's artifacts into tourist attractions. In Williamsburg, Rockefeller oil money preserves colonial candleworks; in New Mexico, government billboards direct motorists to Indian ruins. Such exhibits protect modernity in two ways: by confirming the optimist's belief in progress and by distracting the pessimist with the unattainable past.[1] Where modern and traditional societies are contemporaneous, the search for the past is a weapon of change. European tourists modernize Kenya; vacationing Australians develop New Guinea. When the car usurped the train, however, the dialectic took a somewhat different turn. Here the future conquered the present by coming disguised as the past.

To auto tourists seeking what nature writer Dallas Lore Sharp called "the Better Country," motoring meant escaping from modern problems associated with the railroad age. The train, not the car, represented modern times. Railroads were part of everyday life, vital to industrial civilization. For motor columnist Robert Sloss, trains were "uncomfortable necessities which must be employed upon occasion because we live in an unimaginative commercial world." To this generation raised on the railroad, the train was the all-too-familiar given. The railroad *was* the industrial establishment—arrogant, impersonal, mechanical, and monopolistic. "At best," wrote motor tourist Theodore Dreiser in 1916, "the railways have become huge, clumsy affairs, little suited to the temperamental needs and moods of the average human being."[2]

If the railroad—Frank Norris's encroaching "octopus"—was the conglomerate present, the car was the New Freedom. It promised a nostalgic return to a simpler age of benignly individualistic operators, an age set before the beginnings of the Industrial Revolution, and thus, before the railroad. Through the early 1930s, touring literature described automotive transport as a revival of stagecoach and carriage travel. Railroads had supplanted stagecoaches and now cars would replace railroads. As *World's Work* editor Henry Norman predicted in 1903, "The stage-coach will be avenged upon the railway by the motor."

Although railroads had brought economic progress, something worthwhile had been lost. According to *American Motorist,* the American Automobile Association (AAA) journal, railroads had "robbed the roads of that picturesque and free means of travel [by stage], and nothing ever took its place until the dawn of the motor car." Henry Norman associated coaching with independence and pageantry—"a fine, manly age, full of splendid horses and vigorous men, redolent of romance and gay with color."[3] Rail travel was too impersonal: anonymous passengers manipulated by officious conductors, unseen engineers, faceless black porters all called *George*. Stagecoach travel, on the other hand, was intimate: only a handful of fellow travelers, healthy fresh air, frequent stops at cozy inns. In this early fantasy stage of automobiling, few worried about the social costs of individualized transport, for cars were frankly portrayed as being refreshingly regressive. Thus it was not at all inconsistent for tourists to liken this brand new gasoline machine to the archaic gypsy wagon. Both were slow and inefficient; both traveled primitive highways; both promised an autarchic alternative to modern mass travel.

Off the Beaten Track

Motoring meant "freedom from the shackles of railway timetables." This image of delightful emancipation from the "thraldom" of railroad schedules pervaded early travel writing.[4] The timetable was one frame of reference against which the car's responsiveness to individual needs could be measured and appreciated. In earlier years railroad timetables had fostered and symbolized a useful standardization, group discipline, and centralization in a chaotically developing society. Standard Time, for example, was an 1883 product of railroad modernization and was hailed as a great reform, allowing people within a broad region to live and do business by the same time. There was also a certain pride in the fact that train schedules were man-made. Arriving exactly on time—say 7:13—on some "crack" intercity express, was taken as a sign of American technological mastery over bad weather, personal vagaries, and hard terrain.

By 1910, however, when trains routinely transported almost a billion passengers a year,[5] auto advocates suggested that modern

Edward Penfield's sketch for an Oldsmobile advertisement, c. 1906, exploited the familiar nostalgia theme. Supplanting the crack train, the automobile returned travel to the challenges and pageantry of preindustrial days. (Library of Congress)

View from the tracks, Dunkirk, New York, turn of the century: the ugly industrial landscape of smokestacks, utility poles, warehouses, billboards, depot hotels. In small towns, trackside commercial houses like the Erie Hotel might be the only accommodations available to motorists without camping gear. (Library of Congress)

society demanded too much conformity. "Gregarious transportation has, of course, made wonderful strides," *American Motorist* conceded, "but the individual has had to sacrifice much of his liberty of action to take advantage of it. He must go with the crowd at the time that the crowd wants to go and by the route the crowd takes."[6] The railroad's authority to set time could seem especially arbitrary in smaller towns, where trains might stop only in the middle of the night.

War worsened the situation. Passengers still had to be ready to board on time, but freight and troop trains preempted crowded track and station space, making it hard for regular passenger trains to keep to their schedules. Moreover, the upsurge in wartime travel—troops, more business, and more freight—forced long-distance travelers to reserve desirable Pullman space. This seemed yet another encroachment on individual freedom. Who wanted to plan far ahead in order to secure space in a crowded, badly ventilated Pullman car?[7]

Auto enthusiasts promised that cars would free commuters from streetcars and tourists from intercity trains. In motoring there were no 1 A.M. departures, no rushed meals at some seedy depot lunch counter, and no rude awakenings by an anxious porter at 5:30 A.M. In a "highway Pullman," the driver was his own station master, engineer, and porter, with no one's time to make except his own.[8]

Like the stage coach, the car followed a more "natural" schedule than the through train, which ploughed through time and space without regard for weather, scenery, or darkness. Driving stopped at mealtimes and at night. Moreover, bad weather, muddy roads, washouts, a fellow motorist stranded ahead were unpredictable events that intervened and forced even the most scheduled tourist to stop, take a breather, meet fellow tourists, and take in the view. In a sense the car freed the motorist not only from the centrally set railroad timetable but from his own internal, work-disciplined scheduling. Faced with a washed-out bridge, the tourist had to shrug his shoulders and be patient. This, too, could seem a bracing return to days when life was more in tune with natural rhythms.[9]

Motorists complained that, in addition to being too scheduled, train travel was too fast. Describing the view from the train as a "blur," passengers resented being "whirled through" at sixty miles per hour, with no time to stop and take in a particularly nice scene, and no time to stretch legs and smell flowers. "As time, tides, and through trains stop for no man, so we flashed by green, beckoning hills that called in vain."[10] For the sake of efficiency, railroad travelers even had to "make miles" while asleep. Nature writer Dallas Lore Sharp found the rush far too disconcerting: "For business the sleeping-car in this country is a necessity; but for real travel it is utterly too violent, the spark of consciousness jumping a five-hundred-mile gap in a single night. You are nearer done traveling by 500 miles, if that is the end of travel; you are 500 miles nearer California. But what about Kansas and Arizona?"[11]

Motor travel was much slower. Given bad roads, low speed limits, and frequent mechanical breakdowns, motorists averaged under twenty miles per hour. Early observers took this to be an advantage. Perhaps the leisurely car trip would counter the modern tendency to sacrifice reflection for velocity. A 1900 *Review of Reviews* article hoped that "many people will prefer to travel from place to place more slowly than at present, . . . rather than to rush blindly along iron rails. And if the automobile does that for us, if it makes us see more of our own country, out of beaten lines, and see it more quietly and sanely, it will have rendered a splendid service to our American life and character."[12] In addition to encouraging deliberation, motoring heightened attention to topographic detail and regional variation. Instead of a fleeting impression, the tourist saw diversity and uniqueness. Motorists actually experienced transitions between sections, "from pine to palm." For Dallas Lore Sharp, motoring restored a sense of gradation and texture lost on the through train's mad dash through the night.

> Every mile by motor is a continuous experience. There are no lapses between twilight and dawn. On the train I have closed my eyes in the early dusk of a winter day to a howling prairie blizzard and opened them the next morning to see cattle picking a desert breakfast from among the soapweeds and prickly pears and dusty sagebrush, climatic zones and geologic aeons apart, a break with the earth so shattering that it can never be mended, at least for that journey and for the sequence of experiences in space and time. . . .
>
> Motoring is liable to violence. Heaven knows, and subject enough to lapses, but lapses not like those of the "limited train." Day in and day out by motor you scarcely average more than a cautious, legal 20 miles to the hour on a transcontinental run; and where you stop for the night, right there you will start in the morning, unless it rains. But no matter how much it rains, you will stay and make your next start there, missing nothing of the road as you do on your flying pillow by train.[13]

Not only did railroads dictate when and how fast you went, they channeled you along defined routes. Rail travel seemed claustrophobic. Before cars, Elon Jessup recalled, "our own open road was usually *hedged in* by two steel rails." While trains were bound to under 300,000 miles of inflexible rail, motorists had almost three million miles of road—mostly dirt—to choose from. Drivers discovered that there was more than one way to get from town to town and that local people themselves were unsure of the way—so conditioned were they to rail patterns. Strictly goal-oriented, trains were "not fond of scenery; the flattest grade is their delight." But cars could travel off the beaten track. "Where the locomotive is *hard bound* to the narrow gauge of a carefully laid out and expensive road, the automobile is free to come and go by highways and byways, up hill and down dale, over stubble field or through morass, unhampered, free, and trustworthy as a faithful hound." For Theodore Dreiser the trip back to his boyhood home in Indiana took on a new significance by car. The same old trip by train had passed by unnoticed, but the rediscovery of travel options by car restored a youthful sense of openness and freshness.[14]

By choosing his own routes, the motorist gained an insider's special access, a more exclusive insight. "The motor car can be induced into localities inaccessible to railroads, and the delights of getting into the primitive, away from the toots and hoots and howls and clangings of up-to-date confusion, is immense." There was a delightful reverse snobbery to this: The train may have been faster and more expensive, but only the motorist got to see the best spots. Climbing the breathtaking Raton Pass, for example, was impossible for those who stuck to the valley-clinging railroad. "Only by motor car can you climb such heights and halt where you will and as long as you will, then flit away as fast as you will over a land as immeasurable in terms of human feet as America."[15]

All writers agreed that America was best seen from the road. Cars broke the railroad's monopolistic hold over American geographical consciousness. Intimacy was the key word, found again and again in travel accounts. Effie Price Gladding's 1914 cross-country run left her with the "precious possessions of memory, the choice intimate knowledge to which the motorist alone can attain." Transcontinentalist Hamilton Laing agreed: "He who runs by rail but makes an acquaintance; he who runs by road makes a friend—or sometimes an enemy; he at least gets intimate."[16] For Americans fearful of the isolating, insulating qualities of mass society, a special closeness was attractive for its own sake.

Seeing the Real America

What exactly did motorists see that their rail predecessors had not seen from the parlor car window?

Of railroad tourists to the West in the late nineteenth century, Earl Pomeroy wrote, "Witnesses tended to describe themselves, their aspirations, fears, and intellectual backgrounds as much as the new lands they visited." The same principle applied to early automobile accounts, but they reflected antimodernist interests.

This was most evident in their idealization of the West, the small town, and the "olde."

Transcontinental motorists—the most publicized tourists—saw a different West from their nineteenth-century rail predecessors who had tended to look for evidence of European and eastern civilization in their western travels. The raw, violent frontier days were too recent, too controversial to be romanticized by genteel Americans. The Great American West—that broad section between Kansas and California—was more terrifying than exciting, a long desolate stretch to be sped through at night, with a minimum of stops. Tourists wanted to see America's Alps (the Rockies), America's Mediterranean (California), America's ruins (the Southwest), and then take refuge in San Francisco's French restaurants and New York-style hotels.[17]

As part of the See America First movement, which began around 1906, early automobiling reflected an anti-European nationalism that took pride in American differences. The real boost came in 1914, when Americans were cut off from Europe. "At last we are delivered from the tyranny of the Chateaux of the Loire, the canals of Venice, and the glaciers of Switzerland," one *New York Times* writer exulted. Travel writers urged tourists to pay more attention to American uniqueness in quality as well as sheer quantity of attractions. "America can raise more scenery to the acre than any other place on earth," raved one southwestern promoter. "Not only can the U.S. duplicate practically everything in the way of mountain and lake scenery which is to be found in the Alps or the Highlands of Scotland, but it has many of a more or less exclusive character." Americans discovered the arid Southwest, Petrified Forest, and the Grand Canyon. "In natural scenery, 'Seeing America First' means seeing many things which can nowhere else be found. Mount Rainier is finer than Mount Blanc; the Yosemite far surpasses the Engadine; Niagara has no rival this side of the Zambesi."[18]

In effect, by playing up American superiority, these "See America Firsters" were as imprisoned by the European model as was the Victorian American abroad comparing the Columbus, Ohio, capitol building with the Vatican, or the western rail tourist looking for "Europe in the Wilderness." This was a familiar debate, and after the war many Europe-conditioned tourists returned to Europe for the real thing.

Where automobilists really differed from their rail predecessors was in their attitude toward the urban West. Rail tourists had welcomed the cultivated manners and up-to-date (that is, *Beaux Arts*) architecture of western cities as signs of civilization's progress over barbarism. Only a few jaded European aristocrats had found the *other* West's primitive roughness attractive. After 1900, however, middle-class easterners wished to avoid reminders of home. Noting Cheyenne's neoclassical library, movie theaters, and society balls, they regretted the eastern pretensions, for they wanted a different West. "It was the *West,* the great free, open West we had come to see," wrote New Yorker Emily Post. "Ranches, cowboys, Indians, not little cities like sample New Yorks."[19] But the need for contrast went beyond familiar cowboy and Indian stereotypes. If anything, tourists were disappointed by these carefully staged sightseeing attractions.

Motorists were more impressed by the open sky, informal dress, and generous hospitality of ordinary westerners. These qualities were most striking in the region that had most terrified rail passengers: the great dry plains of western Nebraska, Wyoming, and eastern Colorado. Enroute to Denver and San Francisco, trains sped through this area, often at night, leaving passengers with an impression of flat, unpopulated desolation. Auto tourists also headed for mountain and coastal destinations, but along the way they took time to marvel at the "awful immensity" of the great treeless plains. And they also stopped in the towns. For rail passengers these whistle stops had seemed backward and forlorn; for motorists they loomed as welcome oases. Here they met farmers, ranch hands, and garage mechanics who seemed infused with "a cheerful spirit and a hearty readiness to do for you any favor possible."[20] Unlike the more class-conscious eastern laborer, these independent businessmen considered it beneath themselves to charge for information or for fixing a flat tire. "You bet," rather than "how much," seemed to be their motto. To New York aristocrat Frederic F. Van de Water, western garage men seemed remarkably "unafflicted with their eastern brethren's combination of misanthropy and dyspepsia."

We had lived on Manhattan Island so long that we had come to consider all America suspicious, hostile, abrupt, insolent. Through Red and the farmer and the garage man and a score more of unconscious teachers we learned that New York and all it signifies, while geographically of the nation, are no more intrinsically America than a monocle is part of the optic system.[21]

So what if service was slower or if everything shut down by 6 P.M.? Breakfasts may have been plain, but portions were immense, food fresh, prices low, and tipping virtually unheard of. And the countryside was not quite as unpopulated or as ugly as the train ride made it appear. On the road one constantly met helpful local people, and there was an appealing dignity in their apparently uncomplicated struggle in the majestic open stretches.

California, too, contrasted favorably with the East. Emily Post considered New York "the princess of impersonality, the queen of indifference. . . . You can come or go, sink or swim, be brilliant, beautiful, or charming, she cares not a wit." With its "millionaires' palaces, its flashing Broadway, its canyon streets, its teeming thoroughfares, its subway holes-in-the-ground into which men dive like moles, emerging at the other end in an office burrow," her home city was "omnipotent," but ultimately decadent. Californians, on the other hand, seemed "merely happy—happy about everything, happy all the time." "'Welcome to the Land of Sunshine!' says smiling California. 'If your heart is young, then stay with me and play!'" In this magic place, people worked less and enjoyed life more—the gypsy life-in-residence. Post's contact with the West Coast left her with "a more direct outlook, a simpler, less encumbered way of life," a vast improvement over her "Eastern hidebound dependence upon ease and luxury."[22]

Appropriately enough, whereas rail travelers had generally preferred neocosmopolitan San Francisco, automobile tourists were equally impressed with southern California, with its lower density and fabled Garden-of-Eden abundance. Here was the ultimate in leisure-based living. Los Angeles seemed to prosper not from manufacturing or trade but from the "sale of climate" to retirees from the eastern rat race. Known for its good dry roads, year-round touring, boosterish auto clubs, and relative scarcity of rail alternatives, Los Angeles became the "Mecca of West Coast tourists."[23]

In all, the motorist's West stood for the same qualities associated with vagabondage and stagecoach days: independence, open space, simplicity, a more leisurely pace—all in direct contrast with the crowded, frenetic, compulsive East.

Although the transcontinentalists were the most publicized motorists, their widely read accounts forming the roots of a burgeoning motor literature industry, only a few Easterners actually motored to California before 1920. The early cross-country trip could take a month one way, and affluent motorists sometimes shipped their cars back by rail or sold them in California. But motorists with less time and money could achieve many of the same goals by staying closer to home. Indeed, Malcolm W. Willey and Stuart A. Rice would argue in their 1933 contribution to *Recent Social Trends* that cars may have initially strengthened provincial rather than national ties.[24] Vacationists no longer had to take long train trips to crowded resort areas. Resort operators complained that many families now seemed to be staying in town, taking a suburban cottage on a nearby lake and making short weekend runs to outlying sights. Roadhouses within a few hours' drive of the city experienced new prosperity, while hotels farther out suffered. City newspapers and local touring guides emphasized the motorist's ability to explore nearby country villages and back roads. Since suburban roads could be just as rough and as exciting as many western trails, there was little need to go far for adventure, and the natives one met could be as colorful as any Wyoming ranch hand.[25]

Nostalgic motorists gravitated to picturesque villages. For long-distance tourists and Sunday drivers alike, the city was a disagreeable obstacle on a sentimental journey between small towns. Few tourists wanted to see the industrial landscape of modern cities. Here the car seemed a decided improvement over the train alternative. Trains created an intense wasteland along their tracks. Train passengers rarely saw the city's best face. The same was true in smaller towns and, indeed, in rural areas. Farmers' backyards were cluttered with equipment, discarded furniture, trash, and the ever-present barn billboard. Julian Street described the view from the train as it sped towards New York in 1914:

Towns and cities flash by, one after another, in quick succession, as the floors flash by an express elevator; and where there are no towns there are barns painted with advertisements, and great signboards disfiguring the landscape. There are four tracks now. A passenger train roars by, savagely on one side, is gone, while on the other, a half-mile freight train tugs and squeaks and clatters. When the porter calls you in the morning, and you raise your window shade, you see no plains or mountains, but the backs of squalid suburban tenements, with vari-colored garments, fluttering on their clotheslines, like the flags of some ship decked for a gala day.[26]

An occasional visitor—usually European—might enjoy this honest glimpse of teeming cities, factories, and commercial ingenuity. "Is there not a picturesque side to the triumph of civilization over barbarism?" asked Englishman James Muirhead, whose Baedeker guide, *The Land of Contrasts,* was an incisive portrait of turn-of-the-century America. By civilization Muirhead meant not the reassuring baroque city halls and romanesque train stations but the industrial America best symbolized by the tracks themselves. "Is there nothing of the picturesque in the long thin lines of gleaming steel, thrown across the countless miles of desert sand and alkali plain, and in the mighty mass of metal with its glare of cyclopean eye and its banner of fire-illumined smoke, that bears the conquerors of nature from side to side of the great continent?" For a functionalist like Muirhead there was a stark beauty to everyday, working America.[27]

More often, however, the industrial landscape seemed a jarring intrusion on the sightseers' fantasy world of rustic peace and village charm. A 1908 letterwriter to *Scribner's* wondered why trains had to enter each town through the ugly back door. "Entering almost any American town, big or little, is in fact entering by an unkempt 'postern.' The railroad itself seems to have an unfailing instinct for the slum, which it customarily creates." Not ready to be reminded of the economic and environmental dislocation wrought by the train, this traveler found orderly European villages more attractive. Yet, as Edith Wharton wrote, rail tourists there, too, had to arrive "through the area of desolation and ugliness created by the railway itself."[28]

Cars changed this. Now one could drive down Main Street, past well-kept front yards and store fronts, away from the warehouses and tenements of trackside Front Streets. To Emily Post it seemed that motorists now had front row seats for the best part of the performance. "We are seeing our country for the first time. It is not alone that a train window gives only a piece of whirling view; but the tracks go through the ragged outskirts of the town, past the back doors and through the poorest land generally, while the roads become the best avenues of the cities and go past the front entrances of farms." Theodore Dreiser agreed that car travel exposed travelers to the timeless, pastoral calm, the "human scale" of village and farm order.[29]

Yet tourists were selective in what they considered a picturesque village scene. A New England square, an 1820 mansion with well-kept lawns and rose-covered white fences, a Revolutionary War bridge, all qualified. A few tourists were excited by the booster spirit, the naive commercialism of small-town businessmen, with their welcome signs and imposing bank buildings. It was pleasant to motor through "thrifty" Ohio towns, but few visited a Pennsylvania mining town or, for that matter, a western ghost town. The demand was for the "successful" and the "historic," and history stopped before 1865. Later buildings and landmarks were just old. A colonial church was inspiring, but a late Victorian mansion was "an eyesore."

Where an edifying relic had never existed or had long since been torn down, civic clubs, local governments, philanthropists, and individual entrepreneurs sought to remedy the deficiency. This was a period of widespread historical renovation—old mills, Revolutionary era houses, battlefields, and, in the late 1920s, Williamsburg. Antiquarians refurbished old inns for the motor trade or sought to convert long-neglected roadhouses into "wayside tavernes" suggestive of coaching days. Roadside mansions and farmhouses became tearooms with names like Ye Ragged Robin, The Tally-Ho, and Pine Tree Inn, offering "heartye fare," "olde-fashioned hospitality," and antiques for sale to motor-wayfarers. Architects designed gasoline stations to look like Tudor cottages or like colonial Spanish missions. City traffic departments erected wrought iron street signs topped by silhouettes of stagecoaches or with inn-like wooden placards that swung freely from chains. Road crews constructed white-washed, round-topped milestones—"a return to the methods of other days

when the highways were, as now again, through routes of travel."
Oil and rubber companies sponsored billboards describing local
colonial or frontier history. Early bus companies likened their
interminable, depot-to-depot journeys to "a revival of the
stagecoach posting from inn to inn." The most durable commercial elaboration of this trend would come in the late 1920s, with
the development of tourist cabins that seemed to restore the intimacies of "old coaching days and old coaching ways."[30]

Reviving the Strenuous Life

In early automobile touring, the physical experience of driving
strengthened the sense of nostalgia. This was perhaps its most
important contrast with train travel. Like the Victorian parlor, the
rail coach was consistently warm—overheated in winter, poorly
ventilated in summer—but otherwise well protected from outside
hazards and obstacles. The result was a fairly smooth, well-
insulated ride.

Motoring was a step backward in terms of modern comforts.
Touring in an open car, with meager springs and little padding,
on rough roads, was an arduous, bumpy, drafty ordeal. All early
accounts detail the trials of soft summer mud, tortuous mountain
rocks and grades, perpetual dust, lost directions, and mechanical
breakdowns. Mud was especially troublesome in the Midwest
just after the spring thaw and in the dry plains after a summer
storm. Near Pierre, South Dakota, Kathryn Hulme found that
mud "was a predatory vampire, insatiable, long armed, wicked to
a bottomless depth." Motorists argued energetically over whose
"gumbo" was worse—Kansas or Iowa, or maybe Missouri.
Guidebooks advised prospective tourists to pack for all sorts of
emergencies: block and tackle for mud, at least two spare tires for
rocks, a decent set of tools for carburetor and engine, flares, and
so on. "Make sure your automobile is fit to fight a long hard
battle," was Frank Brimmer's advice in 1923.[31]

But writers turned difficulty into virtue. The 1915 Lincoln
Highway guide warned that the journey was "still something of a
sporting trip, and one must expect and put up cheerfully with
some unpleasantness, just as you would on a shooting trip." Here
the road adventurer could overcome obstacles with gentlemanly
bravado. The easy train trip, on the other hand, was too soft, too
effete, too familiar. "Those who want luxury and ease should
take a deluxe train," the guide sneered. "To those who love the
wide spaces, who enjoy exertion in the clear ozone of the great
out-of-doors, the trip is a delightful outing."[32] Motoring thus an-
swered Theodore Roosevelt's call for a revival of the "strenuous
life" that had supposedly preceded turn-of-the-century deca-
dence.

Railroad passengers sat while all the work was done for them and could do nothing if the train was delayed. In motoring, however, drivers might have to build bridges, dislodge tree stumps, drain ditches, and pull each other out of the mud. If the car was not suited for American roads—as was the case with many European luxury cars—the driver had to learn to compensate. A low, heavy vehicle with little clearance, Emily Post's foreign car was fine for smooth French roads but was out of place in the West. In crossing New Mexico's heavily rutted, rocky roads, her son E. M. had to back up, jack up the car, build up the road bed by hand with a spade carried precisely for that purpose, fill in holes, and forage for wood to ford ditches—in short, to show "great skill and no little ingenuity." But this was the point. Driving was a skill you sought to perfect for its own sake. E. M. advised drivers to buy an American car for such a journey but otherwise not to worry about obstacles ahead, for "the experiences he may have will prove an incomparable school for his driving and for his ability to tackle new problems with the means at hand."[33]

For autocamping tourists, living outdoors added the problem of devising ways to cook, clean, and perform everyday domestic chores. This, too, was approached as a challenge, a deliberately self-imposed hardship. "There is joy in doing the work, away from modern conveniences, away from usual surroundings, [in] the exactions of camp life, where it is sometimes more difficult to accomplish ordinary undertakings."[34] At a time when growing specialization seemed to threaten individual autonomy, autocamping offered training in traditional values of self-help and all-around dexterity.

The trip could also be a spiritual test. As Emily Post reminded worried readers, ordeal was good for character. "I have found it a splendid idea when things go very uncomfortably to remember—if I can—what a very charming diplomat, who was also a great traveler, once told me: that in motoring, as in life, since trouble gives character, obstacles and misadventures are really necessary to give the *trip* character." Sturdy travelers had to tolerate uncertain accommodations, bad food, sleepless nights, and hard roads. Autocamping doubled the hardships. For naturalist John Burroughs, out on a widely reported autocamping trip with Henry Ford, Thomas Edison, and Harvey Firestone, the ordeal was a welcome escape from luxuries that alienated modern man from "first principles." "Discomfort is, after all, what the camper-out is unconsciously seeking. We grow weary of our luxuries and conveniences. We react against our complex civilization, and long to get back for a time to first principles. We cheerfully endure wet, cold, smoke, mosquitos, black flies, and sleepless nights, just to touch naked reality once more." Autocamping taught urbanite Melville Ferguson that the normal bourgeois

Pioneer transcontinentalist in-
spects a midroad boulder on
the way to Gore Canyon,
Colorado, 1912. In overcoming numerous road obstacles,
early drivers had to show
"great skill and no little
ingenuity." (Bureau of Public
Roads, National Archives)

Fixing a culvert, near Mack, Colorado, 1912. Road delays fostered "remarkable pal-ship and cooperative democracy" among motorists. (Bureau of Public Roads, National Archives)

criteria for well-being were surprisingly dispensable, "that it is not fatal to have wet feet; that pneumonia, or even a cold, does not necessarily follow the discomfort of undressing occasionally in a shivering haste to crawl under warm blankets; that a bath in a bucketful of tepid water is sometimes a luxury; that the overtures of annoying insects are at least friendly in intention, and may easily be endured."[35] If the experience was not intrinsically enjoyable—and many found it hard—there was at least the satisfaction of suffering stoically with the shoulder-shrugging aristocratic attitude summed up in Beatrice Massey's title, *It Might Have Been Worse*.

As evidence of suffering and triumph, early tourists decorated their cars with banners—"Kansas City to Los Angeles," "Ocean to Ocean." Proclaiming distant origins and even more distant destinations, these appropriately worn pennants showed, in effect, what pioneers had been through.

Sad-faced banners are they too before their duty is done. Flailed in the wind and the rain, burned and bleached by the desert sun, coated and overcoated with road dust from a dozen states, they eventually arrive bearing the marks of the fray, honorable scars indeed, and so are properly hung away by their owners as souvenirs—or more properly as battle-scarred ensigns, emblems of victories won.[36]

Dusty tonneau, battered fender, travel-stained khakis, weather-beaten canvas, these, too, were evidence of having gotten through. Dust was a particularly welcome symbol, a theme of many motorist signs, like the humble "Just a Little Dusty" scrawled on the rear of a road-weary Model T or the polite but proud "Pardon My Dust." Some autocampers mounted tin cans on radiators as emblems of their ascetic but functional diet, their worldly vagabondage, their defiance of more pretentious standards. In addition to physical documentation, tourists savored impressive stories of hair-raising escapades, near-collisions, and ingeniously repaired radiators, to be recounted with relish and embellishment to fellow wayfarers at garages, camp fires, and hotels, or to envious neighbors at home.

For the sake of memory alone, it was good to have trouble. "The peaceful motorist who has no major trouble has a pleasant enough time," Emily Post allowed, "but after all he gets the least out of it in the way of recollections."[37] Proud of having overcome difficulties, some tourists had their recollections privately printed and copyrighted; for example, Hugo Alois Taussig's *Retracing the Pioneers from West to East in an Automobile* (1910), or Paul H. Marley's *Story of an Automobile Trip from Lincoln, Nebraska, to Los Angeles* (1911). Having been advised to "Kodak as you go," they also took pictures of muddy roads, steep grades, formidable boulders in the middle of the road, hairpin curves at ten thousand feet, thrilling fords through rushing streams, the inevitable farmer's team extricating a hopelessly mired Packard, the Olds overturned in a ditch, and, very rarely, some unidentified roadster at the bottom of a deep canyon—ghostly proof that roads could be treacherous, indeed deadly.

More than a badge or tool, the road-weathered car became a living partner in the struggle. Unlike the train—a huge machine that belonged to a distant corporation—the car belonged to the tourist and was in fact the trip's focal point. In early touring the sights were often just excuses for being *in* the car. Autocampers slept in cars, cooked on radiators, and used running boards as headrests for their autotents. Since most cars—especially the Model T—were simple enough to be tinkered with, the average motorist could feel that in case of breakdown he had at least an even chance of fixing it. Early cars, moreover, were very frail, fallible machines—not at all like mighty locomotives. Cars were as dependent on owners as owners were on cars. Mutual reliance led motorists to name cars for women or small animals—Lizzie, Bouncing Betsy, and the Galloping Goose. Noting this convention, the iconoclastic Kathryn Hulme deliberately chose a male name, Reggie, with medieval knight connotations. "It suggested gallantry and courage and iron strength under a glossy exterior." Once on the road, however, Reggie was no superman, but his vulnerability made him even more lovable, like a close male friend who was not afraid to admit weakness.

Reggie very soon became much more than an automobile to us. It is impossible to hum along day after day, week after week, panting across the blistering flatness of endless prairies, roaming up to the dizzying heights of innumerable mountain passes, and not conceive of some sort of hero-worship for that car that carries you. For there is about machinery a fidelity transcending all human faithfulness. There are heart-rending moments, too, when your car coughs to a halt and looks mutely to you to right the intestinal disturbance—and you peer under the hood and find perhaps a loose connection or a flapping wire; with what sympathetic fingers do you feel your way through the black grease to the ailing part to fix it! And then, when you're humming along again, there is a tenderness mingled with your hero-worship, for you've found that your car has become a person whose tissues are not infallible but oh so willing! They say that personifying inanimate objects is a trait of the aboriginal mind, but those who talk so have never crossed the continent in a car.[38]

No haughty, mysterious, anonymously controlled supermachine, the car was a friend—helpful, yet humble. More reliable and powerful than a horse, more personal and approachable than a train, the automobile seemed to restore a human scale to machinery that had been lost with the onset of the steel age.

This machine also brought strangers together, but more selectively than did the train. Train travel was commonly portrayed as a disagreeable, even dangerous, social experience. Passengers competed for the more comfortable lower berths and window seats and fought over whether windows should be raised or lowered. Separated at night by thin curtains, they tried to sleep to a chorus of whispers, coughs, and snores. In the morning they lined up to use the common washroom. Bemoaning the "grotesque publicity" of the average sleeping car, *Outlook*'s "Spectator" observed that "surely average humanity is never so eminently seen at its best and at its worst as in a sleeping-car at the moment when it turns out in the morning." Fresh air reformers worried about dangerous "microbes" exchanged in "unduly intimate" sleepers and coaches, especially in those carrying emigrants. Coach passengers complained of malodorous salamis and ripe bananas consumed by those unable to afford eating in the dining car. Etiquette manuals advised female travelers against unguarded acquaintances with salesmen in the next seat, and Travelers' Aid Society officials warned that ingratiating strangers could be con artists or white slave agents. Among themselves, railroad men agreed that too many ticket clerks took bribes, too many conductors were unconscionably rude, and too few porters understood basic sanitation.[39] In all, the population of the rail car seemed like that of the city: at best, diverse and colorful—at worst, "unscreened" and hostile.

On the road motorists met other motorists, especially at large mudholes, washed-out streams, and crossroads garages. Here travelers interacted not as suspicious, passive passengers but as a community of independent but like-minded engineers who could help each other. One traveler even welcomed a delay at a washed-out Florida road, for it "demonstrated the remarkable pal-ship and cooperative democracy which have developed among American automobile drivers." Fifty cars were backed up; everyone had to get out and help. "Can you visualize any other exigency besides motoring which would make businessmen and professionals unaccustomed to manual work step down into the mud and put their shoulders to dirty wheels?" For this motorist, this unforgettable incident recalled the democracy of the trenches. "Friendships were formed and tempered in heavy service over that detour which out-rivaled the worst in France during the world war."[40]

Kathryn Hulme, too, welcomed the South Dakota "gumbo" and Montana "toothpaste," for mud served to bring tourists together. "Between us and every other motorist on the road, it was the bond that made friendship instantaneous. It made 'How's the road?'—the earnest salutation east of the Mississippi—a delightfully absurd expletive that chirked up sagging spirits when mud rivalled a bulldog for tenacity." So universal was this concern for road conditions that some commentators wondered whether tourists saw anything else.

Play honest eavesdropper to any two auto-loads of travelers at the filling station and what are they discussing? Not the beautiful scenery of the hill country of Pennsylvania, not the grandeur of the snow-caps towering about the Colorado Rockies, not the marvelous sunsets of the painted deserts of Nevada, but the perfectly rotten time they had negotiating the mud of Iowa, the narrowness of the mountain road up to the pass, the pitchholes and dust of the god-forsaken dry lands, or perhaps the size and ferocity of the skeeters of Illinois.[41]

With few accurate maps or guidebooks, this casual shop talk was quite functional. Indeed, it was a cardinal rule of motoring to "pass it on." Just as tramps informed each other of hospitable farm houses and hostile police, tourists talked of bad roads, bad hotels, and dishonest garages. Road talk also sharpened one's skills as a worldly traveler, for tourists learned quickly that not everyone knew the right directions and that fellow motorists tended to exaggerate hardships.

Every man tells his very worst. You meet an easy-going tourist in say, Nevada; you are having a rough time with the weatherman and mention the fact. "Ah! Wait til you get into the mountains and then you will have something real to do!" is his consolatory message. . . . The traveler soon learns to calculate, discount mentally on a liberal percentage, and proceed undaunted to face the horrors.[42]

Essential to the battle-scarred veteran mystique, exaggeration imparted "a tinge of heroism, an agreeable smack of daredeviltry." Learning to be skeptical was part of the "transcontinental game," the process by which novices became seasoned old-timers. Meeting "misdirectors" and "road liars" also added to the desirable kaleidoscopic quality of road life—the feeling of having met all kinds. And for patriots, it was the conversation itself—the *freedom* to talk, to boast, even to lie—that confirmed the belief that the road was the real, democratic America. "With the freedom established by their membership in the great motor fraternity, they voiced the talk of the road." Only on the highway—"America's Main Street"—could comradely Americans "rub shoulders and fenders" and talk.[43]

The road ordeal and road contacts ratified sightseers' faith that only by motoring could one see the country. Hardship validated pride in having "been there." To use Daniel Boorstin's distinction, taking the train was *tourism*—easy, packaged, modern, superficial; motoring was *travel* in its literal, traditional sense—"travail," hard work that paid off handsomely in adventure, new insights, a changed outlook, a special intimacy.[44] Beatrice Massey exclaimed, "You will get tired, and your bones will cry aloud for a rest cure, but I promise you one thing—you will never be bored!" There was no challenge in train travel. Being "tunneled through" on a limited train left a traveler unchanged. "The steel-walled Pullman carefully preserves for you the attitude you started with," wrote Emily Post, who welcomed motoring's "invigoratingly delicious" hardships.[45]

The ordeal particularly confirmed motorists' belief that the West was the bastion of true comradeship, since vulnerable tourists *had* to cooperate in the West's empty plains, rough mountains, and forbidding deserts. Even the gentle, aristocratic, hotel-hopping Massey felt changed by the western ordeal. "Unless you really love to motor, take the Overland Limited. If you want to see your country, to get a little of the self-centered Eastern hide rubbed off, to absorb a little of the fifty-seven (thousand) varieties of people and customs, and the alert, open-hearted, big atmosphere of the West, then try a motor trip." Frederic Van de Water experienced a similar conversion on his 1926 autocamping trip. After five weeks of sun, dust in the Corn Belt, alkali in the desert, and irregularities in the highway, he felt transformed from a provincial New Yorker to a broad-minded American. Upstate New Yorker Mary Crehore Bedell, suffered much discomfort for the opportunity of getting close to "the people of this great democracy" but returned home "a broader, more confident, immensely heartened person." America seemed a good place after all.[46]

The revival of bourgeois consumer loyalties was another function of the ordeal. Having suffered and changed, one could go home feeling that it was a good place, too. "One must have been bumped black and blue in the Devil's Cañon, one must have breakfasted and dined for days on attenuated slices of fried meat, on muddy coffee, and the eternal hot biscuit, properly to appreciate civilization."[47] Van de Water's wife could not control herself when, after those five weeks on the road, the family finally checked into the St. Francis Hotel in San Francisco:

"Oh," she babbled hysterically, "the beds, the beautiful beds, the white soft beds! And the sheets! And white blankets that haven't got bits of grass sticking to them. And the lovely closet and oh, the bathroom, and a bathtub! And there's hot water and you can use all of it you want. Isn't it beautiful? Isn't it exquisite? Isn't it the most beautiful thing you ever saw? White sheets and hot water—"[48]

Melville Ferguson found Seattle's factories, stores, traffic, and bustling crowds surprisingly pleasant after the long drive through mountains and desert. Mary Bedell felt the same way. A year-long autocamping trip had more than satisfied her longing for the vagabond life. "When we started on our trip I wondered whether we would become discontented with our home and surroundings upon our return; whether the lure would prove to be too great for us elsewhere, to settle down as comfortable house-holders again." After a hundred different camping spots, numerous mishaps, ten thousand miles, many memorable encounters, home looked good. Virtually all motorists agreed with Bedell and the AAA poet that, after the hard joys of the road, it was good to be back, cured of viral restlessness—at least for the coming winter—by this strong dose of motor medicine.

I love a road of romance
That speaks of mighty men,
A road that leads me somewhere
And then back home again.[49]

Autocamping versus Hotels

Back to the Family Homestead

Living on the road by day, autocampers tented by the roadside at night. Autocamping thus had two components: touring and camping. The train was the frame of reference for the former, the hotel for the latter.

All motorists shared the sense of liberation from trains, but not all took camping equipment and slept in tents along the road. In fact, after a hard day's drive, most early tourists welcomed a hotel's soft bed, hot bath, and prepared meals. For a Beatrice Massey, Emily Post, or Theodore Dreiser, the ordeal of the road was bearable partly because they knew they could escape it at night. Although these tourists did complain of hotels, most were too committed to comfort to forsake hotel bed for camp cot or dining room for campfire. Only with the cabin camp of the late 1920s would the fastidious consider a roadside alternative. Until then, they continued to frequent the three major types of hotels built to serve railroad tourists: summer resorts, big city commercial hotels, and small town drummers' hotels.

For a small but visible and articulate minority, however, gypsying meant a *total* break with restrictive institutions. As a creature of the railroad, the hotel seemed to inhibit individual freedom every bit as much as the iron rail. Autocamping maximized independence, removing what one advocate suggestively called "the hotel question, the bane of the automobile tourist."[1]

As with the motorist's case against the train, autocamping was pictured as a quest for lost virtues. If the car restored the hardy stagecoach, the roadside campsite revived the pioneer homestead, where ascetic self-reliance and warm family fellowship were said to reign.

3

Roadside Self-Service

Against the moralistic charge that a car was a costly bauble that would encourage middle-class extravagance and lower-class jealousy, early automobile proponents insisted that motorists actually saved money. They presented the car not as a spendthrift's folly—the latest incursion of wasteful consumerism—but as a democratic, efficient, and indeed frugal alternative to existing transportation.[2] Autocamping advocates took the case one step farther: motor camping was cheaper than staying in hotels *or* at home. Virtually every account written during wartime and postwar inflation maintained that autocamping was a sure cure for the rapidly rising cost of living. Professor William Kitchin reported that by taking advantage of opportunities to buy milk, butter, eggs, and vegetables from farmers along his route, his cost of living was frequently less than at home. Mary Bedell allowed that there were expenses in running the car, "but food and clothing cost less and with no rent or electricity to pay for, one should be able at least to come out even." For journalist Harry Shumway, writing during the Red Scare of 1919–1920, the supposedly low cost of such a vacation seemed almost socialistic. "Ah me," Shumway sighed, "when one stops and thinks of these things, one gets Bolshevik goose flesh."[3]

The cost actually depended on the type of trip. If tourists stayed within a few hundred miles of home, car operating costs were comparatively low. A totally self-sufficient tour, averaging under one hundred miles a day and requiring only a few staples and gasoline could run under $1.00 a day per person; some estimates went as low as fifty cents a day. Staying occasionally at hotels to clean up—as many long-distance tourists did—could increase costs to $2.50 a day per person. The comparable resort cost was $3.00 to $5.00 a day per adult and $2.50 a day for each child, *plus* clothing and railroad expenses of two cents a mile per passenger. Tourists relying solely on hotels could expect to pay $5.00 or more each for three meals and a room each day.

For campers the single most expensive item was gasoline, which ranged from twenty cents a gallon in metropolitan areas to fifty cents a gallon in the desert. On good roads the average car might get twenty miles to the gallon, but much less in mud and on rough grades. Oil cost fifteen to forty cents a quart and was used profusely. Tires were expensive and wore out easily. One tourist estimated that a trip over rough roads cost two cents a mile for tires alone—the same as for gas and oil. Early transcontinentalists had additional expenses: Many shipped their cars across the Rockies, and most returned from California by train. In 1915 it cost $60 to ship a car back from Oakland to Chicago if the car was part of a lot—$136 if alone.[4]

Like many automobile enthusiasts, writers probably under-estimated expenses. Few included the price of a camping outfit, which could run over one hundred dollars. Since campers commonly liked to add new gear each year, the initial outlay was not necessarily spread over several years. Few expense sheets listed depreciation, insurance, or the cost of supplies taken from home. The savings, then, were probably more modest than claimed. A longer rail-hotel trip might average three cents a mile per person; a 3,000-mile car trip two cents a mile per person, or $2.00 a day each. In 1922 a *New York Times* writer estimated that a two-week summer resort vacation for a family of four cost $310, and a two-week autocamping trip cost $200.[5] Yet even a $100 trip was beyond the range of the average family with an annual income under $1,500. Certainly the writers of these accounts and most early car enthusiasts could afford hotels. Accustomed to a high standard of living, it was easy for them to see two dollars a day as cheaper than home.[6]

For the purpose of promoting autocamping, however, accurate accounting was less important than the vague impression that escape somehow made economic sense. Writing for a middle-class audience that was only partially assimilated to the emerging leisure-on-credit ethos, proponents shrewdly referred to traditional values of utility and thrift. The dollar-and-cents factor added a nice concreteness to the automobile's case. But cost was usually mentioned only as the clinching argument in a long series of hotel comparisons designed to show how eminently practical and healthy this return to self-reliance actually was.

For example, autocamping advocates carried the case against the dictatorial timetable to its logical conclusion. Like the train, hotel travel entailed a schedule that, if not quite as arbitrary as the rail timetable, still restrained spontaneity. Summer resort rooms had to be booked well in advance, and with the wartime increase in travel, reservations also became necessary at city hotels. As automobile touring became more popular, even small town hotels began to fill up by late afternoon. To assure a room, motorists had to hurry ahead, perhaps cutting short a visit or skipping sights. Even if they had reservations, they might have to speed ahead to make town before the hotel dining room closed; in small towns they closed quite early. Before registering, patrons had to find a parking space at the curb near the entrance, unload their luggage, and drive to a garage several blocks away—all tiresome and time consuming. Before dining, dusty motorists had to bathe and change. Autocamping promoter Frank Brimmer argued that motoring between hotels differed little from train travel, for one had to rush along "the appointed highway, running on almost trainlike schedule in order that we might go through the orgy of unpacking unwrinkled clothing and getting through the toilet in time for dinner."[7]

The dining room might not open until after 8 A.M., taking away valuable road time. Lunch at hotels also required scheduling as there were few restaurants outside major cities, and many small hotel dining rooms were open only for one or two hours at noon. Once seated, motorists might have to wait a long time for service, for in the name of graciousness, hotel service was frequently slow. Rail depot restaurants were not any better. They were geared to incoming trains, could be very crowded, and force-fed diners in twenty minutes flat. In all, travel by hotels left less time for whims. Motorists were advised, "If you are so keen about traveling on a railroad-like schedule, better travel by railroad and have done with it."[8]

In autocamping motorists simply carried their hotel with them, and they could linger without having to think about finding a place to eat and sleep. "The constant worry to reach good hotels at noon or night that has marred your previous trips is a thing of the past," *Motor Car* rejoiced. A good picnic or camping spot could be found along the road, in a field, or in a schoolyard. "What matters it if night finds one in the center of an expansive desert many miles from the nearest hotel?" Elon Jessup asked in *The Motor Camping Book.* "In five minutes you set up a hotel of canvas that is much more satisfying than any builded of brick and stone." In the morning motorists cooked breakfast, packed up, took off. "No more hanging around on a dewy morning waiting for a cafeteria to open, or the sleepy garage owner to appear and release the family Lizzie. They arise with the lark, or a few jumps ahead of him, hustle the breakfast without regard to fletcherizing, dismantle camp, and are on their way once more."*[9]

If hotels had been pleasant, tourists might not have minded the inconveniences of scheduling. Staying in a packed hotel had some distinction, but in this seller's market crowding and high prices did not automatically signify quality. As one writer put it politely, hotels tended to "shame nature in their variance." In *Free Air,* a semi-autobiographical novel about a 1916 motor trip, Sinclair Lewis captured the uncertain prospects facing tourists reliant on hotels in the Midwest.

The state of mind of the touring motorist entering a strange place at night is as peculiar and definite as that of a prospector. It is compounded of gratitude at having got safely in; of perception of a new town, yet with all eagerness about new things dulled by weariness; of hope that there is going to be a good hotel, but

*Popular dietary reformer Horace Fletcher (1849–1919) advocated eating only when hungry and chewing very small bits of food very slowly.

small expectation—and absolutely no probability—that there really will be one.

The "unsavory probabilities" made hotel touring anxious and troublesome.[10]

To be sure, motorists could probably count on decent accommodations at deluxe summer resorts and first-class city hotels, but these very expensive hotels were not sufficiently off the beaten track. Tourists who wanted to see the real America of the West, the small town, and the countryside had to stop at small town hotels.

At first, romantics had high hopes for the small hotel. The big-city hotel was too impersonal and modern. In registering, a San Francisco editor complained, "the guest feels that he is applying for a job to the personnel director of a big corporation, or asking for admission to a clinic."[11] With Europe closed off by war, travel writers predicted that the new automobile trade would encourage rural hotel keepers to emulate the clean, deferential efficiency of Swiss and English innkeepers. Or, in line with stagecoach imagery, they hoped that smart entrepreneurs might restore roadhouses and taverns with their traditional amenities; there travelers might find the legendary, ever-genial Mine Host of caravansary and colonial inn days. A *Christian Science Monitor* article drew on this nostalgic imagery:

"It is a far cry from the luxury of modern hotel life back to the days when the stagecoach rumbled up to the door of the tavern beside the turnpike and footmen in small clothes aided dusty passengers to alight, and genial landlord met them at the door stone and ushered them into the great hall, in whose broad fireplace the embers-like symbols of hospitality for long years never ceased to glow."[12]

Motorists did occasionally find such places. In New England the tradition almost fit. Some genuine colonial inns were restored; wayside mansions and farmhouses were renovated as tearooms and "motor lodges." One traveler praised a converted New Hampshire commercial hotel for its "fraternal spirit" and easy ambience fostered by "a landlord whom prosperity had not spoiled." Here lonely traveling salesmen had been replaced by affable vacationists who met in the lounging room and talked heartily of the road. Mary Harrod Northend's *We Visit Old Inns* described a few dozen eastern hostelries with cheery landlords, wrought iron signs, crackling fires, tankards of ale, and mellow good cheer in low-ceilinged rooms.[13]

Most small hotels, however, were old but not historic. Relics of the post-Civil War era of small-town boosterism and rapid rail expansion, many were now hopelessly run down. A few small hotels were converted to suit the fantasies of motorists, but most remained hotels for drummers who were commonly portrayed as cigar-chomping wiseacres who made uncouth remarks as self-conscious motorists passed through the lobby. Guests often ate boarding-house style—in a hurry, and in a manner offensive to more polite tourists, especially women. English visitor James Muirhead wrote that "The manners of the other guests are apt to include a most superfluous proportion of tobacco-chewing, expectorating, an open and unashamed use of the toothpick, and other amenities that probably inflict more torture on those who are not used to them than would decorous breaches of the Decalogue." The *Nation* reported that the "second class" country hotel was little more than an "overgrown boarding-house in which the maid seats you 'where the reaching's good, sir!' "[14]

Interiors generally remained unchanged from the 1870s. To 1914 eyes this meant shabby, overstuffed Victorian parlor furniture and faded green wallpaper. Many tourists could easily identify with the claustrophobia of Sinclair Lewis's motoring heroine, Claire Boltwood, when she arrived at Gopher Prairie's only good hotel: "In the hotel Claire was conscious of the ugliness of the poison-green walls and brass cuspidors and insurance calendars and bare floor of the office; conscious of the interesting scientific fact that all air had been replaced by the essence of cigar smoke and cooking cabbage; of the stares of the traveling men lounging in bored lines; and of the lack of welcome on the part of the night clerk, an oldish bleached man with whiskers instead of a collar."[15]

Upstairs, bedrooms seemed hot and stifling; their cramped furnishings accentuated the poor ventilation. James Muirhead reasoned that mid-Victorian Americans had deliberately overheated and overstuffed hotel bedrooms and sleeping cars as an insecure expression of conspicuous consumption. Also, many had tended to fear drafts; hence the tight, airless feel of their bedrooms. After 1900, however, more casual home decorating standards prevailed. Designers urged readers of women's magazines to paint walls white, to expose wood beams, and to replace old, heavy drapes with light, gauzy curtains. Most suburban homes built between 1900 and 1920 had sleeping porches, for fresh air and outdoor sleeping were now valued as cure-alls for "jaded nerves and tired bodies."[16]

Lacking funds and adaptability many drummers' hotels did not bother to keep up. At Cedar Rapids's commercial house, Emily Post was almost tempted to turn back when she saw the bottle green wallpaper, stained carpeting, broken plumbing, and the "cowpath surrounding my big bed in my narrow room." James Montgomery Flagg's room in Lyons, Kansas, was a "dreary, little hole with a window overlooking a battered tin roof, grimy cheap lace curtains, one hanging electric light bulb decorated with greasy finger smudges, and a rolling prairie of a bed, clean but spartan." In some hotels, guests could not even count on a clean bed, for linen might be changed only once a week.[17]

Run by the unimaginative heirs of a better age, like the decaying Willard House of Sherwood Anderson's Winesburg, Ohio, these small hotels were doomed by marketing changes that made it unnecessary for drummers to stay overnight in every town. Catalogs allowed country people to send away for manufactured goods. Automobiles ensured their demise, for by switching to cars commercial travelers could make several towns a day. And because consumers could drive to larger marketing centers, drummers skipped many small towns entirely.[18]

For tourists seeking European or American colonial amenities, the reality could be very disillusioning. "Whether it is a newly furnished and refurbished Olde Humbugge, or merely plain Drummers' Hotel," *Country Life* observed, "it is sure to be lacking in the atmosphere of country comforts and fittingness that our country hotels should offer just as surely as do the unforgettable inns of England and the tiny wayside hostelries of France." Yet motorists without camping equipment could do little but put up with this trial of early travel. Unlike other aspects of the road ordeal, however, this inconvenience had little redeeming spiritual value. Worse, such places often charged tourists more than regulars. Auto clubs talked of listing rates in guidebooks, but in a seller's market, with few alternatives, this had little effect. In the memory of many early autocampers, then, was the picture of an "unsavory wayside inn" where they had paid "first-class prices for fourth-class accommodations."[19]

In addition to their dissatisfaction with hotel scheduling and atmosphere, autocampers complained of unreasonable dress codes, hostile service, and bad food.

The clothes issue illustrates how inadequately hotels served new touring needs. Not every hotel required evening attire, but clean, conservative street dress was compulsory. Even the more informal West required white shirts, collars, ties, and business suits for men and skirts and blouses for women. Eating out at a hotel was more formal than daily family dining. Hotel men considered dress an essential ingredient in a hotel's high cultural tone; since the mid-nineteenth century, hotels had served as primary public arenas for display of good manners and fashionable dress. Even in the rough Southwest, Fred Harvey's hotel restaurants required coats and ties well into the 1920s. In upholding the coat rule against a motorist's challenge in 1921, an Oklahoma judge put the case in a broader perspective:

Society in America has for years assumed jurisdiction to a great extent to dictate certain regulations of dress in first-class dining-rooms, and these conventions of society can not be entirely ignored, without disastrous results to those who serve a metro-politan public in such capacity. . . . Man's coat is usually the cleanest of his garments, and the fact that he is required to wear a coat serves notice that decorum is expected and creates a whole-some psychological effect.[20]

To an increasing number of middle-class Americans after 1900, however, these dress rules seemed artificial and anachronistic. Many no longer valued the hotel's role as a forum for conspicu-ous show. On vacations they wanted to escape convention. They particularly resented the coat rule at the shabbier mid-Victorian drummers' hotels, where such strictures seemed especially for-malistic.

Even if motorists were willing to carry an extra suitcase in order to change clothes for dinner, the initial arrival was something of a trial, especially for self-conscious travelers. Motoring was messy. Cars were open and roads were alternately muddy and dusty. "You go out to drive feeling clean and immaculate," Beatrice Massey reported, "and you come in with smuts and soot on your face and clothes, looking like a foundry hand."[21] Since motorists were still a minority at hotels, the arrival of a touring party in splattered motoring garb attracted considerable attention. A traveler's dress was a clue in the "sizing up" process by which doormen, bellmen, waiters, and clerks gauged their service. Un-kempt motorists felt they received inferior service because of their appearance; at best they sensed the secret scorn of ever-calculating servants. When bad weather forced his family to take refuge at a good Harvey House in New Mexico, Melville Fergu-son felt very embarrassed:

I feel yet the flush of shame that suffused my cheeks under that thick layer of dust as the bellhop held open the door and eight grimy intruders marched in, single file. Had we been clean, we should still have been objects of hostile suspicion, owing to our bizarre camping togs. But the bellhop, whatever his mental reac-tion, let us in, and we slunk off to our respective washrooms.[22]

Motorists felt even more misplaced at summer resorts where guests commonly changed dress three times a day.

Autocampers, on the other hand, enjoyed a freedom from the conventions of proper dressing. The privacy of the roadside camp did much to facilitate informality. In sociologist Erving Goffman's terminology, the autocamper rarely left the "back-stage" area of private family life, even as he traveled in the larger world. Having escaped both resort tuxedo and business suit, men relinquished stiff collars, ties, and shined shoes as well; women did not have to worry about soiling a clean blouse or

Atlantic City, New Jersey,
summer 1903. Urging a de-
centralized camp or cottage
vacation, *Ladies' Home Journal* asked: "Do you want your
children to be on dress
parade, continually strutting
as proudly as peacocks on
congested boardwalks?"
(Library of Congress)

keeping children out of the mud. Men stopped shaving; women left hair uncombed. Having traded "starched boiled shirts" for soft flannels, Dallas Lore Sharp felt like he "had split and shed the false front . . . as a cicada sheds its skin." At first tourists felt self-conscious about wearing khakis and old shabby clothes in public and often took along a set of respectable clothes just in case. But gradually they came to delight in flaunting tired protocol, especially as they moved westward. Thus Sharp did not discard his regular dress until Kansas. It is still a matter of controversy, however, whether the West *was* more informal. Historian Earl Pomeroy argues that westerners were as decorous as easterners, and that eastern tourists brought their hunger for informality—as well as the styles—with them. Projection or adaptation, the autocamper's casual dress seemed a refreshing alternative to hotel practices.[23]

Camping also spared tourists contact with disagreeable hotel personnel, especially clerks. Hotel chronicler Jefferson Williamson set 1840–1890 as "the Augustan age of the hotel clerk." Said in nineteenth-century myth to wear diamonds, the clerk held a desirable entry-level position into the privileged white-collar class. Often the sole small-town contact point with arbiters of good taste from the East, the suave, well-dressed hotel clerk transmitted genteel tastes and manners to uncouth country people and exerted a strong "cultivating" influence on the timid provincial guest. By the turn of the century, however, with more rail travel, the availability of other media for transmitting sophistication, and the depreciation of clerical work, the hotel clerk seemed more a mannerless despot than an authority; yet he still had the power to size up guests, delegate rooms, and humble the unwary. Unlike the European clerk, who was merely a servant, the American clerk considered himself an official, a member of the managerial class. "In America," Kathryn Busbey complained, "to ask the price is to court a stony stare or a haughty response of the maximum and minimum cost of accommodations, and you take what the clerk considers your appropriate tariff."[24] Well into the 1930s writers decried "supercilious" hotel clerks whose unmerited arrogance angered sophisticates and intimidated novices.

Tourists also complained of "tip-hungry bellhops," "gouging waiters," and "over-bearing baggagemen."[25] In a 1917 letter to a large hotel chain, a veteran traveler voiced the common complaint about hotel servants:

People in hotels want a cordial welcome, a kindly atmosphere and human warmth, which you do not give them. I found two things in your inns, obsequiousness and indifference. The porter was very anxious to carry my little valise that weighed ten pounds. The cloak room girl insisted on checking my hat and cane which I could easily take care of myself. The waiter manifested a lively interest in my wellbeing only at the crucial moment when I was counting my change. Venality and subservience stuck out all over these persons. Their acts and manner dumbly shrieked, "How much is this fellow going to give us?" The impression I got was not that I was there to be made comfortable, but was there to be fleeced. I was not a guest, I was prey.[26]

Unless they were especially seasoned, most motorists did not know the art of tipping. Critics of the practice argued that human beings should not have to bow and scrape for a living; rather, service should be included in the price. One also suspects that servants, being Americans themselves, were insufficiently deferential to those they served. Tourists objected to the "surly" waiter who seemed to expect a good tip regardless of service, as if it were his right. Such "insubordination" increased as war and restricted immigration reduced the supply of unassimilated domestics; yet tourists also distrusted the excessively subservient like the black or immigrant porter whose wide grin seemed to mask resentment. If nothing else, motorists were reluctant to entrust new cars to bellboys or doormen because they were notoriously hard on other people's cars. In wartime, patriots added fuel to the anti-tipping campaign by attacking it as a corrupt European vice and by demanding that hotel flunkies be drafted first. Several state legislatures outlawed tipping. During Prohibition bellhops and waiters were further discredited as known purveyors of illegal liquor.[27]

Long bothered by the tip problem, railroad and hotel men began to hire female bellhops and waitresses, who could be tipped less. A few considered eliminating tipping altogether. E. M. Statler, the hotel industry's Henry Ford, built giant hotels that specialized in gadgetry that reduced employee-guest contacts. In 1919 he introduced the servidor, which consisted of a compartment set into a door, with hinged panels on both the inside and the outside of the door. Able to set out and retrieve their laundry without facing a bellhop, guests were not required to leave a tip.[28] But even Statler could not eliminate servants or tipping. Priding themselves on full service, hotelmen employed large staffs at low wages. Barring an unlikely increase in wages, hotels could not get extra effort without the tip incentive. Indeed, western hotels that had avoided tipping before the war were now forced by economics to institute the eastern custom—ironically at the same time that European hotels began to adopt a standard 10 percent service charge.

For tourists annoyed by the hotel obstacle course of unfriendly clerks and outstretched palms, modern technology offered a return to pioneer autarchy. In an age proud of its labor-saving innovations—cafeterias, Piggly Wiggly groceries, household appliances that displaced maids, and, of course, automobiles[29]—the self-contained gypsy caravan inaugurated roadside self-service. By hauling almost everything they needed to live on the road—shelter, cots, food, transportation—tourists were virtually self-sufficient. An autocamper's outfit was an instant hotel to which one had to add only water. "Just back off the main road, in a little grove of white birches on the bank of a noisy brook, which will furnish water and perchance, fish enough to fill the breakfast frying pan!"[30] Like hotel guests, only more so, autocampers loved gadgets. Collapsible equipment that minimized work and space could be purchased or designed at home. Bolted to the running board, an auto tent unfolded almost automatically into a full-scale shelter complete with cot, springs, and headrest—the running board itself. An *ABC Sleeper* converted a car seat into a Pullman-like berth. An auto kitchenette carried everything from pots and pans to eggs and stove in a compact box. Most elaborate were the two- and four-wheel trailers: trim wagons that miraculously mushroomed into bungalows with beds, stove, table, and screened windows. The more ascetic camper might reduce his outfit to a frying pan, bed roll, and a few cans. Either way, self-reliance was the aim and result.[31]

The ability to cook one's own food was another reason to go autocamping, for hotel food was under attack at this time. "On the subject of [hotel] food," Emily Post wrote, "the cumulative effect of a traveling diet is queer. After many days of it you feel as though you had been interlined with a sort of *paste*. Everything you eat is made of flour, flour, and again, flour." Pasty sauce dominated city and country hotel menus because most dining rooms tried to be continental. The French menu had been a major innovation of the Boston Tremont House in 1829. At that time it was hailed as a cultural improvement, a sign of America's entry into the civilized world. By midcentury most hotels had adopted the French menu and often combined it with the native American practice of offering a staggering variety of dishes. The inevitable result was great quantity but mediocre quality. By the century's end European visitors and eastern hotel reformers questioned such "mongrel French" cuisine. A Philadelphia journalist called the standard menu "a dream of polyglot vocabular horror," a "linguistic free for all" with *huites sur coquille* followed by stuffed olives, then "saddle of mutton" and *pomes croquettes*. Why call a *canvas back duck*—a native American dish—*canard canvas-back*? Hotel progressives called for shorter menus, simple food, and plain English; others regarded the pretentious dining room as a source of pride, especially in small towns. Thus motorists usually had to endure an unpleasant dinner "where good food was manhandled by a foreign-born chef," or worse, by a local cook trying to be French.[32]

City hotels did little to improve food either. Even if they avoided the continental model, dishes tended to be overspiced, overcooked, and heavy on meat and potatoes. Hotel restaurants generally made money not on food but on the bar trade, and heavily spiced meals went well with liquor. Women travelers objected to "chophouse" fare that catered to male dining habits. At the same time, middle-class Americans were becoming more conscious of the need for more healthy, balanced meals, with fewer courses, less red meat and spices, more vegetables and salads. The hotel restaurant was no place for touring families, and few hotels made any effort to attract them until Prohibition.[33]

All hotel tourists complained of bad tasting hotel food. Emily Post deplored the Cedar Rapids menu of "anemic chilled potatoes, beans full of strings, everything slapped on plates any which way, and everything tasting as though it had come out of the same dishwater." At Gopher Prairie, Sinclair Lewis's Claire Boltwood ate the customary dinner of cold salty ham, acidic beets, bitter peas, and lumpy mashed potatoes. At another small midwestern hotel, James Montgomery Flagg washed down "a poor meal of half warm dishes" with a "Roman Punch" of "pink hair tonic and water slightly, not to say parsimoniously, frozen"—a depressing throwback to the 1880s. Advocating a roadside picnic, another tourist recalled the "soggy potatoes, congealed gravy, and leathery pie of the average village inn."[34]

There were few alternatives. In many small towns the hotel had the only public restaurant. On the outskirts of major towns roadside tearooms offered dainty little dishes that hardly whetted the appetite; as the female equivalent of a chophouse, the tearoom was not a suitable place for the whole family. In large cities, motorists had little energy after a tough day on the road to register at a hotel, change clothes, and then search for a restaurant outside. Many country hotels and summer resorts operated on the American plan, which required guests to take at least two meals in the dining room. In all, the hotel restaurant was another monopoly against which autocampers declared their independence.[35]

Autocampers insisted that their meals were both healthier and more convenient. According to popular nutritional theory, fresh air primed the palate—an important consideration at a time when a poor appetite almost automatically suggested a bad illness, especially tuberculosis. According to the AAA camping guide, an invigorating ride in the "ozone" was "a mighty spur to create a healthy appetite, to increase the good one into ravenous proportions, and to incite the jaded one into most unexpected relish of the plainest of food and plenty of it." "The appetite is like

Drummers, clerks, and bellhops at the Hotel Beale,
Kingman, Arizona, early
twentieth century. Women
motorists felt particularly uncomfortable in such tra-
ditionally male places.
(Library of Congress)

Hotel Champlain, Glens Falls, New York, 1890. Beginning in the 1890s, resort guests complained of pretentious food served by obsequious waiters in excessively formal hotel dining rooms. (Library of Congress)

"Eating catch-as-catch can, without table or napery." A family picnic near Yellowstone Park, 1923. (Library of Congress)

Topsy," wrote autocamper Harry Shumway, "it just grows and grows. About the sixth day out you want to throw bricks at all the doctors' signs. At the end of two weeks you will place a good bet that you can lick all the doctors in the state. . . . This is the kind of appetite that makes you want to eat eggs with the shells on and chew the bones of a chicken to a frail powder."[36]

Most autocampers cooked bacon and eggs, canned beans, and fried meat and potatoes, supplemented by fresh produce and milk purchased from farmers at cheap prices. In feeding themselves, autocampers delighted in taking the path of greatest convenience. The culinary equivalent of camping anywhere was opening a can and eating without elaborate preparation. A can took only a minute to heat up on the car radiator or over a small fire. Bacon and eggs or fried steak took only five minutes. A pot of beans could last a week. Convenience maximized time for the road or other camp activities. Also, travelers with fussy food tastes could be assured of food that was more familiar than hotel fare. Romantics extolled smoky campfire banquets of brook trout à la wayside and eggs à la trailer. As a backhanded slap at hotel pretensions, and as a symbolic link with the ever-practical hobo, canned food advocates called themselves tin can tourists. Finally, in contrast to formal hotel dining rooms where respectable middle-class families felt obliged to act politely even if drummers behaved boorishly, autocampers sprawled on the ground and ate "catch-as-catch-can, without table or nappery." In public restaurants little children had to behave like adults; in camp parents could behave like little children. "This terrible appetite seeks to overthrow all the pretty tricks that imported butlers have so patiently taught us," wrote Shumway. "Nobody waits for anything or anybody."[37] In this return to frontier manners, campers ignored both public proprieties and everyday domestic decorum.

The Camp as Family Reunion

The suspension of normal etiquette was vital to autocamping's well-publicized role as a unique family reunion, an occasion when family members got "reacquainted" under special circumstances. Hotels did not meet this need. Rather, they tended to *divide* families. This was perhaps the autocamper's most serious objection: nineteenth-century hotels did not suit twentieth-century families.

In orientation, hotels were either "commercial hotels" for men or "vacation hotels" for women and each sex felt out of place in the other's domain. In effect, this division institutionalized the Victorian "separate spheres" scheme, by which men worked full time so that their women and children could enjoy the finer things in life—that is, leisure. This system had been appropriate to an age of rapid industrial expansion requiring total male devotion to production. Woman's role had been to ameliorate this imbalance through devotion to higher ideals. The separate spheres bespoke a profound ambivalence about the nature and consequences of industrialization, but it also reinforced a basic commitment to those hard gains. The sacred home, presided over by a "cultured" woman, served as refuge for the working male. Knowing that such a place existed, and that he paid the bills, he could throw himself into the economic battle with even greater energies. Thus, through the family division of labor/ leisure, brutal economic gains seemed to be translated into humane ends. This division was most visible in the summer: While self-sacrificing husbands remained in hot, unsafe cities and took meals at commercial hotel restaurants, wives and children escaped to breezy country hotels and played. The commercial hotel served production, the summer hotel consumption. Through acceptance of these separate worlds, families held together—in symbiosis.

By 1900, however, the symbiotic spheres seemed to be breaking down. Insisting on a more active public life, many women were no longer content to remain decorously idle. With entrepreneurial independence giving way to bureaucratic discipline, many white collar males found less satisfaction at work. And given rapid technological and organizational change, the new world seemed to belong to children, whose values and education came increasingly from associations and institutions outside the home. According to the emerging "companionate" family ideal, middle-class families would be held together not by Victorian specialization, but by mutual, voluntarily given affection. Parents and children would relate as friends, companions. Recreation would play a vital new role in this scheme: families who played together would stay together. All members would play, not just women and children.

Although this concept actually signified a dawning "postindustrial" economy based on mass consumption, it was frequently perceived as a return to an earlier age when families cooperated on isolated homesteads, free of dangerous cities, bureaucratic pressures, and encroaching institutions. The suburban house where families communed with nature in pastoral isolation was one expression of this ideal. The ruggedly self-sufficient automobile tour was another. When families went touring, they did so as a closely bound unit; yet when they arrived at a hotel, they encountered an anachronistic institution that did not serve their companionate needs.

Whether city skyscraper or small town inn, the commercial hotel was a male institution. As late as 1919, according to *Hotel Management* editor J. O. Dahl, most hotels were occupied largely by drummers, and less than one percent of their guests were women. Hotel services catered to male needs: barber shops, meeting rooms, central business location, clerical help. As indicated earlier, hotel food was considered male in taste: much red meat, starch, spicing. What dining rooms lost on food, they frequently made up on liquor.[38]

A woman could enter almost any commercial hotel, but she did so under definite restrictions. Etiquette books advised women entering this hostile male territory to dress inconspicuously and keep to themselves. Women traveling alone faced special restrictions. Until the First World War, only unaccompanied women had, as a rule, to make reservations. The public lobby, with its coterie of traveling salesmen, was off limits to respectable unaccompanied women; many hotels provided separate ladies' entrances and waiting rooms. Women traveling with husbands remained at a discreet distance from the main desk, out of public view, while husbands registered. Until the 1920s few women signed hotel registers. Clerks made the official notation for women traveling alone. Except at a few fashionable metropolitan hotels, the register was not considered suitable reading for the gentler sex.

James Muirhead considered such separate female space a blessing, for in Europe unaccompanied women were more exposed. "If there is anything the Americans pride themselves on—and justly—it is their handsome treatment of women. Every traveler reports that the United States is the Paradise of women." To Muirhead, handsomeness of treatment was measured by the degree of segregation. As an unusual and therefore doubly vulnerable figure in the world of commercial hotels, the woman deserved special attention; thus chivalry confirmed and glorified the separate spheres. "Man meekly submits to be the hewer of wood, and the beast of burden for the superior sex." Muirhead reserved his scorn for those "indecent" provincial hotels that lacked such facilities. There women travelers faced certain embarassment.[39]

As more women began to travel after 1900, the first institutional response was to accommodate them in separate facilities such as New York's Hotel Martha Washington, the first female commercial hotel. According to one sympathetic observer, the Martha Washington was established in 1903 to meet the lodging needs of those women "who are, it would seem, going out into the world more and more, and away from occupations purely domestic. It is only just that such places should be provided where such women can have the care and attention that has almost universally been denied them in ordinary hotels." Similarly, women dining in public frequented female-oriented and frequently female-operated, tearooms and soda fountains, while the male chophouse remained off limits. Railroads added special tearoom cars and ladies' observation cars to parallel all-male smokers and club cars. As etiquette writers called for a revival of chaperonage, the Travelers' Aid Society stepped up efforts to protect female travelers from unscrupulous predators. Thus social change was channeled into traditional categories.[40] By 1914, despite much notice of the professional New Woman, the woman worker was only slightly less restricted than her mother:

If she goes to a state convention of her profession, she preferably goes with some other woman; if she stays at a hotel it is best for her to have some other woman with her. She shuns the hotel lobby and public restaurants and theatres in the evening, especially if she is alone. She hesitates to engage a man in conversation on the opposite side of a public table or on a train, or to invite a male friend to dine at a hotel or to go to the theatre with her. And yet a man may do any of these things as naturally as he would ride in a street car, and without giving the matter a second thought.[41]

With Prohibition, large commercial hotels did try to make up for lost bar trade by catering specifically to women with lighter meals, more female employees, and homelike decor. Grillrooms became coffee shops and tearooms; railroads integrated smokers. But to hotel people the most easily served, the most welcomed guest was still the traveling salesman. Lack of experience in sizing up women guests was a major reason for the strange looks clerks gave them upon registration. "Of course, I know our regular women patrons," one city hotel clerk confided in 1922, "but I confess that I can't remember them as easily as I can the men," who were easier to categorize. "I can tell a salesman the minute he comes to the counter; in fact, I can generally spot him clear across the lobby. He walks as if he knew just what he meant to do when he got there. . . . He knows all the ropes—and he likes to show that he knows them." Men further showed their sense of territoriality in the way they ogled women as they entered lobbies. Thus to the notoriety of being a dust-covered motorist in a rail-oriented hotel was added the incongruity of being a woman in a male arena. This sense of being out of place discomfited women travelers well into the 1930s, especially in provincial hotels where tradition died slowly.[42]

Unlike the forbidding male world of commercial hotels, the Victorian resort hotel was the woman's place. Here women practiced the cultivated arts of fancy dress and leisurely conversation financed by their husbands' hard work. As Thorstein Veblen noted, woman's office was "to consume vicariously for the head of the household."[43] While men remained behind in the city—"American fathers are never counted in the summer plans beyond figuring as the source of supply"[44]—lady guests sewed in the mornings, changed their clothes several times a day, and took long naps. The important thing was that idleness be purposeless and repetitive, the opposite of economic activity: "day after day, rocking and talking; and going in bathing, and coming out to lie on the sand until the hair is dry; a little nap, a little bridge, more rocking and talking, and then to bed." Even conversation was intentionally inconsequential; one disgruntled male likened it to the French *blague*—"the empty, amusing, good-natured talk that comes from nothing, and leads back to the home of its origin by a thousand devious routes." Another bored male guest characterized this resort routine as "miscellaneous idling."[45]

To devotees and critics alike, the veranda symbolized summer hotel life. Here guests rocked, sewed, talked, and watched the children or the view. If talking to strangers was proscribed in commercial hotels, such conversation was mandatory on the veranda. Ideally it was to be on a high plane, in keeping with woman's cultivating role. In practice, however, veranda talk also covered more personal topics. What the smoking car, the saloon, and the hotel lobby were to male culture, the hotel veranda was to the female sphere: an arena for casual intimacies among members of the same sex.

The dining room was another important focus of resort life. In commercial hotel dining rooms women were advised to dress inconspicuously. At resorts each meal required a change of clothes, for resort life dictated fashionable display. Some women were said to shop for months before heading off to the country.

Men dutifully visited families every couple of weeks, perhaps staying for a two-week stretch during the season. But if men knew how to act where business was transacted, they were uneasy outsiders at resorts, where idleness ruled. Dress requirements, in particular, were dismissed as onerous chores. While women projected individuality in the varied clothes they wore, men wore a uniform—the same dinner attire every night. Here *men* remained anonymous. Veranda conversation seemed like just idle chatter or, worse, vicious gossip; politics and business were not to be discussed on the veranda. Resorts like Saratoga that did try to accommodate male tastes with casinos and racing thereby lost their family hotel status. More than one wife questioned the eagerness with which men approached the Sunday evening trip back to town. The resort served the businessman mainly as evidence of his ability to support his family in a state of conspicuous indolence.

Back home the summer bachelor might actually enjoy his seasonal respite from genteel domesticity. Music critic Carl Van Vechten wrote that before World War I respectable women deserted New York and left Manhattan "a paradise for men from the end of May to the middle of September." The extra time at the office or in card games was his equivalent of the woman's veranda relaxation. His temporary exemption from family routines paralleled her release from housekeeping duties. At the end of the nineteenth century, when men began to take vacations, they frequently did so separately, in an entirely masculine camp environment, and engaged in such appropriately acquisitive sports as fishing and hunting. When a wife occasionally went along on such an outing, it typically ended with vows of "never again," reinforcing the belief that men and women had to go separate ways.[46]

Children belonged with mothers in this summer scheme. In line with their mother's display role, little children were dressed cutely, almost as an extension of their mother's wardrobe. Resorts also gave youths an opportunity to learn adult roles. Teenage girls were given full reign to practice feminine arts of display and idle chatter. The seaside resort was dominated by the "summer girl" in alluring bathing costume, followed by her "attendant swain." One typical mountain resort account sentimentalized the usual group of summer girls who were, of course, "anxious to breathe into one another's ears the confidences of young girlhood"—the idle chatter role—"or the tender messages of gentle souls that seek a mating." Young men, for their part, were supposed to court suitable young virgins and to learn how to act as gentlemen in society. For this they were best left to the company of women, who knew the rules better than their absent fathers.[47]

As an institution, the large summer hotel began to lose hegemony in the 1890s. In part, vacationists worried about heavy food, outmoded sanitary facilities, hot, ill-ventilated bedrooms, and, worst of all, the omnipresent fire danger. Designed to earn a year's profits in three months, many of these hotels were flimsily built. Virtually every major summer colony could record a recent disastrous fire. Also, some women began to complain of the old-fashioned idleness and hankered for more activity. "It has been neither profitable nor stimulating," wrote one dissatisfied woman, "to sit on hotel piazzas and listen to conversation seldom above the level of domestic difficulties."[48] Heralding the breakdown of the separate spheres, these women took to bicycling, hiking, and travel.

Furthermore, some old hands were disturbed by the latest wave of nouveaux riches flooding fashionable resorts. Since the 1830s, fancy resorts had served the upwardly mobile as useful arenas for status-confirming display and marriage brokering. The old-timers of the 1890s had been newcomers themselves in the 1870s, displacing the nouveaux riches of the 1850s, and so on. To established patrons, these obviously wealthy and ambitious new "types" seemed very vulgar. "They know absolutely nothing outside the narrow limits of their own vocations," observed one veteran, of an Atlantic City throng. "They represent crass materialism in its most helpless form; since they do not even know that there is any other life outside and beyond the life they live." Whatever beauty still remaining in genteel standards seemed hopelessly lost when subjected to the coarse mimickry of the new, socially mobile "masses."[49] That many of them came from immigrant stock made the new patrons even more objectionable to some old-timers. Thus, one convert to autocamping asked, "Why stick in one place, at fifty a week, keep dressed up like a circus pony, squat on the veranda, listen to the old and young maids ladle out the current scandals, observe Mrs. O'Goldburg try to out-dress Mrs. Sullivanstein, etc., etc.?"[50]

Easy veranda talk became impossible. In the old days, wrote one saddened commentator in 1914, the resort had served as Henry James's "social arena," a congenial place where one could look forward to "scraping up an acquaintance" with new people of "assured mutual social authenticity." "You chose a resort where nature smiled and where 'nice people' gathered." But now, with the more mixed clientele, sociability had given way to "armed neutrality." A fear of contamination caused women to erect barriers previously reserved for commercial hotels and passenger coaches. The best attitude at "public resorts," etiquette expert Marion Harland advised, was to be "pleasant toward all, and intimate with none"—the essence of "armed neutrality."[51]

Resort critics worried especially about the effects of such a crowd on the young. To Ladies' Home Journal editor Edward Bok, it seemed that one no longer met the "best" people anymore, only those who could afford it, "and quite as often as not these people and their children are not the people whom parents feel are the 'most desirable' either for their own acquaintance or for their children's." Mothers on the veranda could not screen their children's playmates, who might be a bit too "cosmopolitan" for safety. "Every phase of life at these hotels has in it a possibility disastrous to formative thoughts and principles." Where parents had once seen a certain cuteness in the way their well-dressed children imitated adult models, now the model seemed debased by the eagerness with which newcomers pursued it. The old ideal therefore became artificial. Fancy dress, once a sign of allegiance to a cultivated elite, was now just a fashion show. "Do you want your children to be on dress parade, continually strutting as proudly as peacocks, on congested boardwalks?" It all seemed too "commercial," too "make-believe," too "sensational." To Bok, democratization had rendered formality superfluous. What was left was mere faddishness and formalism.

"There is all the slavery of dress and none of its freedom."[52]

Travel was one alternative. Since the 1840s, successive waves of displaced resorters had toured Europe and, after the Civil War, the American West. As in the resort pattern, husbands frequently stayed home—or went as wearied chaperones. Just as men were unexcited by veranda life, they were portrayed as intolerant travelers. As a form of high cultural display, nineteenth-century travel remained within woman's sphere. The travel alternative was very expensive, however.

Beginning in the 1890s, some families turned to more remote farm boarding houses, smaller hotels, and summer cottages. Against the larger hotel's "herded life," the decentralized vacation spot offered private pastoralism. "The summer is not for the summer hotel," Bok wrote, "it is for the closest possible association with Nature." Against the "absolute restless discontent" of "flashy and unsatisfactory summer hotels," the cottage or farm stay promised tired mothers fresh air, a vegetable garden, long walks in green fields, restful naps "amid the sweet scent of clover." Bok hoped that city people would benefit immensely from contact with plain rural folk, whose old-fashioned values contrasted sharply with city ways. "The sanest, the highest lives are led by these people, and yet in our narrow horizon we think their lives are contracted. The fact is that we are narrow; not they. It is *their* lives that are *real;* not ours."[53] Bok's disgust with the ways of his own society and class signified a new form of alienation. Seeking authenticity, the modern bourgeoisie would now turn to the distinctly non-bourgeois—the simple rustic, the black "primitive," the timeless vagabond.

Children, too, seemed to need a less civilized summer vacation, not only because of the cosmopolitan invasion, but also because a new idolization of youth favored postponement of entry into full adulthood. Given adult doubts about modern society, children were best left in a more natural state. Since adulthood, with all its attendant confusions and frustrations, would come all too soon, childhood was to be savored. "Don't take all the pleasures out of his freedom-loving life by trying to make him conform to the routine life of a fashionable hotel," *Good Housekeeping* advised. "Ahead of him stretches many a day of restraint and convention."[54]

Moreover, given the uncertain direction of modern life, perhaps the young needed pragmatic self-reliance rather than genteel grace. The notion of socializing teenagers at resorts seemed out-of-date. To motorist Theodore Dreiser, a summer hotel scene of breathless young maidens pursued by earnest young men seemed "so naive, so gauche, so early Victorian." Writers now satirized the "silly flirtations" fostered by the "idiotic admiration" of idle women. The ideal of summer romance remained, but imagery became less Chesterfieldian, more Teutonic, and its locale shifted from veranda to forest:

Where two can wander and be quite alone, where the twilight keeps its secrets well, and where the breath of evening is full of soft suggestion—it is here that the true summer types are found—the clean limbed, graceful girl who feels the mysterious influence of that companionship of the open air which is the most sane of all the *philtres d'amour* that human magic ever dreamed of.

Contrast this with the effete types now seen likely to spend vacations in "seaside resort revels": the boy, "soft and flabby in his tissue, wears the spick and span garments of the young men of polite society," a precocious, effeminate, "supercilious mollycoddle." The female counterparts—"dainty little creatures, tied up in silk, silken gowns, and pink ribbons"—were spoiled, helpless, and self-centered. Progressive thought favored farm or wilderness, where children could relive the strenuous life of a more robust era.[55]

The summer farm or cottage also attracted tired, overworked husbands. A modern, consumption-oriented economy required that both sexes consume leisure. By 1900 domestic commentators agreed that men could not live by work alone, and, more important, they needed to play with wives and children for the sake of family unity. Here was the beginning of the companionate, recreation-based family. Writers for ladies' magazines worried about the bad effects of the separate spheres on home life. Wives were urged to drop their Victorian "reforming institution" role and become "pals" with husbands, lest they lose their restless men to clubs, saloons, or, worse, office stenographers.[56] Discussions of the "summer problem" painted dire portraits of what happened when husbands were left free in the city. For example, *Ladies' Home Journal* printed a letter from one woman confiding how she "preserved" her husband in the summer by staying home:

Privately, but none the less firmly, was I determined not to turn that admirable husband of mine out to bachelor grass. I've seen it done, too many times, with disastrous results to family happiness, to imitate the example of my women friends. A summer in town, with only club friends for companionship, the restaurants for a dining room, a house like a tomb for lodging, places so dangerous a strain on digestion and home influence that I did not hesitate to put my moral foot right down.[57]

If Prohibition was one expression of this "moral foot," the new summer ideal was another. Each aimed to save the family.

Men, for their part, were urged to take greater interest in their children, lest they lose all contact. Boys, in particular, were said to need a man's influence; yet they were unlikely to get it at home, with fathers absent all day, or in school where most teachers were female. "We are just beginning to realize that leaving the job of training young children almost exclusively to women as we Americans do, is not altogether a good thing," began one 1914 *Good Housekeeping* treatise. "The responsibility is heavy on mother, the extensive feminization of the teaching force is unfair to the children, and the monopolizing by women of the broadening effect of parenthood is unfair to the father."[58] By necessity, however, father's involvement had to be confined to leisure time and vacations.

The cottage or farm thus suggested a suburban-type solution. Here families could play together in a natural setting more secluded, casual, and restful than any large hotel.

Continued reliance on trains, however, hampered summer dispersion. Except for the very rich, who could afford overpriced cottages near railroad stations, most vacationists had to seek out boarding houses and small hotels near the village. Many of these places overcharged for facilities inferior to large hotels. Smaller hotels overadvertised their attractions while doing little to safeguard health. The annual search for a satisfactory small hotel came to be known as "the summer experiment." Popular literature caricatured the summer boarding house with three words: "flies, fleas, and mosquitoes."

Autocamping advocates eagerly exploited the wide gap between expectations and realities. To Frank Brimmer the resort was a place from which "you generally come home more exhausted than you went, more fly-smitten than a sailor ashore in Panama." Another autocamper reminded *Motor Camper and Tourist* readers of similar experiences: "You know what I mean, . . . one of those traps that advertise excellent boating, bathing, and trout fishing; and when you get there you find nothing more than a large mud-puddle—entitled Beauty Lake—well stocked with both plain and fancy mosquitoes, and where the last trout was captured by the late Monsieur Christopher Columbus."[59]

Behind such sarcasm stood the collective, occasionally tragic experiences of thousands of would-be health seekers. Well into the 1920s state public health journals reported worries about summer hotel sanitation, particularly typhoid. Noting the general longing "to get away from the city and to spend the summer in some shady rural retreat," one health official lamented that "too frequently the realization of this happy anticipation is a hasty return to the city and a long stay in the hospital, to be followed, perhaps, by the death of some loved one." Smaller, less expensive hotels, moreover, were not immune to undesirable "types," who were as eager to escape city heat as everyone else. One journal writer suggested that the "unscreened character" of some hotel guests could be as responsible for disease as rural ignorance.[60]

Enter the automobile. For some vacationists the car meant a wider choice of resort hotels to visit. If one seemed unsafe or too expensive, another down the road beckoned. Farmers' wives in areas once inaccessible by railroad began to take in automobile boarders; farm journals predicted a revival of New England farm prosperity based on summer boarding and land sales. Cars opened up cheaper land, far from rail depots, for cottage developments. Some cottages were built close to town so fathers could drive out nightly to rejoin families; a few talked of moving out there permanently—the beginning of auto-oriented suburbia. Instead of taking one extended vacation trip, the family might take several weekend jaunts through nearby countryside.

Yet reliance on "unsavory" wayside inns and fading drummers' hotels could mar such excursions. Moreover, the rest of the time, mothers were left with housekeeping chores, children played by themselves, and fathers remained commuting outsiders. And for many middle-class families the cottage was still more expensive than the summer boarding house or small hotel.

In effect, the roadside tent was a cheap summer cottage. As a "family affair," autocamping offered something for everyone. Brimmer pointed out that autocamping combined all previously separate vacation experiences into a single trip:

Does father crave to fish for trout and bass and pike and musky? Take him auto-touring. Does sister want to dip in the surf, or study art, or see the world? Take her automobile vacationing. Has grand-dad the "hoof and mouth disease" so that he craves the green of far-away courses? Auto-camp him to a dozen golf-courses. Does mother sigh for a rest from daily routines? Take her touring. Does Jack-the-Scamp weep, like Alexander the Great, for new worlds to conquer? Well take him tour-camping with you. Does baby need fresh mountain air far from flies and heat? Take him auto-camping.[61]

For women autocamping offered respite from housekeeping and an opportunity for sightseeing. Since cars carried more equipment more conveniently than trains or trolleys, camping wives were promised more comfort than in previous "never again" outings. At the same time, they were spared disagreeable commercial hotels. By preparing family meals, they could guarantee a healthier, more familiar diet than the average hotel fare, yet cook food less complicated than at home.

For children autocamping combined a summer camp and a summer school, for it was both primitive and educational. Instead of the questionable clientele of summer resorts, they met farmers and small-town folk. Instead of foppish manners, they learned history. Instead of being left to mother's care, they could fish and build fires with father. To Elon Jessup, author of *The Motor Camping Book,* this was the most important autocamping innovation:

"O, daddy, Look'et." [a child points from the car]
The particular object which Daddy is called to look upon is of no special importance. The fact of his being where and as he is, however, is a matter of utmost importance. In fact, from a recreative and educational standpoint, one might even call it in some respects the biggest event of the decade. Daddy, be it known, is a motor camper, sometimes generally referred to as a "tin can tourist"! Mommer and the whole canned family are with him. They always are.
It's nice to have daddy along. He's great fun when you get to know him. Always before he's gone off on fishing trips with somebody else. Yes, indeed, this is the first time the family's been all together on a vacation. They don't know just where they are going, but they're on their way.[62]

For fathers, autocamping offered unquestioned family leadership, both as camper and camp guide. Tent, khakis, and camp fire, all were comfortably within the male sphere. Motoring was also more producer oriented than veranda rocking or passive rail travel, for there were miles and sights to make.

Best of all, autocamping forced families to cooperate. A family on tour spent a great deal of time together. Six or eight hours a day might be spent in the car, a cramped space with no individual privacy. Life in a small, flimsy tent put a premium on harmony and selflessness. Setting up camp, preparing and eating three meals, sitting around the evening camp fire, these were all done together. The AAA's 1920 *Official Manual of Motor Car Camping* outlined the principles in pitching camp:

Each member of a party should have his or her allotted task. Thus, while one gets out the tent, erects it, and prepares the cots and bedding, another will get the stove, if one is used, ready and unpack the pots, pans, dishes, and food, while still another, if there are that many in the party, will hustle the wood, light the fire, and bring the water. Should there be a fourth member, it will be his or her lot to wash the dishes and pots when the meal is over, a task which had best be shifted from time to time as nobody likes to wash dishes.[63]

"Woods housekeeping" had always entailed a systematic division of labor, but in autocamping, with its daily making and breaking camp, efficiency was especially important. Each family had to work out its own system to minimize work and maximize time on the road. Generally it took several hours to make camp the first night, for everything would be packed wrong. Within a few days, however, as the trip took on its own special rhythm, the group would have its routine well in hand. "We soon learned that camping parties must be organized as well as big corporations, so each of us had a certain amount of work allotted to us, and after we had been out a week we could pitch camp as quickly as the old-timer." "We were to learn many new kinks," another autocamper wrote, "and each day's experience taught us how to improve upon and expedite the camp routine."[64] This successful adaptation to the demands of road life was one means by which novices became professional travelers.

If the touring family resembled a well-drilled army unit, the worst thing was to have a slacker along. "A slacker is sure to spoil the good comradeship which should prevail in order to make camp life thoroughly enjoyable."[65] Every member was intimately involved from start to finish. The trip was a closed set of experiences, different for each group, with no possibility for disengagement once home was left behind. Father could not go to the office; children did not go to school. As strangers in unfamiliar territory, the family had to draw together for security, subsistence, and companionship. Novelty and hardship made the trip unique. Preparing for the trip, as well as reliving it afterward, joined family members in common cause and experience.

In characterizing this intensified intimacy, some campers wrote of rebellion. Modern life, they argued, threatened family vitality. While the commercial octopus kept fathers in the office, schools raised the children. Large corporations dictated what families ate and wore. Transit companies and railroads dictated where they could live and play, herding them into apartment blocks and crowded vacation places. Mass magazines, movies, and, after 1920, radio dominated leisure. The hectic pace and distractions of modern life sent family members on their separate ways. All that remained was the brief summer interlude, when families might get reacquainted. Thus, the resort hotel that divided families even further was the last straw in a year-long battle against family erosion, "the climax of social negativeness," as one angry father put it.[66]

Autocamping seemed to restore family cohesion. If family ties were tenuous at home, on the road they were very strong.

Joyfully do parents and children flee at length from the Gomorrah of profiteering landlords [of apartment houses] to the fellowship of the roadside camp-fire. And the soul of the whole matter is this fact: [autocampers] sacrifice their home ties lightly because they bind them lightly. Only in song do they pay tribute to the theory of there being "no place like home."[67]

Indeed, life in this self-contained, self-sufficient roadside homestead seemed warmer, more communal, more homelike than home itself. "If the home is where the heart is (and it is) then the

Motor Camper who takes wife and children on the camping trip finds home in the car and wherever the car may stop. That place where camp is set up for the night, there is 'Home.'" Alone in nature along the timeless, boundless open road, campers hoped to regain the "free cooperation of individualized family life" of a bygone age.[68]

From Fad
to Institution

Municipal
Autocamps,
1920–1924

It is an irony of modern travel that those who flee off the beaten track often beat a path for those they flee. Students of mass tourism have noted that in the evolution of a popular attraction the initial discovery is usually made by eccentric "drifters" who deliberately seek to escape crowded, overly institutionalized vacation places. In a democratic society of romantic individualists, however, the ability to be a nonconformist cannot long be confined to a small elite. Moreover, an economy increasingly reliant on the consumption of leisure requires an expanding consumer base. But democratization and expansion inevitably change the travel experience. With numbers comes a specialized tourist infrastructure to control, service, and exploit the increased flow.[1]

Autocamping began as an anti-institutional sport. Autocampers delighted in breaking out of familiar summer patterns, escaping crowds, going anywhere without having to make detailed arrangements or join a group. The fellowship of the road had no membership list; one's roadside apartment had no mailing address. It was not quite anarchy, for the road had its rules and its society, but road life was still relatively unorganized, decentralized, nomadic.

This random squatter stage lasted only a few years. By the early 1920s autocampers generally stopped not along the roadside but in public campgrounds in municipal parks. Somewhere between 3,000 and 6,000 autocamps existed in the country. In 1922 Minnesota had 150, Colorado 247. Wisconsin claimed 300 (1923), Indiana boasted 233 (1926), Texas 174 (1924), Florida 210 (1925).[2] Some were very small, entertaining only a few autocampers. Others were veritable cities, like Denver's Overland Park, "the Manhattan of auto-camps, the middle-western metropolis of the thermos bottle and khaki lean-to." Established in 1915, this

4

"Motor City" was the recognized "progenitor of the autocamping park." Spreading over 160 acres along the Platte River, its 800 lots—each 25 by 30 feet—accommodated over 2,000 autocampers. Each lot was no more than 150 feet from a hydrant and was lighted by electric bulbs. A three story central club house had a grocery, kitchen and grill, steam table, comfort stations, showers, barber shop, lunch counter, and laundry room with eight tubs. Seattle and Omaha had similar "metropolises." Indeed, enthusiasts reported that almost every town, big or small, seemed to have a free autocamp. By 1923 a municipal engineer could see a general tendency toward standardization of camp conveniences. The average small town camp on a main road could expect 50 to 60 cars a day. The 10- to 15-acre camp offered, as basic necessities, good water, maintained privies, electric lights, wood- or gas-burning stoves in a central kitchen building, a lounge area, cold showers, a caretaker, and a laundry room with tubs and washboards.[3]

Simple autocamping had obviously grown quite elaborate. Actually, the process of elaboration began with the very first articles praising roadside gypsying. Early autocampers wrote with missionary zeal. Flaunting eccentricity, they sought popularity. By 1920 they had achieved it. "Motor Car Camping Grows More Popular Each Year," was the title of one *American Motorist* survey that year. "Camping is getting all the rage," noted autocamper Harry Shumway in 1921. "I suppose we'll see tents and wood fires in Central Park if the thing keeps on. Here's hoping." Camping promoter Frank Brimmer found the attention especially satisfying, for autocamping could no longer be dismissed as a fad. It was now "established as a tried and seasoned American avocation—nay an institution," which was about the greatest compliment to be paid in a country often said to be lacking established institutions. "The sport is national in scope—it may become *the* American sport," wrote another enthusiast. "Get out on the highways and you will think everybody is doing it." In 1921, when President Warren G. Harding joined Henry Ford, Thomas Edison, and Harvey Firestone on one of their closely reported autocamping trips, it seemed that everybody *was* doing it.[4]

Even the arduous transcontinental run, once an option only to the adventurer, seemed an everyday occurrence—an extended Sunday drive. Elon Jessup estimated that 20,000 Americans drove cross-country in 1921, compared to only twelve in 1912. That so few actually did it was less important than that everyone *could* do it: "Cross country motoring is no longer reserved for the daring few doers of stunts, questers of thrills, but democratically speaking, it is now the divine right of any and all Americans who possess anything that rolls on wheels."[5]

Promoters used statistics to suggest the magnitude. Jessup es-

"Everybody's doing it." A widely reported autocamping trip, 1921. President Harding is just to the right of center. Thomas Edison is just left of center. The first man to Harding's left is Henry Ford. (Library of Congress)

In autocamping, "the main thing is that everybody is a good fellow, willing to do his or her share." Henry Ford chops wood. (Library of Congress)

timated that 9 million Americans would go motor camping in the summer of 1921. *The New York Times* guessed that out of the 10.8 million cars on the road in 1922, 5 million would be used for camping. At an average of three passengers per car, this meant 15 million autocampers. The Chicago Auto Club put the figure at 10 million autocampers in 2 million cars in 1923. "The national horde of motor campers mounts higher!" exclaimed one writer that year.[6] The *Saturday Evening Post* put it at 15 million people in 5 million cars for 1924. The slightly more cautious AAA estimated 12 million campers in 3 million cars for 1926. Generally the figures ran between 10 and 20 million autocampers for the mid-1920s. Perhaps the only certain figure was that car registrations increased from 6.7 million in 1919 to 17.5 million in 1925.[7] It seems reasonable that the number of autocampers increased at least proportionately, and given tremendous publicity, improving roads, and, most important, well-equipped municipal autocamps, the increase was probably much greater.

The story behind this increase involved the interaction of three parties: local government, town businessmen, and tourists.

Government Intervention

The free campground was the first roadside institution designed to balance public order, private profit, and tourist comfort. In the beginning order was the major concern. The fact was that even before 1920 roadside autocamping was getting out of hand. Growing numbers of campers after 1920 made matters worse.

The root of the problem lay in the libertarian appeal of gypsying. Autocampers sought to escape authority. "Freedom from" was a major attraction. By 1920 it appeared that the intimacy with nature so attractive to autocampers amounted to full-scale appropriation of flowers, trees, farmers' crops, and private property. Only a few orthodox wilderness buffs carefully left sites as they found them. Most autocampers viewed nature as a resource to be manipulated rather than as a treasure to be preserved. Tourists also misconstrued the openness of the public road. They did not realize that the roadside itself belonged to neighboring property owners.[8]

Farmers and other roadside natives had trouble with automobilists from the very start, but this was primarily near large cities, where affluent day-trippers tangled with resentful country folk. For a brief while, when autocamping was just beginning, outlying farmers were more sympathetic. Here was a new market for home produce as well as an opportunity for outside contact. By the early 1920s, however, many rural areas had had enough. Roadsides were strewn with garbage, especially with tin cans, the autocamper's emblem. "We are living in the tin can era," *Outing* noted, "and like the antediluvian beasts, the can is leaving its imperishable records in every geological strata on the earth today." Tourists broke off fruit tree branches to decorate their cars or graft at home, picked flowers, corn, apples, and even milked the cows. Schoolyards were left a mess. "Their carelessness in the use of public property is atrocious. Instead of cleaning up the litter and refuse they have made, and properly leaving the premises, they leave the yard strewn with refuse and paper," bemoaned an autocamper about the "shortsightedness" of many motor campers.[9]

Some responses were voluntaristic. The Motorists' League for Countryside Protection, formed in 1923, pleaded with autocampers to be careful. "The motor camper has got to take hold of himself." The AAA issued a "Courtesy of the Camp" code asking tourists not to leave trash, not to pull up flowering bushes by the roots, not to leave fires burning, and more. Frank Brimmer's 1923 guide, *Autocamping*, devoted a chapter to autocamping ethics, warning of legislative restrictions if campers did not take care. Brimmer's Golden Rule was: "Autocamp upon others as you would have others autocamp upon you." Tourist magazines tried to shame offenders with sarcasm: "They are pioneers, explorers all. Yea, some of them may be termed vandals, slaying and burning as they go, bringing down upon innocent Nomads of the road the justified wrath of injured farmers."[10] But the problem could not be solved so simply. Too many motorists were out on the road, and being on the road meant freedom from constraints.

Farmers took matters into their own hands, posting no trespassing signs and standing guard with shotguns. "Sunday is not a day of rest for any farmer living within 100 miles of a fair sized city. It has become a day of increasing vigilance, for the crops must be protected from the pillaging auto-tourists or auto-riders." One "Notis" outside a San Diego ranch angrily warned that "trespassers will B persecuted to the full extent of 2 mongrel dogs which neve was over sochible to strangers and 1 doubl brl shot gun which ain't loaded with sofa pillors. Dam if I ain't gotten tired of this hell raisin on my place." School boards closed their yards and local police began to ticket blatant offenders, but motor campers who exploited the easy anonymity of nomadic life were hard to catch. "Tourists, like gypsies, frequently leave disorder and perhaps disease in their wake," *Minnesota Municipalities* noted. "They appear in early evening and depart at the first streak of dawn, and none knows whence or whither. We only know that they have been."[11]

In their desire to move and camp without constraint, many campers also failed to take adequate safety and sanitary precautions. All guides reminded tourists that a good camping spot was not simple to find. A summer thunderstorm could turn an idyllic trout stream into a raging river. Moreover, some campers used streams as toilets, or failed to locate their makeshift latrines far enough from drinking water. Everyone wanted to drink clean stream water—a major part of the outdoor experience—but many streams were polluted by nearby towns, industries, and other campers. Despite their concern for health, campers were soon exposed to dread diseases like typhoid that by 1920 were no longer found in cities. The growing numbers of inexperienced autocampers worsened the dangers. By 1924 wayside camping entailed carrying your own water.[12]

Establishing and subsidizing free autocamps could be justified on purely defensive grounds: to keep tourists and natives separate, and to protect tourists from themselves. This conservationist-segregationist rationale guided state and national parks in setting up special, controlled campgrounds. Well publicized in municipal management journals, these early public camps induced some progressive park boards to follow suit for public safety reasons alone. According to one Denver official, a municipal camp would "discourage indiscriminate roadside camping," preventing "the camper from 'squatting' where he is not wanted."[13] In many towns, however, public authorities were as interested in local profits and publicity as in regulation.

Boosters

The earliest and most telling evidence of autocamping's commercial potential was the move by local business groups to cash in on this new tourist trade. Local businessmen viewed autocampers not as ascetic campers or as eccentric gypsies but as affluent tourists who, although capable of paying hotel rates, were tired of shabby, crowded accommodations. Establishing a free camp, boosters argued, would not take away hotel business because these vacationists disliked hotels anyway. In some cases, the camp was proposed as a temporary expedient while a better town hotel was being built. The inadequacies of most drummer hotels—particularly in the West and Middle West—were widely acknowledged, and the 1920s were years of widespread hotel renovation. Encouraging people to camp in the middle of town in the interim would recapture tourist dollars that would be lost if campers stayed by the roadside. Hotels might even benefit indirectly from the general prosperity to be created, for many campers did like to stay in a hotel every once in a while just to clean up. "The general tendency of tourist camps is to encourage tourist travel by automobile," went this optimistic argument. "The hotel man profits by this increased tourist travel, as a portion of the increase results in at least occasional patronage."[14]

As in many towns, the citizens of Ashland, Oregon, decided to establish a free municipal campground for autocampers "with a view to getting some of the dollars they were leaving as they went through."[15] Because estimates of potential tourist expenditures tended to reflect past experiences with affluent rail tourists, they were often very optimistic, ranging from $1.00 to $5.00 a day per person. At the very least, tourists would buy gas and oil, food, supplies, and souvenirs, and perhaps these receipts would trickle down to the general good. Farmers, too, would be profitable campers, for they often combined a short touring vacation with the business of buying major supplies and equipment. One widely cited article pointed to a touring farm family who despite owning a shabby Ford, spent $1,900 on supplies while staying in a town camp. Even the lowest estimate, $1.00 a day per tourist, indicated a good investment. From a few hundred dollars spent on basic facilities, the smallest town might reap several thousand dollars in shared prosperity. Such windfalls seemed plausible given reports that one Lincoln Highway town counted 764 tourists in one day in the summer of 1920; that Cheyenne, Wyoming, hosted 2,540 autocampers from 31 states in *one day* that same season; and that Coeur d'Alene, Idaho, entertained 1,382 campers in 439 cars in August 1920.[16]

Sometimes a civic club or chamber of commerce sponsored the public camp. In most cases, however, boosters looked to the town government—usually the park board. To attract tourists to downtown stores, camps would ideally be situated in a centrally located town park. Generally responsive to business interests, public authorities accepted the responsibility. Also, with growing acceptance of the ideology of mass leisure in the early 1920s, establishing free parks was politically popular. To have a municipal recreation program just like Denver's or Seattle's was to be truly up-to-date. Furthermore, an old-time booster idealism mixed with expectations of profit. Camp backers commonly included women's associations, scouting groups, churches, and municipal reformers as well as self-interested garage men, highway associations, and merchants. In these glorious years of unquestioned automotive expansion, it was an honor to be chosen as a point along a national route. To play host to automobile tourists was to participate in an important new movement, to have special contact with the outside world. "An auto camp, in my judgment," wrote a Denver civic leader in 1920, "is just as essential to any city, town, or community that wants to thrive and prosper and keep ahead of the times, as a railway station."[17]

Knowing that tourists commonly exchanged information about roads, sights, and pleasant towns, boosters hoped for good publicity from an attractive free park. A Michigan handbook for "progressive communities" interested in establishing autocamps promised that every well-treated transient "proceeds on his way with a feeling of pleasure and satisfaction, thus unconsciously becoming a perpetual "booster" for the community." To be known through the tourist grapevine or tourist magazines as an "enterprising community" was a great honor. "You could not conceive of another advertising medium that would stand for as much for the upbuilding of your community as a well-conducted autocamp," wrote one Portland, Oregon, man.[18]

So, like nineteenth-century boosters who had competed for rail routes by sponsoring attractive hotels, towns vied for motorists with attractive campgrounds. "When the new khaki-clad gypsies approach a town," *Illustrated World* observed, "they see various signs inviting them to camp overnight, or 'stay as long as you like, stranger and you'll not be a stranger long.'" South Bend, Indiana, claimed to have a fully equipped facility for campers, with water, stoves, and firewood. Entertaining 2,000 visitors in the summer of 1924, the free camp of Beloit, Wisconsin, boasted of two wells "of unexcelled spring water," camp sites with wood tent floors to smooth out bumps and to keep water out, brick ovens at every site, a full-time custodian, and a community house "of generous proportions" with showers, toilets, and lounge area. The camp in Lebanon, Indiana, offered cold showers, free wood, a community building with flush toilets, tables and benches at each site, and a full-time matron to greet and serve autocampers.[19]

Western camps generally offered the most, both because hotels were worse there and because many western towns hoped to convince affluent tourists to invest or settle permanently. On the West Coast, Melville Ferguson found, "they pamper the camper." Ashland, Oregon, advertised three kinds of mineral water, playgrounds for children, wading pools, kitchenettes with gas stoves in a central building, hundreds of electric lights with individual switches (so retiring campers could sleep in the dark), a large comfort station "of the most modern type," cement incinerators, a laundry wagon that picked up wash each morning and returned it the next, and a nearby grocery store stocked with all the necessities. The free "wayside auto inn" of San Bernardino, California, had twenty concrete tables, stone barbecue pits, a post office, and checker tables in addition to such standard amenities as showers and flush toilets. The "come-in-glad-to-see-you-spirit" of California camps confirmed one tourist's impression of the West as a more friendly, comradely place. "The most conspicuous thing in the West now is a sign, 'Free Municipal Camp Ground, One Mile,'" *Nation* reported.[20] Eastern towns, on the other hand, lagged behind, confirming the image of eastern stinginess. Here rail and hotel interests were stronger, and boosterism played a smaller role in local affairs. But pressure built through the tourist grapevine, and the first New England free camp opened in 1921.

By 1924, the move to channel autocampers into regulated campsites was generally successful—from a management point of view—for tourists could not find sites along the roadside. Where they did not find no-trespassing signs, they found barbed wire. Yet, despite this restriction on road freedom, most auto-campers applauded the change.

Motor Hoboing Deluxe

Roadside autocamping may have been the most romantic way to go, but it had its problems. Because the municipal autocamp seemed to resolve these problems, it was warmly received by both veterans of several seasons and other vacationists originally put off by the difficulties of gypsying.

In equipping themselves, for example, many autocampers never attained the desirable balance between "going light" and being "at home" on the road. All guidebooks admonished autocampers to go light. The ideal was a neat looking, simple camping outfit that served all of one's needs, yet could be unpacked in fifteen minutes. Such an outfit maximized road time and minimized work time. A well-designed, well-packed outfit merited respect and admiration. "To step up to the old car and fish out from somewhere the right little 'jigger' to meet the situation—yet apparently to have very little 'duffle' on board—that's the mark of a veteran."[21] The ability to move comfortably yet easily in the world was one sign of being a traveler rather than a tourist. Experienced voyager Beatrice Massey boasted that from the uncluttered appearance of her car she might have been shopping on Fifth Avenue rather than motoring cross-country. Just as seasoned hotel travelers knew how to pack one small suitcase, practiced autocampers were supposed to know how to simplify gear. But the guides were not particularly specific. "Unburdened, yet we camp comfortably," was one vague rule of thumb. "Fully, but not elaborately equipped," was another. Or, "Go light, but right."[22] In the end autocampers had to learn by trial and error.

Achieving the elusive balance between necessities and luxuries was one ingredient in developing the right system that bound the camping family. The first time was the hardest. It took time to figure out how many dishes or blankets one might need; at home one was rarely so calculating. The prospect of driving through unfamiliar territory made things even more complicated. Novices approached the first auto tour with the understandable insecurity of one about to enter a region inhabited by wild natives—if inhabited at all. Although there was some basis for

At home in a public auto
camp near Yellowstone Park,
1923. (Library of Congress)

Doing chores, Colorado forest camp, 1923. (U.S. Forest Service, National Archives)

A well-equipped campsite, Colorado, 1923. (U.S. Forest Service, National Archives)

this, given poor roads and uncertain garages, emergency services did exist in most areas. "Get over the idea that you must pack a ton or two of freight to guard against emergencies," an early guide advised. After his trip from Chicago to Los Angeles in 1921, Vernon McGill reported that it was unnecessary to carry a gun. Others advised, quite seriously, that one could buy groceries even in Nebraska; telephones existed in North Dakota; farmers played jazz in Vermont; Wyoming cowboys knew all about carburetors.[23] Nevertheless, many campers piled it on:

Some people just keep piling on odds and ends of camping junk until it runs over the sides and even the top of the car. I have heard many a flivver squawking under an overload on a hill; until I have wished one of those Humane Societies would "get after" the driver. There ought to be a law against loading more than the furnishings of a three-room apartment and two families on one flivver, or four-lunged car of any kind.[24]

Some tourists found this sight more pitiful than amusing. Beatrice Massey exclaimed that a traveling circus was an "orderly, compact miniature" compared to the "two-ton equipment enthusiasm" she saw on her 1919 run.[25] Campers most afraid of seeming to be "traveling grocery stores" went to hotels, but those wishing to avoid such places tended to pack something for every contingency. Later, most narrators sheepishly agreed that they had taken far too much.

Behind the problem of carrying too many supplies lay a serious contradiction inherent in the very principles of autocamping: the gypsy delight in rootless mobility conflicted with the bourgeois delight in a sport that promised home comforts in outdoor life. One goal of gypsying was to get out from under "the absurdity of material things which clutter up life; the clocks that do not run, the old hats, the faded embroideries, the pictures no one looks at, the wrapping paper and string, the boxes that may some time be needed."[26] Campers complained of being "roof ridden" before their vacations; theirs was an almost claustrophobic sense of being buried by the elaborate equipment and furnishings that crowded the upper-middle-class home. Gypsies were enviable because they got along with just a small wagon load of goods, rather than a ten-room house crammed with furniture, decorations, and clothes. Tramps seemed to survive with even less—a small sack. By using cars as caravans, vacationing motor vagabonds hoped to achieve some of the same mobility. Once they packed their caravans and slammed the door of the house, they had no choice but to live with what they had. Packing only what they absolutely needed imposed limits, and limits paradoxically meant more freedom—freedom to play with families, to move, to see new sights. In gypsying they escaped not only hotels, fixed routes, and beaten paths but also the distracting materialism of everyday life.

Yet it was precisely the autocamper's ability to tour in a "home on wheels" that made the sport more attractive than earlier wilderness camping. Earlier campers had been forced to rough it because they could take only so much by train, but autocampers did not want to suffer like regular campers. The hard wilderness camp was a thing of the past. Campers took gas stoves, heaters, and lots of blankets. They sat at collapsible tables instead of on the ground, slept on spring beds instead of in bedrolls. This was the suburban, compromise nature of car camping: to go "hoboing de luxe," to be "as primitive as Robinson Crusoe, with gasoline trimmings," to "revert to nature with a car and teabasket." The well-equipped autocamper could live "in a roadside apartment as cozily and comfortably as at home." Writers frankly acknowledged and praised this unprecedented ability to combine modern conveniences and outdoor living.

Modern science and invention have joined hands in smoothing the road to the enjoyment of outdoor life in a way that we seldom stop to understand. Anything that makes for a greater opportunity to get closer to Nature, to seek her out in all her beauty and vigor, is something to be appreciative of, and there are many of us who would lack the courage or the inspiration to get far out of doors if the way were not cleared, as it were, and made easy by the addition of comforts that belong essentially to civilization.[27]

As Harry Shumway noted, this was "pretty soft rough stuff," but Adelaide Ovington justified such comforts on the grounds that everyday city life was hard enough. "We do not go into the woods to rough it, we go to smooth it. We get it rough enough in town."[28]

In a sense, motor gypsies were caught between what historian Arthur O. Lovejoy has called hard and soft primitivism.[29] The former idealizes the stoic, ascetic, disciplined simplicity of more "savage" people—in this case, the road-weathered vagabond. Calling for greater self-sacrifice and fewer luxuries, hard primitivism is the over-civilized man's longing for a less effete, more virtuously virile life-style—Theodore Roosevelt's "strenuous life." Soft primitivism, on the other hand, is more hedonistic and pastoral. Its model is not the Spartan camp, but the Garden of Eden, where men lived effortlessly off nature's generous bounty. It is the nostalgia of the overworked. Although autocampers did write favorably of road hardships, as recreationist consumers they tended to lean toward the soft ideal, which better fit the new ideology of affluence; that is, through democratic technology and mass consumption, modern capitalism would create a leisure society where people would work less and enjoy life more.

By 1920 commercial equipment manufacturers offered gear designed to resolve the dilemmas of packing by maximizing collapsibility: gear that served several purposes, folded up, and was easily unpacked. The municipal autocamp took the solution one step further by providing domestic apparatus that tourists would no longer have to carry: fireplaces, picnic tables, coin-operated gas stoves in community kitchens, electric lights; tent floors (and occasionally tents as well); recreational equipment like swings, slides, and balls; emergency shelter and wood. The nearby grocery and gas station made carrying fifty pounds of food or a full box of tools unnecessary. Since tourists still pitched their own tents, cooked their own meals, and developed their own system, they could be both comfortably at home and independently mobile. And like camping gadgetry, autocamp equipment had its own fascination. Campers soon talked of the latest conveniences offered at one camp, or the failure of another camp to keep "up-to-the-minute." Finding what each camp had to offer became part of the sightseeing experience.

Well-equipped autocamps also helped to resolve a major question in family autocamping: How do you keep wives happy? According to convention, camping was fine for men, who liked to play at being little boys again, but it was unattractive to women. "In summer, man's thoughts turn to the great outdoors; woman's to a fashionable resort with wide verandas and a jazz orchestra,"[30] yet the companionate ideal urged women to go along with husbands. Although roadside autocamping was billed as being easier than traditional wilderness camping, many women remained unconvinced. There was still too much difficulty.

Sensing that the sport would grow only if they could overcome lingering female doubts, after 1920 equipment manufacturers pitched their appeal mainly to women. Women were described as being especially afraid of crawling insects, cold, and ground moisture; hence, the appeal of big tents, folding beds, and auto beds that could be set up right in the car. Frank Brimmer attributed the spectacular growth of the camping goods industry in the mid-twenties partly to the participation of comfort-appreciating women. Women were particularly responsible, Brimmer noted, for the rising sales of camp beds with springs (instead of plain cots), air beds (instead of cotton pads), and elaborate kitchen kits (instead of the old frying pan and tramper's pail).[31] As part of this effort to attract the family trade, municipal camps offered clean privies, showers, and rain shelters to appeal specifically to women's needs.

Wives also had to be accommodated as camp workers. Women usually did all the cooking. Early autocampers generally stuck to traditional male camping fare—beans, fried food, bacon and eggs, and canned food—because it was fast and convenient. But after 1920 writers noted that many women hesitated to camp because they disliked such a monotonous, indigestible diet. This was a serious problem, for it was woman's role at home to safeguard family health. Proponents therefore sought to convince prospective autocampers that they could eat as well in camp as at home. For chefs tired of canned milk, tinned goods, smoked and salted meats, dried fruit, and stale hardtack, *Motor Camper and Tourist* regularly printed recipes for pancakes, omelets, poached (rather than fried) eggs, meat loaves, macaroni, salads, roasts, and breads. "It means a little more thought and a little more time when you are planning your eats," one adviser allowed, "but it makes all the difference between fussy, tired, sick children, and children who are full of pep and joy. And you know yourself how much better you feel when you don't wake up with a dark brown taste in your mouth."[32]

But eating this way required more work and more equipment. It was hard to cook a wholesome meal over a simple wood fire. "The difference between the men I have camped with and myself, generally speaking," Mary Roberts Rinehart wrote, "has been this: they have called it sport; I have known it was work." For wives' sake, therefore, convenience tended to outweigh picturesqueness; autocampers took along gasoline stoves, Dutch ovens, portable refrigerators. "It may not be romantic to cook over gasoline, when all the traditions of camp life call for a glowing fire," Mary Bedell admitted, "but remember, we were *modern* Gypsies, and found some recent improvements of great advantage in a life such as we were leading."[33] Such improvements added still more weight and bulk to the car's pack. Organized campgrounds thus balanced the needs of mobility and domesticity by providing gas stoves, ovens, and sometimes iceboxes, as well as such household niceties as steam irons and wash tubs.

Anxious to ease the transition, writers depicted the move from primitive roadside camp to more comfortable organized autocamp as a sensible switch. Men had had their fling with romantic gypsying; now it was time to sober up and face facts: the health dangers, the hostility of farmers, the discomforts that were hard to gloss over. "Quite often," one woman wrote, "the men say that they want to camp wherever they happen to be when evening comes. When we first started out, we thought the same way. So one night we selected a beautiful spot. No sooner had we got in bed than we were pelted with rocks by a gang of ruffian boys." Another night they slept on the ground—or tried to. "A small pebble the size of a hickory nut feels like a football by about 2 A.M. We slept little and got home as quickly as possible." Her husband wanted to cook over a wood fire, but she had to remind him that it might rain, or that the wood might be wet.

Some places did not allow fires at all. After that they stayed in a safe municipal camp, slept on a cot, and cooked over a convenient stove. Noting the "complications" inherent in taking a wife along, Fred Smith cautioned would-be ascetics of the consequences: "Remember the old adage that one man's charm is another man's harm. Try it for yourself, if you will, but for the other half of the family, remember that auto beds or camp cots can be had for the buying. And these things are cheaper than a divorce."[34]

Through the 1920s, in pursuing the family trade, equipment manufacturers, private roadside entrepreneurs, and public camp managers all spoke of the need to please wife and mother, for she was considered the final arbiter. Toilets had to be clean, cooking facilities convenient, grounds neat. But it would be wrong to overemphasize gender differences in the demand for comfort. Some women suspected that despite the daring male talk about sleeping under the stars, pitching a tent near an isolated trout stream, and cooking over a glorious wood fire, many men secretly welcomed the female presence as a good excuse to get more comfortable facilities than were customary on all-male camping excursions.[35] The focus on feminine comfort thus reflected the primary role given to women as purchasers of consumer goods for the whole household.

In addition to helping families, the organized campground also served the frenzied driving styles that began to emerge in the 1920s. Rather than "lazing along like gypsies," tourists became obsessed with "making miles." This was another inner contradiction of roadside gypsying.

Autocamping was supposed to free tourists from schedules, from being rushed along by trains, from being hemmed in by flexible rails. Car touring was to be leisurely, unstructured, freewheeling, unshackled. The autogypsy hoped to leave behind the everyday time fix, the achievement orientation, the anxieties. Early enthusiasts hoped for a slower, more attentive pace. This was central to the idea that only the motorist could really see America.

Yet tourists noticed almost immediately that driving seemed to impose its own special momentum. Even with the many new sights, drivers could not help but want to go faster, to move on, regardless of immediate attractions. "We certainly won't be 'educated' if our chauffeur [son E. M.] can help it!" sighed Emily Post in 1915.

He is exactly like the time lock on a safe. Only instead of being set for the hour, he is set for distance. At Erie, for instance, he throws in the clutch, "Cleveland?" he asks, and snap! nothing can make him look to the left or the right of the road in front of him.

"Oh, look! That's the house where President Garfield—"
Zip! we have passed it!
"Wait a minute, let me see that inscription—"
We are half a mile beyond! We arrive in Cleveland, when click goes the lock and he stops dead, and nothing will make him go further.[36]

"There seems to be a certain irresistible impulse within us to keep moving on," wrote one autocamper who was not pleased with the discovery. "We have vowed to curb this impulse. Just why a person should travel miles to see Niagara Falls only to remain about one hour and fail to get a full appreciation of this wonder of nature, is more than I can understand. Yet, we all have been guilty of this very thing." By the 1920s this mysterious urge to move on assumed the status of conventional wisdom. "A vacation is a time of release for uninhibited impulses," wrote one newspaper editor; "it should be a wandering where fancy dictates." Countless articles and guidebooks admonished tourists to slow down and see the country. *"Take time to see things!" "Stop and appreciate it while you can!"* Yet all too often the auto vacation wound up as a "hurried drive toward a given objective."[37]

Early tourists blamed their chauffeurs—hired foreigners interested mainly in getting there rather than in sightseeing—for this hurried touring. "His dream of perfect bliss is a mathematically-straight French road and forty miles per hour—with you holding your hair while the landscape cinematographs by in a pale-green blur." But wider car ownership soon showed that all classes were infatuated with speed and straight roads. Another writer cited railroad precedent: with all their disgust for rail timetable shackles, Americans had always been upset with train delays, even if they occurred in scenic territory. Perhaps this obsession with making time was the just revenge of the locomotive on the motorist. Maybe it was just part of the nomadic instinct that made driving so attractive in the first place. Or perhaps it was the American character. To humorist James Montgomery Flagg, this perpetual auto-motion befitted a nation known for rocking chairs and chewing gum.[38]

Or maybe it was that, given bad road conditions, drivers *had* to be obsessed with the road. This was certainly true in the mountains. "For the driver," wrote Melville Ferguson, "looking at the scenery in the sort of country we had been traveling [the Rockies] is a privilege. Only a few can do it with impunity. We saw the wrecked cars of many who had tried, lying in ditches and at the bottom of embankments." But what about the straight, flat stretches? Even that most attentive of sightseers, Emily Post, became enthralled with "making up lost time easily" on Nebraska's fast roads.

What if your engine is barely capable of forty miles an hour, that miraculously fast stretch magically carries you at the easiest fifty. If you have a big powerful engine, you forget that ordinarily you dislike whizzing along the surface of the earth, and for just this once—even though you think of it more in terror than in joy—you are approaching the raceway of America, and you, too, are going to race![39]

As roads improved in the 1920s, tourists discovered that all highways were potential raceways.

Men in particular may have enjoyed this chance to cover ground. Male-oriented touring articles emphasized the car's obedience to will and the technical mastery involved in driving. The active, producer-oriented nature of mileage-making was an obvious contrast to passive rail travel and the aimless tenor of resort veranda life. Perhaps leisurely sightseeing was more a female interest. Women collected postcards, attended travel lectures, wrote travel guides, and supported highway beautification in the 1920s. In line with the separate spheres, female-oriented autocamping articles played up the quieter, aesthetic features: the "soft-glowing camp fire," the "silver radiance of a summer moon playing upon the sands," the "soft mellow qualities" of a sunset seen from the road.[40] Women may have preferred scenery to speed, but in most cases men sat behind the wheel.

For manufacturers, speed and movement had been priority objectives from the start. Cars attained sixty-mile-per-hour capability long before roads could handle that speed. The sixteen-mile-per-hour average of early touring allowed a better view of the countryside, and innumerable road delays facilitated intimacy with natural obstacles and fellow tourists, but one suspects that many felt restrained by this. Maybe the praise for leisurely car touring merely made virtue of necessity. While travelers rationalized the spiritual ordeal of bad roads, they also pushed for smooth, good roads. Similarly, while they praised the intimate contact with dust, fresh air, and bumps, they also welcomed closed cars that allowed more insulated, faster travel.

Indeed, even early roadside autocamping was compatible with mileage-making. Pioneers discovered that the best time to drive was in the early morning, when drivers were the freshest. "You can never compensate for a late start by a longer driving period in the afternoon," wrote Frederic Van de Water. "It's the mileage turned back by noon that counts." By camping along the road, tourists did not have to wait for the hotel dining room or garage to open. Rather, they breakfasted at sunrise and took off. Using the car as a trunk saved packing and unpacking time. Eating the heaviest meal in the evening rather than at noon, opening a few cans or frying a steak, having collapsible equipment and an efficient system, all these added time for the road.

Tourists demanded greater efficiency so they could be on the road more. Autocamps provided this efficiency. Electric lights permitted campers to drive later and set up camp after dark. Established, graded campsites let them set up right away, without having to find a level, well-drained, safe spot and clear away rocks and debris. Gas ranges facilitated a quick, hot dinner without having to gather wood or set up a fire. A hydrant yielded water faster than a stream. Some camps were located near gas stations that stayed open all night, so motorists could have their cars greased and fueled while they slept—ready for an early start.

Security was also an issue, for anxiety had crept into roadside autocamping. Originally, camping anywhere was supposed to relieve motorists of the insecurity of having to make a particular hotel before it filled up. But as farmers and school yards posted no trespassing signs, would-be waysiders struggled to find good spots with fresh water. The search might have to begin soon after lunch, thus cutting into valuable road time. Armed with auto club road guides, autocampers knew exactly where camps were and what to expect.

Beyond efficiency and security, autocamps provided much-appreciated comfort. Despite better roads and more insulated cars, tourists were worn out from making miles on straighter, faster roads and looked forward to the comforts of the autocamp. Replacing the earlier image of the road-battered, dust-covered yet exhilarated pioneer, was the new image of the weary, enervated, slightly cranky tourist. "The almost monotonous travel of improved roads, with never a bump or a detour, becomes irksome when you are driving day after day," wrote one tourist who regretted the passing of the earlier outing ordeal.[41] Driving still had character-building qualities, but the heat, stiffness, and boredom were better cured by a shower, a cold drink, and a cozy armchair in the community building, than by a manly handshake with fellow suffering frontiersmen at a washed-out bridge.

The progress in daily mileage was slow but steady: about 125 miles a day in 1916, 170 in 1920, 200 in 1925, 240 in 1928, 300 in 1931, 400 in 1936.[42] In theory, this increase was not inevitable. With better roads and faster cars, motorists could have traveled the same 150 miles in less time, with more opportunity for leisurely sightseeing. In practice, however, as tourists became more road wise, the intrinsic pleasures of being on the road, no matter where, tended to wear off. It is amazing how quickly Americans became accustomed to their cars and the road. In a way, this had been an aim of early gypsying: to be at home on the road, with all the easy familiarity of a world traveler. Yet familiarity meant that motorists soon took the road for granted. Motoring emerged as a means to get somewhere rather than as an end in itself. Moreover, with increasing numbers of motorists came complaints of roadside ugliness: traffic jams, litter, billboards, ramshackle food stands. The view of roadside America as a tawdry bazaar was well established by the early 1920s.[43]

At the same time, steady improvement in road quality enabled them to cover a greater range of spectacular sights, and many new tourists on two-week vacations simply had no time to wander. Earlier autocampers had more time and more money, and had already visited many of the main attractions by train. For the less affluent traveler who may never have left home, getting to Niagara Falls, the Wisconsin Lakes, Yellowstone Park, or a once-exclusive resort area was more important than taking in less well-known sights along the way. Also, in a country of emigrants, many tourists used automobile vacations to visit distant friends and relatives. In their case the car's utility in maintaining extended family ties took precedence over its recreational role. This has been an enduring pattern: recent surveys reveal that the majority of vacationing motorists still name friends and relatives as the main factor behind their choice of destination.[44]

As touring became more goal-oriented, tourists needed itineraries. Knowing the location of established autocamps helped motorists maintain schedules. Guidebooks distinguished between through camps—designed for overnight stops along main routes, catering to the efficiency and comfort needs of tired, harried autocampers; and destination camps—located in traditional resort or sightseeing areas, where tourists sought time-honored relaxation and fantasy. In one ironic sense, tourism rapidly returned to a resort-railroad mode: fast, utilitarian travel between stereotyped spectacular sights. Tourists now bought colorful stickers at souvenir stands near major attractions for their car windshields; the road-flailed banner, on the other hand, went out of style.

Railroad and hotel men noted this irony right away. Hoping that autocamping was a passing fad, they predicted that as tourists came to prize travel comforts over camp novelty, they would flock back to traditional travel institutions in greater numbers. In straight competition over comfort, who could do better than the first-class hotel? What could be more insulated or goal-oriented than the crack limited train? True, trade journals admitted, sub-par competitors—bad country hotels, antiquated day coaches, and discourteous employees—were forcing tourists into cars. But the rail and hotel *industries* were sound, the argument went. Progressive, better-educated managers could win tourists back. After all, comfort and service were what these men knew best. All they had to do was clean house and wait. In the 1920s few went further. It appeared that since autocampers were coming their way anyway, all they had to do was improve service and facilities. Evolution in touring habits would take care of the rest.[45]

There was some basis to such reasoning: autocampers were getting softer. Building new small-town hotels and designing new rail passenger cars would relieve some of the conditions that had contributed to autocamping's rise. Yet it was a mistake to assume that the evolution would be circular. Autocamping was evolving toward efficiency and comfort, but in a new form appropriate to car travel and to the widening market of car tourists. Americans would not return to older ways. Indeed, as in the gypsy stage, proponents of free autocamps took great pleasure in contrasting their way with hotels. First, camps were free. Autocamping was still the cheapest way to travel; for an increasing number of Americans it was the only way to tour. Moreover, autocamps facilitated car travel better than hotels. Autocamps provided comforts, but these were self-served. A West Coast camp was described as "the cafeteria idea raised to the nth degree."[46] Dislike of hotel clerks, bellhops, and other servants continued through the 1920s, as more new travelers, unaccustomed to being helped, took to the road. At a municipal camp you did not have to tip a maid if she drew you a bath; you simply stood in line and took a shower. Food was still prepared by each family. Eating was still informal and private. Autocamps made it easier to park and to pack. In all aspects—self-service, parking, eating— autocamps saved time and dignity. Hotel men, struck by the noticeable elaboration in camp comforts, assumed that this would lead inevitably to hotel-like service. But tourists wanted convenience, not service.

Hotel spokesmen also failed to account for the ability of autocamping proponents to make centralized camps seem as attractive as roadside camping. The municipal camp could be romantic, too, though in a different way. The earlier tent by the road had been the individual pioneer's sanctuary, his hard-pitched declaration of temporary independence from society. But there had also been a social dimension, a sense of solidarity in shared experiences of hard driving, road talk, banners. Municipal camp romantics built on this side of the autocamping mystique: delight in a road community. Perhaps the wayside campsite had been a bit too lonely.

From this perspective, the municipal autocamp increased options. For the orthodox wilderness camper—the traditionalist seeking to be alone with family and car in difficult terrain—the solution was the national or state forest, where one could still camp along remote, unpaved roads. The organized camp better suited the more numerous tourist-campers who wanted to be in an outdoor setting for essentially social reasons: to meet others and enjoy the middling virtues of campfire sociability. To one exceptionally idealistic magazine commentator, the tourist-camper was mainly interested in the "inspirational comradeship" lacking in normal life. At home "no one cares who lives next door, or dies there. The strain of modern economic life is forcing us to seek relief in strange and hitherto untried ways." Autocamping seemed to be one such search. "Those who drive mattress-gorged cars through our streets are on a spiritual quest. What they are seeking is not material but spiritual shelter."[47] In the well-advertised community of the autocamp, they seemed to be finding that refuge.

The Camp Melting Pot

Touring literature emphasized that autocamps were remarkably democratic and open. Writers earnestly reported friendly encounters with "all kinds" of people. "There is a great free masonry and democratic fraternity in autocamping," wrote promoter Frank Brimmer. "The camp as an institution is very democratic and there is more of a democratic feeling among the tourists than will be found among the rank and file of American people," a sympathetic sociologist agreed. For *The Saturday Evening Post* the tourist camp was "one of our greatest modern let's-get-acquainted institutions."[48] Here was a true melting pot, a regenerative social harmony of which every host town could be proud. After visiting several midwestern camps, a Floridian wrote, "Nowhere have I seen a more apparent feeling of kinship, or more willingness to offer a helping hand, than in the tourist camps along the main highways." New Yorker Van de Water discovered "a comfortable feeling of solidarity with the rest of America." The "absolute democracy of camp life" was a marked contrast to the normal hotel, where guests were "deprived, chief of all, of the priceless, heartening contacts with fellow Americans." To Dallas Lore Sharp, the autocamp suggested a medieval caravansary: open, friendly, informal, heterogeneous, intimate—all very appropriate to the "better country" that was the open road.[49]

Such fraternal feelings confirmed popular belief that outdoor sports promoted healthy nationalism. At a time of heightened Americanization efforts, outdoor recreation would consolidate a dangerously segmented society. "There is no better common denominator of a people," wrote President Calvin Coolidge.

In the case of a people which represents many nations, cultures, and races, as does our own, a unification of interests and ideals in recreation is bound to wield a telling influence for solidarity of the entire population. No more truly democratic force can be set off against the tendency to class and caste than the democracy of individual parts and prowess in sport.[50]

Of all sports, camping best promoted national integration because it brought urban people in contact with timeless, yet characteristically American, values of nature. The city could never Americanize the immigrant or tame the street urchin; autocampers generally agreed on that. The melting pot of the autocamp was distinct from the ominous diversity of the city neighborhood. New Yorkers, in particular, were sure to point out that the America they found in camp was quite different from the pluralism at home. "Having seen Americans, the ordinary rank and file of this land," Van de Water wrote, "we have no desire to be known as New Yorkers."[51]

Tourism seemed an especially useful agent because it brought together people from many regions. "By ruining sectionalism, it is transforming the provincial-minded man into a national-minded one," *Motor Camper and Tourist* observed. "Therefore, it must aid Americanization and the nationalization of the people at large." With so many involved, See America First now had a positive, upbeat, nationalistic ring—less a rejection of Europe than a search for uniquely American values. With politicians in disfavor, perhaps the car culture could unify the country. " 'Seeing America First' is a good motto. The automobile is making more patriots for America than all the silver-tongued orators in the land."[52]

In autocamping the conversion seemed direct and personal. Tourists were intrigued by their first contact with motorists from faraway places. The litany of state names had a romantic, exotic ring to people who had rarely strayed beyond their own county. The bricklayer from Kansas City, the lawyer from Pittsburgh, the sign painter from Toledo—all were "neighbors for a night" at Yellowstone's campground. Rhode Island girls bound for California might camp near a "grizzled veteran from Tennessee" or a farmer from Illinois. Autocampers came in contact with "native 'crackers' of the far South, mountaineers of the Alleghenies, ranchmen and plain scouts—more or less on an equal footing." "The North meets the South, and the East greets the West."[53]

Perhaps the greatest geographical mix occurred at large campgrounds in national parks. Here government policy seemed designed to promote national amalgamation and good citizenship. To be sure, patriots claimed a bit too much. Although 40,000 people in 10,000 cars, representing 46 states, camped in Yellowstone in 1919, tourists were more likely to arrive by train if they came from distant states. Most out-of-state motorists came from neighboring states. The same was true of town camps. Thus, of the 3,063 cars at Denver's camp in 1917, 1,011 were from Kansas, 606 from Nebraska, 368 from Oklahoma. Yet even if they were in the minority, long-distance tourists were found everywhere, and enthusiasts projected that with better roads and faster cars, a truly representative mix would result. They were right. In 1922, two-thirds of all Yellowstone visitors arrived by

Neighbors for a night at Yellowstone Park, 1923. Note the special auto tents that bolted directly to the car, the chatty sign to be mounted on a rear fender, and the fact that the women are the only ones working. (Library of Congress)

Happy family theme, cover of *Motor Camper and Tourist,* April 1925. (Library of Congress)

car, the rest by rail; a third of New England visitors came by car. By 1926, however, half of all New Englanders visiting the park arrived by automobile. This increase in long-distance travel meant a proportionate increase in heterogeneity at municipal camps on main routes.[54]

Furthermore, there was an important integration of peoples from different cultures within the same region—for example, city folks and farmers. Serving as a "universal solvent for urban and provincial reserve," the autocamp would, it was hoped, banish the rural-urban conflict that seemed particularly intense in the 1920s. The Saturday Evening Post argued that a "lack of understanding" was at the root of this tension; perhaps a "new American democracy" was forming in the simple autocamp.[55]

Even more important than the geographical synthesis was the apparent crossing of class lines. "All kinds" meant different occupations and incomes. "Rich and poor, clodhopper and nobility alike, can indulge to their heart's content in motor camping."[56] A wide spectrum of working- and middle-class people seemed to be represented. A 1921 survey counted four classes of autocampers: farmers out to buy supplies, emigrants looking for new homes, migrant workers, and middle-class tourists. Another cited a "great hegira" of midwestern farmers, transcontinental tourists, wilderness campers, and "plain hoboes."[57] A 1926 survey of Yellowstone visitors counted 380 occupations among party heads. Farmers were first, 6,360 in all, followed by 2,459 salesmen, 2,062 "professionals," 2,035 merchants, 1,817 teachers, 1,455 mechanics, 1,454 laborers, 1,384 students, 1,293 business proprietors and executives, 1,089 clerks, and 1,006 retired people.

The car itself was the great common denominator. Its license plates indicated geographical origins, and everyone looked immediately to that badge. Similarly, the various car makes parked side by side showed the democratic leveling of the autocamp. "They came in anything and everything that rolls on wheels, from plebian Fords to patrician Fierce Sparrows. There were rattletraps of ancient times threatening to collapse at a moment's notice, and aluminum palaces, walnut-trimmed and fitted up like Pullman cars." In camp a forty-horsepower, five-thousand-dollar car might "rub shoulders" with a twenty-five-horsepower flivver. Packards hobnobbed with Chevrolets, ultra deluxe "highway Pullmans" with surplus pup tents. "Just what the stations of life of the respective owners may be, neither inquires nor either seems to care." Millionaires camped next to families going coast-to-coast on $100.[58] Autocamp life seemed to transcend everyday economic conflict.

Even when most autocampers were broadly middle class, there were enough personality differences to make the encounters quite memorable. Indeed, most characterizations were more picturesque than political. "Quaint, queer, and interesting characters we meet," was the subtitle of one article about the "Tin Can Tourist Tribe." The author recalled intriguing meetings with theatrical people, a postcard salesman, a Russian nobleman, a photographer, and several ex-soldiers. The variety of characters enhanced the kaleidoscopic attractions of road life. Even the khaki uniforms could be colorful and diverse, as one survey pointed out:

All types and classes of humanity were represented among them. Many of them were goggled, gauntleted, and knickered. The fat women in knickers added a dash of comedy to the most prosaic of days. In khaki knickers, faded and shapeless, without even a puckering string at the knee, they ventured abroad in silk stockings, highheeled pumps, pink silk blouses, crocheted boudoir caps, and jingling ear-rings. It was amazing what colorful combinations the knickered rovers managed to attain. They wore veils of all descriptions, flowing Egyptian veils and even gas masks. They wore paper hats that tied under their chins, caps trimmed with the tails of squirrels, skins of rattlesnakes, and quills of porcupines.[59]

Or the imagery might be much simpler, yet still warm and pleasant. To one writer a Florida autocamp resembled a transplanted Main Street. Another found Yellowstone's campers to be "pretty good people and, after all, Americans just like you and me." This was a key point: beneath the delight in variety was hope that, exotic or homespun, autocampers were basically alike—just folks. The autocamp thus reinforced a sincere desire to link automobility with fresh intimacies. Celebrants hoped that, by coming together in a new and relaxed environment, tourists might rediscover a common thread broken in everyday life.[60]

How did autocampers overcome normal social barriers?

First, the sport was still new. Though no longer eccentric, autocamping still felt different, even as it consolidated into organized camps. Although estimates ran between ten and twenty million participants for the mid-1920s, AAA statisticians noted that few outsiders seemed aware of the magnitude of the sport. Autocamping was a mass activity—a "national pasttime"—that still enjoyed inside dopester status. "It has increased without the artificial stimulus of publicity," one publicist exulted.[61] By 1924 it was big enough to deserve a New York-based magazine devoted solely to its interests, *Motor Camper and Tourist*; yet this glossy, attractive monthly with a circulation of fifty thousand retained a gossipy, small-town tone in its columns, contests, and cartoons; autocampers contributed stories and photographs. Similarly, the growing number of tourist accounts and diaries retained a sense of novelty and uniqueness.

Sharing the delight in doing something unusual, autocampers lowered their guard. "The sport of motor camping is too new to have been blighted, thus far, by the chill of ceremony," Melville Ferguson noted. Van de Water found that it had, "like most things, not only certain mild hardships and rough spots, but an engaging ingenuousness. Tin-can tourists are too new to the craft to have developed skepticism and suspicion of their fellows. They are friendly, generous, kind-hearted folks, exceedingly easy to impose on." He worried that this lack of established guidelines could leave tourists vulnerable to "bunco artists," but it was precisely this shared vulnerability in a new enterprise that made autocampers so open.[62]

Despite the informality, campers did wear what amounted to a "regulation uniform." Khakis or old clothes—originally worn for utilitarian reasons—took on social significance. Everyday street dress displayed status or at least aspiration. Camp life mocked this show, as campers calmly paraded through camp in bedraggled knickers, night caps, and other outlandish clothing. By suspending conventional standards, informal camp life fostered "a pleasant sense of truancy." "With all the conventions reduced to a minimum, how much easier it is to estimate the real character of a person met casually this way." With no one dolled up, true friendships could result. "There you meet men and women just as the Creator made them, not as man-made conventional veneer has made them." So deep-seated was the distrust of ostentation that Van de Water advised fellow wealthy tourists to have a modest car to match modest clothing. "Thus equipped you raise none of the latent dread of patronage which is a heritage of all Americans. One glance at our disreputable selves and dusty equipment was enough to inform the most insignificant of our roadmates that we were no more, at best, than his equals." Inexpensive, dusty apparel "served as a due guard and sign, admitting us without further questioning into a somewhat nebulous esoteric brotherhood."[63]

Yet autocampers were careful not to overstep acquaintanceship. A definite rule applied: you could tell a stranger virtually anything about yourself, except your name. "We chatted daily with people who knew the salient facts of our history, and told us in return the stories of their lives," Ferguson wrote, "but in very few cases did we learn their names, or they ours." Names, like clothing and manners, tended to place people. At hotels the first thing a clerk sought was your name, and you had to record it in full public display in the register. In camp you remained anonymous. A similar custom prevailed in the hobo jungle, where, as sociologist Nels Anderson found, men might brush elbows for weeks without ever learning each other's names.[64]

No longer a Jones or Robinson or Smith, campers commonly

took their names from their license plates: "Hello New York, you're a long way from home." Or, camp residents might refer to each other by *noms de tour,* appropriate to the particular camp situation, "secretly bestowed upon us by our neighbors, not in malice, but for purposes of identification." Thus, in one Santa Barbara camp, Ferguson met "the Dutchman, the Old Gent, the Woman with the Green Sweater, the Busybody, the Old Hen, Jack the Hatter, the Woman with the Long Skirt, the Red-Headed Woman, Rapid City," and so on.[65] Characteristically, everyone knew a person's camp name except that person—an appropriate reversal of everyday public behavior. Even members of one's own party took on separate road names. Writers of tourist accounts rarely named companions; rather, they referred to "my better half," "the captain," "the nipper." This was an important part of getting away from conventional proprieties and associations.

A key, then, to this fellowship of the road was that it occurred among strangers. One writer perceived the irony in this: "The tourist camp is about the freest and most generous thing in the average town, and yet it is for entire strangers—a curious anomaly." But this was the point. Through limited liability, tourists preserved long-run privacy. There was little danger that a camp acquaintance might look you up some day at home or office, where regular protocol could make the encounter embarrassing or annoying. The temporary nature of a camp stay further safeguarded against discomfort. Since you could always be confident of tomorrow's renewed privacy, tonight you could reveal as much of yourself as you dared. "You seem to dip into other people's lives at odd moments, as if you opened a book at random." Tomorrow "the highway would swallow them up." This was the useful non sequitur nature of road life, the chance encounters, the "brief contacts, the sudden intimacies that dissolve forever at dawn."[66] With this limitation well understood, autocampers could afford a good deal of public exposure.

"One's peculiarities, especially if external, cannot long be concealed in camp," wrote Melville Ferguson in explaining the basis for many camp names. In the campground everything normally private and personal became impersonally public. A week after leaving New York, Van de Water found himself sitting within six feet of the main street of Lyons, Iowa, shaving in plain view of the townspeople, while his wife calmly put up her hair at his elbow. Surprisingly, the exposure was not distasteful.[67] Camp life had traditionally blurred the boundaries between front and backstage behavior, but only within the camping family. Now hundreds of strangers all lived backstage together. For Victorians used to hard distinctions in domestic matters, this blurring could be jarring but also regenerative. Living in canvas homes, using public showers and toilets, sharing cooking facilities, all served to break down restraint. Even a genteel urbanite like Chicagoan Gula Sabin could find herself rather unwillingly "melted" while cooking in the community kitchen—a major forum for sociability:

I found myself running back and forth over this great stretch of lawn to get a fork or spoon. I remembered criticizing a friend who was entertaining at dinner for calling to the maid in the kitchen, "Bring some more potatoes," or "Pass the rolls again," and here I was yelling across a block or two of space, "Charles, bring me the paring knife."
Was I deteriorating socially, and joining the ranks of the flivvered, breakfast-capped camper?[68]

While Sabin did not particularly appreciate the publicity, other women did find the the communal cooking experience more pleasant. If nothing else, it relieved them of the isolation customary on more traditional camping trips or in roadside camping, where husbands went fishing or exploring while wives stayed near the tent and cooked.

But woe betide the wife who tried to pull rank, even inadvertently. The wife of New York aristocrat Van de Water got along very well with comradely wives in the group laundry until she wistfully mentioned her laundress at home. "Conversation stopped and she was ostracized—as though she had uttered some highly colored obscenity." In autocamping you had to be openly domestic, you had to "work your own passage. Otherwise you don't belong." The camper who brought, or even referred to, servants would never be accepted. "The democracy of 'tin can touring' is a jealous and sensitive thing." There was still some necessary discomfort and inconvenience in setting up camp and living outdoors, even in the most up-to-date autocamps, and democrats valued the ordeal. To be colorfully weather-beaten you had to suffer a bit, but it earned you respect. The best autocamper was "always willing to lend a hand, always cheerful in his self-imposed sacrifice of modern conveniences."[69] If you dined with millionaires, you were not supposed to know it until later, if at all.

For men, the equivalent forum was the evening inspection of camping gear. While autocampers had always eyed each other's equipment, the campground provided an especially convenient arena for display. And display it was, but of a different sort from that at resorts. Art historian Siegfried Giedion writes that camping equipment reflects the vernacular patent furniture tradition which emphasizes multifunctional designs, free of useless ornament. This no-nonsense approach can stimulate great ingenuity and creativity. "Collapsible, transportable camp furniture opens a wonderful playground to fantasy. All must be encompassed within a slight bulk and combinations of different utensils must be packed into the smallest space with the barest reliance on mechanical impediments. Every idea must find its most direct expression." Giedion argues that this acute utilitarianism characterized much of household furniture until banished from the middle-class parlor by genteel ruling taste in the late nineteenth century.[70] In the autocamp, however, where parlor dress and manners were out of place, utilitarian standards prevailed.

The earliest roadsiders often invented their equipment: collapsible auto beds, trailers, equipment racks. One 1909 gypsy modified his car into a "lodging house on wheels": the front seat, on hinges, lowered to form a bed; the back seat was replaced by a portable refrigerator and "gypsy kit" (cooking utensils); his wife made curtains for the windows. A Californian devised a "Combination Car": a truck outfitted as a "Pullman on wheels," with beds, kitchen, sitting room. Out of such home experimentation came the early commercial outfits and trailers.[71] Even as manufacturers made inroads in the early 1920s, there was still room for private ingenuity. Store bought equipment could still be modified, and manufacturers themselves could not agree on what constituted standard equipment. "With so many ideas of personal comfort and convenience to be taken into consideration," *Popular Mechanics* noted in 1924, "it is manifestly impossible to lay down any set rules and regulations for construction and arrangment." The key word was "individual." No two outfits were alike. "Motor camping is an individual problem that must be solved by the individual," wrote Elon Jessup in *The Motor Camping Book*.[72]

Autocamping thus relied on personal experimentation and inspection, trial and error, word of mouth. Home inventors exchanged their "handy kinks" in special columns of *Motor Camper and Tourist, Popular Mechanics,* and the auto club journals. Touring the campground was another way to exchange information. "A tour of any of the big camps brings out the oddities of conveyance and equipment, for each tourist has his own ideas and works them out in his own way. . . . Of types there are countless to suit the party of every size, every taste or idea." Some inventors went so far in their search for the perfect kit that their creativity served as a subject for satire. "In the interests of convenience and efficiency," went one mock advertisement, "this camper's children are trained to fold up." Another article described "one of those new automatic affairs that fall into place in about ten seconds. You just tie it onto the running board of the car, and when you get to the dump where you wish to camp, why, all you've got to do is press the self-erector button and presto!—the tent flops off the running board and erects itself in a jiffy!"[73] There was a leveling, good-natured tolerance behind this self-ridicule. It was fun to invent—or even buy—labor-saving equipment, but it was important not to take it too seriously. An expensive, custom-built highway Pullman merited universal envy, but the cherished badge of a seasoned veteran could be won with just a little skill and resourcefulness. The criterion for acceptance was utility. If you could get along with a pup tent and frying pan, so be it. The only camper who might be scorned was the over-equipped novice who could not set up camp right. Greenhorns were ridiculed mercilessly, but this began the process by which they eventually joined the group.

The camp fire was another opportunity for sociability. Cooking and eating out in the open welcomed public notice and participation. Campers invited each other to dinner or passed around surplus cookies and fruit. National parks featured special fire circles for after-dinner story-telling and marshmallow roasting. In more elaborate municipal camps tourists could relax and chat in indoor community rooms, with fireplaces and easy chairs. Generally, however, groups formed spontaneously at a particular camp fire.

Wherever they met, campers spoke their own language. Much of this was an extension of earlier road talk in which motorists traded information and stories while waiting at road delays and filling stations. Road talk supplemented the incomplete information of Blue Books and maps: How many miles to Centerville? What's the best route to Carbondale? How's the road? To these questions autocampers added topics of special interest, particularly equipment.

Of course, the auto-tourist campers are still more violent than the golf bugs when it comes to arguing about the science of equipment. They will sit for hours on a rainy day discussing with considerable heat the relative merits of lean-tos, palmettos, autobeds, air-mattresses, khaki, corduroy, square umbrellas, balsam beds, dingle sticks, Indian fires, cot beds, hammocks, and a thousand other subjects close to the heart of the camper.[74]

Other topics included narrow escapes, recipes, weather, mosquitoes, and the world situation, but not specific political or religious issues.

Most important was "verbal advertising" about other camps: what conveniences they had, recent experiences, and what to avoid. As with so much road talk, information was to be discounted liberally; yet each camp's reputation took on a life of its own—a fact of life for booster groups anxious to establish their town's good name. One engineer, in dealing with the specifics of setting up a municipal camp, took special pains to emphasize this fact:

It has been demonstrated repeatedly that an attractive camp conveniently located will be advertised from one end of the country to the other. After a camp has been established a few seasons a large part of its patronage will be made up of previous visitors and those who have learned of the camp's merits from friends of the road. Poor camps are also given free publicity, but it is not of the sort desired by the community.[75]

Tourist talk, even if accurate, made roadside business very insecure. A well-run camp could earn nice publicity for its town, but even good camps could be threatened if some other town down the road had more conveniences. News spread fast, and tourists soon demanded to know why this camp had only cold showers, while the last had hot and cold. A once-deserved bad reputation could live on long after inadequacies had been remedied.

Along with the specialized autocamping magazines and manuals, camp talk now constituted a principal source of autocamper information and intimacy. Having been banned from random roadside exploration, autocampers now inhabited a segregated tourist world with its own concerns, routines, and institutions. Using sociologist Erik Cohen's terminology, this specialization was part of the process by which individualized "drifter tourism" evolved into institutionalized "mass tourism."[76] The original drifter autocampers sought unstaged encounters with unsuspecting natives outside the dominant rail-hotel establishment. But such spontaneity could not withstand the weight of numbers. Tourists upset natives; natives reorganized their world to accommodate tourists.

Despite the loss of freshness, such reorganization had its attractions, for it better served tourist needs and expectations. If the open road was not quite as free and open as originally hoped, at least the autocamp was. If the roadside was not as homelike as vacationing families had hoped, the well-equipped autocamp was. If not all natives were comradely, generous, and easygoing, at least other autocampers were. In this separate autocamp world, tourists talked to tourists about matters of mutual interest.

Such a community could be quite pleasant, but, ironically, it was vulnerable to the same tension that had produced it: popularity.

Limiting Access

Pay Camps, 1923–1926

The free municipal autocamp was even more short-lived than the roadside camp. Indeed, at the same time that eastern towns were first channeling motor gypsies into free public campgrounds, western towns were taking steps to separate "better-class" tourists from "undesirable" tourists.

From the beginning, an uneasy tension had existed between democracy and discrimination. Early roadside autocampers had welcomed the easy accessibility of the road, the vernacular simplicity of camp equipment and dress, and the informal democracy of road contacts; yet they had also sought escape from vulgar *nouveaux riches* flooding once exclusive resorts and from the uncomfortable proximities of the rail coach and hotel, where immigrants, blacks, and lower-class whites were employed. While claiming that they had found the real America, they shunned cities and the industrial landscape in favor of a more reassuring view of Main Street, the West, and the preindustrial past.

A similar tension held at the free municipal autocamp. It was free, open, accessible to all travelers who happened to be passing through. Tourists took their chances with the types of people camping nearby. Their lives could be enriched by such encounters. This was the camp-as-melting-pot, a roadside re-enactment of the assimilationist myth. Yet, as with the myth itself, there were limits, subtle assumptions about the kinds worth melting with. Writers tended to like fellow campers who conformed to pre-established images of the real America. In early motoring one was most likely to meet the more prosperous farmers, small town merchants, professionals, suburbanites—each of whom had secure home ties and conventional middle-class values. The occasional eccentrics—circus people, peddlers, Russian noblemen, cowboys, wandering poets—added a picturesqueness that enhanced the sense of archaic vagabondia. The independent mechanic or artisan added a comfortable democratic glow. But, in the end, autocampers emphasized respectability over eccentricity and democracy. If romantics hoped to cross class lines, it was the line between the middle and upper classes; now the moderately well-off could do what had once been reserved for the very affluent. The Pierce Arrow thus received more attention than the Ford, for the rich man's car—not the poor man's—legitimized the sport. Pleasantly informal contact with the "better sort" seemed to confirm the classic bourgeois dream that the rich were, in the end, just everyday folk who shared middle-class values.

But in the 1920s many other people were buying automobiles. Registrations quadrupled from 4.6 million in 1917 to 19.2 million in 1926. Although many of these car buyers were middle class, others were more economically marginal people for whom the autocamp was the *only* place to stay. As a result, the camp population became a bit too proletarian for certain tastes. During this time politicians praised the great American melting pot but took severe steps to restrict immigration in order to obtain a more secure blend. The same happened in autocamping. Even as town officials, boosters, and tourists exulted in the unprecedented democracy of free campgrounds, they worried about the changing camp population, especially about a new "class of undesirables," "an undesirable element," a "class of wanderers" who were living in municipal camps.

In order to deal with these "unmitigated nuisances," many towns imposed fees, registration requirements, time limits, and police supervision at their camps. By limiting access, they hoped to attract only the "better class" of paying tourists. Their rationale was summarized by one Texas camp manager in 1924:

The maintenance of a slipshod tourist camp in any city is, in my opinion, bad business, for the reason that the bums and a class of people that are of no benefit whatever to a community use and abuse the privilege. Where you have a well-run, up-to-date large camp, you secure a class of people who are an asset to any community, and by offering these the proper sort of accommodations, a great majority of them, instead of staying one day, stay two or three days. I most certainly believe that a pay camp is the solution to making your city attractive to the right sort of tourists, and that a free camp is an abomination.[1]

This man, president of a profit-making management company, Southwestern Tourist Camps, ran the well-known Camp Grande, in El Paso, Texas. Originally a free public camp, Camp Grande was turned over to private managers in 1923, when the city experienced difficulties with camp clientele. By 1925 most observers agreed that the Camp Grande solution was both inevitable and justified.

"Undesirables"

Who were these undesirables, and why were they so disturbing?

One type was the year-round tourist. Taking automobility to heart, this autocamper traveled more or less permanently, using the free camp as a temporary way-station on an apparently interminable voyage of discovery and adventure. He thus violated the cardinal rule that motor gypsying be a temporary vacation, not a lasting occupation. Although it was exciting to spurn roots and convention for a while, it was considered dangerous to succumb to the virus of vagabondage. The goal of an auto trip was to reactivate one's loyalty to job, home, and family. Few wanted a permanently wandering population. Viewing the restlessness of the auto-borne population in 1925, one writer hoped that behind the ominous flux lay a genuine hunger for roots and stability:

"People want to be settled, but it is only as they are unsettled that there is any hope for them," mused Emerson. In view of this trenchant fact, there must be plenty of hope for these motoring American wanderers. In time, they are bound to find their pot of gold and be transfigured into producers, citizens of worth, voters of understanding, taxpayers of responsibility, and homeowners of moral and financial worth, not just a race of gypsies.[2]

But what if people did not settle down? What if automobiles were in fact creating a new race of gypsies? What exactly was the effect of this intoxicating freedom of life on the road? "Having once started to 'go,' will they ever be content to permanently stop?"[3]

Although tourists frequently asked themselves this question, especially on the first liberating trip out, most found that home looked good after a hard journey. A few kept touring, however, and they received a good deal of attention in national journals. Given the free rent, perhaps it *was* cheaper to live on the road than at home, especially if home was given up for good. Perhaps by rejecting sedentary middle-class life the perpetual camper had discovered something better. A *Scribner's* writer called on Mrs. Fremont-Smith, who shelled peas quite contentedly in her California autocamp home—a tent pitched under a tree near the ever-waiting car. The couple rented out their midwestern house and lived rent-free in the benign Southern California climate.

"We've been traveling for almost a year now," the hostess declared, making a place for her caller upon one of the car cushions. "We started out just to spend the summer, and the people who were in our house would pay twenty-five dollars a month more if they could keep it through the winter. We figured that we could live out this way and save about fifty a month. Henry needed a change anyway, and I was simply sick of housework."

"But what will you do during the rainy season?" The caller

"Undesirables," San Fernando, California, 1935. Farm Security Administration photographers like Dorothea Lange publicized an autoborne migration of the economically marginal that began after World War I. Anxious to keep clear of such "tin can tourists," many middle-class autocampers turned to private camps after 1925. (Library of Congress)

being an adopted Californian dared to hint thus at the possibility of intermittent sunshine.

"Oh, we'll go 'in' for January and February. We have a friend up in San Francisco who will rent us two rooms in his house. But it will certainly be hard to get used to being 'in.' We tried it for two weeks in Denver when the schools first started, and actually, whenever I saw autos go past the window all packed for camping, I just ached to get up and start off somewhere—anywhere, just to be going."[4]

For the *Scribner's* writer the ache made sense. The American home was said to be passing. It was "rapidly becoming merely a service station where we stop only long enough to get supplies for a trip." Children hardly knew their parents. Cities were impersonal and commercialized. Life on the road offered a renewed sense of community. In taking to the road permanently, therefore, the Fremont-Smiths of America simply carried motoring's original promise of social rejuvenation to its ultimate conclusion.[5]

Another writer discerned a similar romanticism in a young couple at Yellowstone who seemed typical of the all-year motor camper. The writer had formerly thought these types were mendicant hoboes, but after several liberating months on the road herself, found them fascinating innocents, "two happy-go-lucky children who adored sunsets and fried trout and long stretches of windy boulevard." The perpetual motor camper had an appeal much like the traditional hobo: Even as Americans feared the tramp, they admired his independence, his ability to work just enough to eat. In his more wistful moments the white collar dreamer could believe that the hobo was, after all, just another good man who had been on the road a bit too long and had yielded to its temptations. Melville Ferguson found himself thus enchanted by the spirit of vagabondage after being on the road for over a year. "The motor camper who wanders long enough and far enough gets to some degree the point of view of the professional tramp. The gap that separates the two is, after all, not so wide. Put a tramp in a flivver, and instil him with some notions of cleanliness and honesty, and you have bridged it."[6]

But the attitude toward regular tramps and gypsies had always been cool, at best. Such vagabonds were acceptable as long as they visited someone else's town. Full-time tourists might be envied as long as they were middle class, as long as they were few in number, and as long as their revolt was essentially romantic. The delicate balance between envy and scorn turned to fear, however, as poor people began to turn to semi-permanent gypsying not for romance, but as a way to deal with serious economic and social problems. By the mid-1920s these transients comprised a visible percentage of many camps' population, especially in the

West, where the first measures to restrict their residence were instituted.

Some sought new homes. Western boosters had hoped to attract new settlers, but it appeared that the good free camps of California, Oregon, and Colorado were housing people who had taken the pitch all-too-seriously. To the chagrin of local people, however, these would-be settlers were not of the substantial business class who might prove a "credit to the community." Rather, they came in the classic emigrant tradition of poor people seeking a new start in a new land. Optimists particularly flooded California looking for the white cottages, free oranges, and plentiful job opportunities advertised by land speculators and work contractors.

Paradise had in fact been oversold. Arriving in a new area after deserting their homes, newcomers discovered that housing and employment were hard to come by. Many settled in autocamps, awaiting a good turn in their luck. Towns enroute to the golden West also became inundated with these migrants. Community bitterness was keen. One Iowa mayor described the change in free camp population in language typical of the mid-20s:

> Ten years ago, or even five years ago, the average tourist was the person who was traveling for pleasure and was a desirable visitor. Today many of the tourists are people with no means whatever. If a tenant on a farm fails to make good, if a businessman fails in business, or a working man gets out of work, he immediately loads his family in a jitney and starts traveling, hoping to get somewhere and confidently expecting to beg or borrow enough gas to keep the machine running, spending a few cents daily for the necessary food. This type of tourist is of no value to any community, and in fact is a liability to any community that he favors with his presence.[7]

Some would-be settlers wound up on charity rolls. Others had to beg for gas, food, and change. A few may have turned to petty crime, or so regular tourists feared. To Van de Water the conversion from respectable settler to pest seemed almost inevitable. Once the frustrated settler "finds that he can earn or beg or pilfer enough to live [sic] and so drifts along from town to town. Gradually the virus of a nomadic life infects him. He becomes a motor hobo, a full-fledged auto tramp who, at times may descend to crime and rarely rises above anything but the most temporary of jobs." This new breed of hobo gave the tourist-vagabond a bad name. A Texan observed that the major problem in tourist camps "is that of the 'hobo' tourist, or that class of traveler who moves from camp to camp in a dilapidated Ford, always broke (both tourist and Ford), always begging and remaining in one city until ordered to move on. These persons are irresponsible vagabonds, who take advantage of the excellent service which has been provided by cities for the accommodation of reputable travelers."[8] For those concerned about a new race of permanent gypsies, the threat seemed real.

Yet many semi-permanent motor campers *did* find work. In fact, their labor was essential. Booster communities may have oversold opportunities for white collar work, but many areas depended on another class of migrant, the seasonal worker. While the auto-borne harvester is generally associated with the Farm Security Administration (FSA) photographs of the late 1930s, the movement actually began around World War I. Some were of the hobo type: single men who followed the wheat harvests from Texas to Canada, now by "fourth-hand" car instead of by rail. Historian Reynold M. Wik notes that "this added mobility brought a sense of dignity to those who shocked grain and pitched bundles during the harvest season." Others were poor families who picked fruit and vegetables. In resort areas like Southern California, the Gulf Coast, and Florida, they might be skilled artisans and servants who worked at fancy hotels. For migrant workers the used flivver meant a slight step upward in the world, for they could travel more extensively by car than by rail. Given the nature of this low-pay work, many did become off-season financial burdens to agricultural communities where they settled. But their work was vital to the nation's farmers, who often encouraged their numbers as a way to keep wages low and unions weak. Indeed, Industrial Workers of the World organizers deplored this trend, charging that it atomized the labor force and gave workers a false sense of upward mobility.[9]

The problem was that many of these workers lived in the same camps as regular tourists. Migrants thus avoided the squalor and tyranny of farm camps and the high costs of working-class boarding houses. Living in relatively heterogeneous tourist camps, migrants could retain a sense of independence and self-respect. But local communities resented the fact that migrants did not spend like tourists; worse, regular tourists disliked the company. Tourists might accept a little integration with transient workers, but only a little. In resort areas tourists and laborers shared a common dislike for pretentious hotels. There was also some sympathy—more pity than compassion—for white collar types who, falling on bad times, had to leave respectable positions and homes. Traveling salesmen and peddlers were occasionally welcome. But class and ethnic differences between agricultural workers and tourists were simply too great; Van de Water found them "a sinister, frowzy, none-to-honest lot."[10]

Perhaps most disturbing was the highly visible automobility of these destitute people. At a time when cars were still considered signs of success, the migrant motorist was an unwelcome reminder of economic dislocation. His dilapidated Ford mocked the studied shabbiness of regular autocampers, for his shabbiness was real. Also threatening was the fact that many migrants took their families along. Autocamping had appealed to a desire to stabilize middle-class families; yet cars seemed to make migrant family life less secure, for migrants did not enjoy permanent homes, schools, or churches. Their lives were often viewed in melodramatic terms, as if the "shiftless" father had "committed his wife and several children to a life of motor vagabondage."[11] In the depression, the FSA photos and John Steinbeck's *Grapes of Wrath* would impart a heroic aura to the migrant family's struggle, but the prevailing moralistic tone of the 1920s did not accept the idea that women and children's labor might be necessary for family survival, or that the shared economic life of these families might actually enhance solidarity.

While migrants were largely a problem west of the Mississippi, by the mid-1920s even tourist camps with few migrant residents were taking steps against riff-raff. Although it is hard to document, since only the middle classes are represented in touring literature, one suspects that even more disturbing than the migrant was the working-class tourist who was out for recreation, not work. For the working-class autocamper, the free camp was the only way to take a family vacation because hotels were too expensive; for him the autocamp was more a melting pot of necessity than of choice. One guidebook cited these two entirely different motives for going to a camp: "Many people of means choose an extended tour, camping along the way, as the most interesting and restful vacation possible, while to many a family of modest circumstances, 'camping out' via auto offers the only opportunity of enjoying an inexpensive rest period." A Yellowstone superintendent found the latter type to be increasing as car ownership spread in the mid-1920s. "The motive of sage brushing is changing. A few years ago it was but a recreation for those who wanted to get away from civilization; they wanted to rough it, eat dirt as it were, and exist for a time without a semblance of comfort. Today camping out is but an economical expedient for seeing the U.S.A."[12] The low-budget camper also differed in his view of autocamping's folksy qualities. For the urbane tourist, camping's well-advertised homey charm had an exotic, nostalgic appeal; for the inexperienced vacationist, the same features had more practical utility. Intimidated by hotel and restaurant rituals, the initiate welcomed the informality and self-service of camping as a relatively painless way to enter the strange new world of travel.

Some of these new travelers were factory workers who used summer furloughs to travel. Since only about a tenth of factory workers had paid vacations, most had to minimize expenses; in some cases, they sought odd jobs along the way to pay for food and gas while living rent-free in municipal camps. Others toured as a way to visit distant relatives. Sociologists found that such family-visiting was inversely related to income; that is, for the less affluent, maintaining extended family ties was more important than sightseeing. These motorists stayed in autocamps enroute. Indeed, some held family reunions in public campgrounds, which were more spacious than the average working-class backyard and more pleasant than a hired hall. Autocamps also accommodated local people for whom even the short trip was out of the question. The nearby free public site offered these campers a convenient weekend respite.[13]

Many glowing articles welcomed the camp melting pot but they could not help but contain a certain ambivalence about the "all kinds." Even the most enthusiastic could betray a bemused condescension toward the lower-class camper, with his funny language, plain manners, and homemade equipment. One *Literary Digest* poem, "An Elegy Written in a Tourist Camping-Ground," typified the literate observer's patronizing attitude:

Beneath those tattered tops, those patent tents,
   Where falls the dust into each sunburned pore,
Each on his folding bed of slight expense,
   The rude explorers of the highway snore.

Let not ambition mock their creaky cars,
   Their khaki clothes, of vintage obscure,
Nor grandeur's view, with hauteur like a czar's,
   The short and simple flivvers of the poor.[14]

By the mid-1920s ambivalence turned to dismay. As noted earlier, enthusiasm over the rich who hobnobbed at tourist camps outweighed the love of beaten-down flivvers. Now the Pierce-Arrowing millionaires began to desert the camp. Complaining of excess publicity, even the ostensibly democratic Henry Ford ceased autocamping after 1924. As one *New York Times* writer put it, "The very fact that all the mechanics, the clerks, and their wives and sweethearts were driving through the Wisconsin lake country, camping at Niagara, scattering tin cans and soda pop bottles over the Rockies, made those places taboo for bankers and chairmen of the board." Some went to Europe; others rediscovered the resort. With the increasing popularity of jazz and active sports, the resort routine seemed less sedentary than before the war. As auto tent sales began to decline after 1925, sales of tennis rackets and golf clubs rose. And with the new sports clothes trend, resorts were less formal. Guests could be both casual and respectably dressy. Khakis and old clothes lost their place as the sole comfortable alternative to business dress and tuxedos.[15]

Where the rich went, the middle class threatened to follow. Worried about losing the middle-class base they had fought hard to gain, autocamping proponents now sought to inject more respectability into their pitch. In the altered vocabulary of the mid-twenties, names like motor hobo, auto gypsy, and motor vagabond took on a negative connotation. Even tin can tourist was left to the riff-raff; camping tourist or motor camper became the preferred title, and some campers removed the old tin can insignia from their radiators. *Motor Camper and Tourist* and other camping publications urged autocampers to take better care of their clothing. The reputable tourist would not want to be confused with the motor hobo, whose "tatterdemalion" appearance indicated empty pocketbooks and questionable morality. To serve the sports clothes market, *Motor Camper and Tourist* hired a fashion editor, Mrs. A. Sherman Hitchcock, who advised readers to look "conservative [yet] smart." "There is nothing more deplorable than a motorcamper whose clothing is soiled and wrinkled and whose appearance is unkempt."[16]

Many campers also became more style conscious about their cars. The age of the trucklike, infinitely modifiable Model T would come officially to an end in 1927, yet its demise was already certain in 1920, with the growing popularity of closed cars. The newer cars had less space for extra gear in the back. A carelessly unpacked tent pole might scratch the paint. An auto tent bolted to the running board spoiled the car's classy lines. Some feared that too much camp equipment might overload springs and strain the engine. Moreover, if one drove with awkward, improvised camping equipment, one risked being taken for a tin can tourist. The image of the autocamper as an unacceptable vagrant with an "old rattletrap car piled high with tents and whatnot" would live on well into the mid-1930s—to be reinforced by photographs of dust bowl refugees who did travel that way. Equipment manufacturers advertised lighter equipment and more streamlined luggage racks that would avoid the "unsightly mess," the "abomination" of excess gear casually strapped on running board and overflowing tonneau.[17]

A 1926 guide "to proper methods and equipment for the successful Tourist-Camper" summed up the rationale for replacing the original idiosyncratic criteria for equipment selection— anything goes as long as it works—with a more discriminating, less faddish approach: "Properly done, motor camping is a pleasant, wholesome recreation; improperly done it is gypsying, with all of the dusty, dirty inconvenience and discomfort of that much over-romanticised life." The sensibly outfitted traveler knew "how to motor camp without hoboism." A *Motor Camper and Tourist* contributor urged a similarly moderate demeanor: "Throw off the restraints of life without discarding your religion.

Get rid of the conventions of civilization without departing from your moral convictions. It is a trick to do it, but it can be done. This is to get the juice out of camping without the jaundice."[18] Other writers reiterated the conservative, recreationist role of autocamping: to relax the tired vacationist in order to revive everyday ties.

Behind this advice was an anxiety that perhaps automobility had gone too far, threatening cherished norms. The 1920s witnessed the rise of the leisure ethic, but it was a transitional period. Traditional values of work and thrift still held sway, especially for middle-class moralists worried about lower-class restlessness. There was something indecent and dangerous about poor people enjoying what had so recently been the prerogative of the upper and upper middle classes. "Fun and funds are intimately related," a *Motor Camper and Tourist* article reminded readers.[19] When a car had been the reward for hard work, paid for with hard cash, it represented success and progress; but when working-class people began buying cheap cars on credit—reportedly sacrificing clothing, homes, their children's education, even food—the automobile seemed more an instrument of corruption. Wouldn't these people, already weakened by easy mobility, be unable to resist the well-known temptations of vagabondage? The virus of gypsying seemed most dangerous when caught by the man of little means.

There is something puzzling about the moralistic reaction against motor gypsies. Even as car ownership broadened, how many poor travelers could there have been? Author of *The Car Culture,* James Flink, points out that only half of all American families had automobiles in 1927; touring remained predominantly middle class. Nor were all migrants and working-class tourists necessarily dirty or immoral. There is no doubt that tourist camp problems—crowding, litter, unsafe sanitation—did increase as more people went autocamping, but who was at fault? There may have been an element of projection at work, a tendency to focus blame on the most visible newcomers. Perhaps fears about the bad effect of automobility on lower-class families reflected new doubts about the car's benefits for middle-class families. Despite original hopes, cars were not holding families together, except during the initial novelty stage, which passed all too quickly. Perhaps fears about the effect of the touring virus on workers' morality reflected qualms about what the installment credit system was doing to traditional middle-class values. Was it the working class or the business class that was being corrupted by the easy credit that facilitated spendthrift consumerism?[20]

By the mid-1920s the car culture was beginning to enter a new stage of consciousness—or perhaps it was a traditionalist backlash. Observers now questioned whether the age of mass automobility would be so golden after all. Cars took city people to the country, but they also killed animals crossing the road and polluted country air. Cars took families on Sunday outings, but they also fostered conflict between parents and teenagers on Saturday night and eroded church attendance. Cars spared commuters the ordeals of streetcars, but they also killed pedestrians—in extraordinary numbers. It was the death toll that most shocked Americans. Over 25,000 people were killed by cars in 1925; almost 70 percent were pedestrians and, of these, a third were children under 15. A war for possession of the streets was being fought in every city, and the car was emerging victorious.[21]

These tensions were the result of rapid, uncontrolled automotive expansion, unhappy byproducts of excessive individualism in the use of a very powerful, dangerous machine. But the public was by no means ready to sacrifice its free-wheeling automobility, or to think in such comprehensive social terms. Instead, blame was concentrated on visible deviants: for example, joy-riding rebellious youth, stone-throwing slum-street children, reckless foreign chauffeurs. It was easier to call for stronger parental authority than to build safer cars, and easier to ban city children from neighborhood streets than to restrict traffic. Rather than face the love of power in every driver, moralists bemoaned the installment credit system that seemed to extend a license to kill to the "irresponsible" poor.

Similarly, as tourist camps entered their mass institutional stage, the problems that tourists blamed on tramps may well have been as much the fault of middle-class tourists and merchant boosters. Just as immigration restrictionists looked for an easy segregationist solution to the complex problems of modern civilization, proponents of tourist camp restriction sought to explain the basic contradictions endemic to mass touring by isolating the newest generation of autocampers.

Camp Problems

For example, many of the better free camps became very crowded because they offered facilities that every camper appreciated; yet when this crowding inevitably led to friction, writers blamed "flivver bums" for the disturbance.

Considering the antiurban bias of camping and touring, the characterization of some tourist camps as motor cities was quite ironic. Denver's motor metropolis housed several thousand neighbors each night in carefully laid out plots along grid streets. Tired, dust-covered tourists generally welcomed its up-to-the-minute conveniences, and through the camp grapevine they pressured other towns to follow suit. But they also came to regret the impersonality, the mechanization, and the long lines. Such features seemed to belong in large city hotels not in friendly autocamps. Small-town camps along main routes also became crowded in the touring season. National and state parks offered impressive facilities, but they too came to resemble little cities, with all the attendant problems of herding, clutter, and noise.

Intimacy now seemed impossible. A uniformed caretaker in a booth assigned numbered plots with no more concern than a movie house ticket seller—or a hotel clerk. With the endless coming and going, grounds became very dusty, and traffic made walking hazardous, especially for children. Firewood for the evening meal or camp fire was hard to find; at national park camps trees were stripped of all usable wood. Moreover, relations with neighbors became strained. Noise alone could disrupt what was intended as a bucolic reprieve; at the very least it made it hard to rest up for tomorrow's drive. Too many tourists arrived after dark and noisily set up camp while others tried to sleep. It was all too common to be roughly awakened at 4 A.M. by a "snorting of autos" out to get an early start. One autocamper suggested lynching "the fellow who comes into camp with a cackling party at eleven P.M. and the one who gets out with a roaring motor at five in the morning. What good is such a person?"[22] All tourists were guilty of the urge to make miles, and hard-pressed travelers with limited funds and time may have been particularly so. Earlier promoters had explained such behavior in terms of a universal nomadic instinct, but elitist critics now cited the "mindlessness" of the newly motorized "multitudes."[23]

Even at idyllic destination camps, where tourists might stay a week, noise could be a problem: the daily racket of playing children, clanging pots and pans, card games, camp fire socials, and, most conspicuous, the squawk of radios and phonographs. Autocampers were equipment minded to begin with—especially the less ascetic recreationist—and it seemed natural to bring music along as another way to mix home comforts with outdoor life. "Taking a radio set along on your vacation is a sure means of varying camp life with some of the peppier of the city's activities," *Field and Stream* proposed. The radio allowed campers to be "far from the cares of city life, but in touch with the finest music the city produces, and the day's news." There was also an adventurous, acquisitive side to finding different stations in each locality. Just as tourists liked to accumulate miles and sights, so with a "Radiola" they could catch stations the way they caught fish. "Radio, when you are on the road, offers new delights," one advertisement observed. "Night after night, as you travel north, south, east, or west, you hear new stations coming in, you hear some stations grow stronger day by day, and others weaker and weaker." Knowing that consumers of one technological innovation were likely to be in the market for others, *Motor Camper and*

Tourist had a regular column devoted to "Radio in Camp." Many camps offered electric hookups, so it was easy to bring along a radio to relieve the "monotony" of a lakeside site.[24]

Radio was still an upper middle-class toy in the mid-1920s. More common were record players—which could be even louder—and musical instruments. Although some tourists enjoyed the cacaphony of phonographs, fiddles, banjos, and radios, others found it annoying. "Phonographs put us to sleep at night and waked us up at morn—and at the dead of night."[25] Some noise may indeed have been caused by those unable to afford more private places for entertaining. Autocamps also attracted local young people who liked to exploit the anonymity of being strangers in an open space. The interests of long-distance tourists thus clashed with those of overnight celebrants. Business-class hunters and fishermen could also be culpable "weekend wild men," and all autocampers could occasionally overstep the relaxed protocol of the autocamp.

Nevertheless, many veterans who were put off by the noise, alcohol, and rowdiness, began to long for the peaceful camaraderie of just a few seasons ago. Many traveled to escape the environmental dissonance of bustling cities. Their move toward smaller, more exclusive facilities continued their withdrawal from the stress of having to tolerate an increasingly diverse mixture of life-styles and values.

The motor vagabond was also blamed for the disturbing sanitary problems of many camps. True responsibility, however, lay with local authorities.

Autocamping faced a serious health crisis in the mid-1920s. Inspectors from the Indiana State Board of Health visited 116 municipal camps in the summer of 1923. Of these, 27 percent had water considered unfit for drinking. Over 50 percent had inadequate sewage and garbage disposal systems. Only 22 percent could be deemed safe in water quality, garbage disposal, clean toilets, adequate maintenance, and mosquito control. A study of 150 Minnesota camps noted that the state had hosted an "army" of 500,000 motor tourists in the summer of 1922 with less care than the U.S. Army had shown a few years earlier in France. Again, the two main problems were unsafe drinking water and improper waste disposal. The chief dangers were typhoid, diarrhea, and dysentery. The state's inability to guarantee sanitary camps for tourists also endangered the health of those living near the camps. Similarly, about 80 percent of Colorado's free camps were said to lack good water and clean toilets in 1924. A 1924 Pennsylvania state inspection of roadside drinking water approved only 38 percent of 875 water supplies, many of these at roadside camps and restaurants. Of 60 Texas camps surveyed in 1924, 85 percent provided water—although of uncertain quality—yet only 38 percent had toilets of any kind. Some 40 percent offered showers, but only 10 percent employed attendants to maintain camp facilities.[26]

And so it went in numerous state health department surveys. Autocampers hit the road in search of rural peace and outdoor health; yet, as one concerned writer put it, "the sorry truth of the matter is that these motorists cannot roam about free from care, if they are to be sure that their vacations will do them more good than harm.[27] Health dangers plagued not only tourists camps but also rural food stands, tourist homes, and filling stations. The whole roadside industry was troubled with health problems, partly because the countryside lagged behind cities in basic sanitation. The same charges were also leveled at country hotels. Roadside facilities were particularly dangerous, however, because they had mushroomed much faster than the ability or willingness of state health officials to regulate them. Only with great reluctance did states acknowledge the need for investigation, and even then solutions were voluntaristic. For example, camps that met basic standards could receive state certificates of approval, but it was still the decision of individuals whether to patronize uncertified camps. Essentially, it was the responsibility of each town to improve its camp. The main incentives were the local profits and good reputation earned from a well-maintained camp.

By the mid-twenties the incentives were not sufficient. For one thing tourists now tended to take conveniences for granted. Whereas just a few years earlier a good camp enhanced a town's image, by the mid-twenties a good camp merely prevented a town from getting the "Indian sign" from tourists, as one South Dakota official put it.[28] Having turned defensive, boosterism was also increasingly expensive. Originally an adequate camp could be established for a few hundred dollars: a few tables and benches scattered over a vacant field, a pit toilet, a well, perhaps a few swings, and a shed for shelter from the rain. But now the tourist word-of-mouth network trapped towns in costly competition to provide the latest in flush toilets, showers, and elaborate community buildings.

Meanwhile, the autocamping market clearly was not going to be as lucrative as expected by town officials. Having justified free camps on the grounds that autocampers were hotel-class tourists whose generous travel expenditures would trickle through the whole community, sponsors now complained that many tourists did not spend enough to merit the town subsidy. A Boston area study found that instead of spending three to five dollars a day per car, most tourists appeared to be spending under one dollar per car—mostly for gas. The city manager of Wichita, Kansas, doubted that even the more affluent tourist spent very much in town. "A person who is touring the country is not on a shopping expedition, and has no intention of making purchases that are not essential for the task at hand."[29]

In one sense, the failure of many tourists to spend large sums of money testified to the success of autocamping as a truly popular pastime. After all, promoters had boasted that autocampers would save money. Moreover, autocamping had clearly arrived as a mass institution. Millions of Americans—by no means the poorest, but not the traditional vacation class either—wandered the road, camped in natural settings, met new people, and saw patriotic sights. In fact, these new customers were essential to the American automobile industry, for they bought the used cars that had become a problem for dealers trying to keep up with the frequent model changes now being instituted by major manufacturers.

But many civic groups felt insulted by the tourists' refusal to hold up their end of the bargain. Boosters of El Paso's Camp Grande complained of a "class of tourists who seemed to realize none of their obligations to the community that was so generous to them." *Motor Camper and Tourist* had to remind readers of the details of that bargain: Since the municipally owned camp was usually supported by the businessmen of the town, it was "only fair that they receive our patronage." Urging tourists to visit local stores, one promoter observed that "no honest camper would want to feel that he was obtaining something for which he was returning nothing." Yet many tourists did seem to insist on getting something for nothing. Indeed, they wanted more even as they spent less. Arguing against free camps, one manager maintained that few "bonafide tourists" stopped there; most were "automobile tramps. . . . boomers who live by their wits."[30]

Booster enthusiasm waned sharply. Many small towns could not afford to subsidize the required improvements: piped-in water, septic tanks, frequent garbage pickups, screens, regular inspection and maintenance. Others neglected their camps altogether. This failure of civic groups and town governments to follow through angered state health officials. "If a community cannot afford to furnish the equipment for a tourist camp, simple or elaborate as it may be," one Minnesota inspector wrote, "it should not advertise the lie that a camp exists. A vacant lot with an adjacent privy and a mud puddle should not be labeled a 'tourist camp.' "[31]

Larger towns might have the funds and the tourist volume to afford basic improvements; in the competition for the up-to-date, the winnings naturally gravitated to larger units, just as large city hotels were generally superior to small town hotels. But tourists could not reconcile their general preference for small-town intimacy with the idea that small towns could be dangerous places to camp, while large city camps, despite their disagreeable crowds, could be the safest. Few were willing to place the blame squarely on the shoulders of local sponsors, where it belonged. After all, the small-town welcome was an agreeable part of the touring experience. And few small-town boosters, for their part, were willing to shoulder the blame. Who could admit to being a "quitter"?

For one *Outlook* writer the cause of health problems was all too clear: "Many a car carries a collection of humanity that seems to have said farewell to all rules of cleanliness, and its occupants leave on the camp their dangerous record." It was very easy to blame the migrant worker, who might indeed suffer from poor health, or the dirty "hobo" or the morally promiscuous "jazz hound." Another writer carefully drew the line between the "bonafide vacation automobile camper" and the "white gypsy:" "The 'white gypsy' is a tramp who has taken over an old car and lives upon the country, preying upon farmers' crops and cutting down trees, breaking up camp furniture, stealing from fruit stands and stores and making himself a general nuisance. Generally he is out of work, so he says, and adds to the tricks of tramping those of the professional beggar." Another blamed local "rowdies" for littering campsites and destroying privies. Reasoning that local poor people resented and envied affluent long-distance tourists and took this resentment out on camp property, he argued for further separation of tourists and natives—perhaps by banning the latter from public camps altogether. For others the solution was even simpler: bar *all* undesirables who, through ignorance or depravity, ruined campsites and thereby drove away "legitimate" tourists who *would* spend generously in town.[32]

Separating "Goats" from "Sheep"

By 1924 a growing number of writers, civic groups, and state officials advocated a user's fee as the best way to upgrade camp facilities and clientele. Given rising demands for comfort and convenience, they argued, how could small towns afford to keep up without charging for services? The free camp subsidized the poor tourist, but serving the cheapest tourist was a disservice to public health. To be sure, a fee would eliminate poor tourists, but it would also finance improvements that would win back more affluent tourists. Few had any doubt that spending tourists did exist, for auto clubs, business magazines, and the U.S. Chamber of Commerce were quoting average daily expenditures for automobile tourists in the mid-twenties at anywhere between $4.00 and $20.00 a car. The AAA predicted that in the summer of 1925 tourists would spend $2.5 billion in communities along the road,

$1.6 billion in California and Florida alone. Another prediction put the figure at $3.3 billion for 1927. These were very crude extrapolations, based on the most affluent tourists, but they received wide publicity.[33] It seemed obvious that money could be made. By imposing a fee, therefore, town officials hoped to attain the goals originally set for free camps: local profits and good publicity. If successful, they would then have a continuing incentive to keep camps well maintained.

In an attempt to favor the "bonafide" tourist some towns stopped short of fees. The simplest solution was to impose a time limit on a stay at a municipal camp. This expedient was particularly popular in through camps, serving as overnight stops for tourists enroute to resort or sightseeing areas. Towns along the Lincoln Highway, Yellowstone Trail, National Parks Trail, and over main highways found that a 48- or 72-hour limit discouraged itinerants, peddlers, migrant workers, and "agents" who tended to stay too long. In one typical sleepy western town a fee was unnecessary because it was a convenient stopping place between two destinations, a day's drive on either side: 150 miles to the north was a national park, 150 miles south was a big city. While tourists did buy fuel and food there, most stopped just for the night, since there was not much to see. Likewise, it was generally assumed in the prairie and plains states that the spending tourist would be passing through on the way to more scenic places. Hence, the time limit—rather than the 50 cent fee—was an expedient popular in the Midwest well into the late 1920s.[34]

In destination areas like the Colorado Rockies, Florida, California, Wisconsin, and the Texas Gulf Coast, however, the time limit was not a workable alternative, for tourists liked to stay a week or two. One scheme set a 24-hour limit for local residents—to discourage the "weekend boozehound" or the migrant worker—while allowing out-of-state tourists a free rein. In Southern California, however, where out-of-staters showed an alarming tendency to become in-state squatters, it was necessary to impose a time limit of four days or a week on all visitors. Those staying longer might have to seek out a private campground. Partly as a result of the flood of would-be settlers, Los Angeles was one of the first places to develop such private camps—over thirty in 1925.[35]

Another solution was to combine a time limit with a registration requirement. For example, Denver's Overland Park instituted a one week camping permit system. If the camper was well behaved, the permit could be renewed for another week. A 1925 Boston Chamber of Commerce study put the case clearly: "We believe that a license requirement would prove a burden and embarrassment only on the undesirable camp and camper, and that it would be welcomed by the higher class camp and the desirable camper."[36] But such permits were too easily obtained—usually by mail from an indifferent government clerk or police sergeant with more pressing business. Many campers were not recognized as "undesirables" until they arrived at camp in run-down cars and shabby clothes. The next step, therefore, was to hire on-site caretakers who could screen applicants as they registered.

Ironically, by requiring on-site registration, camp proponents followed the hotels they claimed to reject. Like the camp, the hotel traced its roots to the legendary medieval inn or caravansary along the open road. Lively and egalitarian, these inns had hosted a diverse clientele of radical thinkers, heretics, and highwaymen. Such gatherings of anonymous strangers had threatened order, however, for local citizens were exposed to foreign, potentially subversive ideas. Town sheriffs introduced the inn register as a way to keep track of possibly dangerous travelers.[37] In its origins, therefore, the hotel register was an instrument of social control, a way for sedentary society to put a brake on road freedom. The autocamp followed in the same direction. Like the license plate and driver's license, the camp register was a move to control excessive automotive independence.

Registrants recorded names, addresses, occupations, and license plate numbers. In part, managers wanted to encourage all to behave more considerately in camp. Camp anonymity, however helpful in encouraging informal give-and-take, had allowed too many campers to litter. Just as hotel registration was one check against theft of towels and sheets, camp identification would protect property. Furthermore, it was assumed that while the "respectable tourist," having nothing to hide, would not object to registration, the "criminal element" would prefer to remain anonymous. The names and statistics would help police and state authorities to check on fugitives rumored to be hiding in the less reputable free camps. Gypsies, hoboes, and migrants would not want to register because they would have no occupations to record. And just as hotel clerks sized up prospective guests, camp caretakers would be able "to separate the goats from the sheep."[38]

The preferred solution for controlling camp population, however, was a camp fee, usually fifty cents, to finance needed maintenance and improvements. Although some resort area camps had charged user's fees from the start, the policy gained wider acceptance only when proposed as a good way to screen out "tramps" and attract the "better class." In defense, fee proponents cited middle-class pride in being able to "pay your own way." In early booster days free accommodations had been a sign of town hospitality, and it was almost one's duty to accept them gratis. Now hospitality towards all comers was attacked as wrong-headed charity that made "a hog out of the tourists." One Minnesota park superintendent argued that a camp's duty was to charge for services. The earlier misguided policy had overburdened the town treasury, and worse, embarrassed the self-respecting traveler. An Iowa mayor agreed that the "better-class tourist" preferred to pay and thus retain his self-respect. "Chief objections come from the hobo class, whose only home is the car they are traveling in," wrote a Denver man, whose Overland Camp experienced a welcomed decline in patronage from "tin can tourist" types when it added a half-dollar charge. Similarly, Oshkosh, Wisconsin, was pleased to report that its fee had eliminated peddlers and "so-called gypsies who have only the barest necessities."[39]

In adding what a Portland, Oregon, pay camp advocate called "the dignity of a reasonable charge for service," the public camp would attract affluent travelers whose patronage would enhance a community's reputation. "The man who travels by motor car should be able to pay expenses just as well as the man who travels by train," wrote one hotel man. The managers of the successful public pay camp of Rapid City, South Dakota, concurred: "The average automobile tourist does not expect to be furnished shelter, food, light, or entertainment any more than the tourist who travels by train expects free hotel accommodations."[40] This average tourist went autocamping not because it was cheap but because it was different, convenient, family-oriented, and good clean fun; after a hard day's drive he was interested more in neat, clean facilities than in social experimentation. The secretary of the Deland, Florida, Commercial Club, which sponsored the local pay camp, urged readers of *Motor Camper and Tourist* not to confuse the well-equipped, well-regulated "modern auto camp" with the discredited free camp:

> As a cussed and discussed municipal institution, the autocamp is in a separate and distinct class, the cussing having mainly arisen from the so-called free tin can tourist camp of the past, which served as a harbor for riff-raff and petty thieves and was rarely patronized by the present day auto tourist who is to be found in all well-regulated Florida auto or tourist camps, comfortably located, having a car in good mechanical condition, and with many ingenious contraptions with which to make himself and party comfortable.[41]

Writing in 1924, this man was a bit too anxious to put the free camp into the distant past—although in the fast-changing world of roadside business, two or three seasons back did seem a long time ago. But in defining the desirable camp patron in terms of a good car and much equipment, he was quite traditional, for boosters had wanted to serve this recreationist, business-class tourist in the first place. Returning to solid business principles—

charging for services rendered—thus seemed the simplest way to salvage that original objective.

Not all municipal officials were convinced that the public pay camp was the solution, however. A few were bothered by this blatant contradiction of public recreation ideals. Although such ideals were still incomplete in the 1920s, some progressive-minded governments had been as interested in the need for public access and control as in the potential for private profit. By banning the "undesirable," wasn't government abdicating its regulatory responsibilities? Where would the poor tourist camp?

Some authorities also worried that rather than reviving sound market practices, the public fee camp violated them. By going deliberately after hotel-class tourists, wasn't the city going into the hotel business? Providing basic facilities for tourist overflow was one thing, but charging for elaborate services was quite another. As early as January 1923, one city manager doubted that a fee system was justifiable, even if it achieved the desired goal of eliminating unwelcome campers. "Why should we go to so much trouble and expense in order to compete with hotel proprietors, restaurant men, and other folks in the community?" In 1923 this argument was premature, for private enterprise still lagged in meeting tourist needs. Although many towns had embarked on intensive campaigns to upgrade or replace inadequate commercial hotels, most remained unattractive, inconvenient, and overpriced. By 1927, however, partly as a result of speculative financing, the small-town hotel market was overbuilt, and hotel men began to complain that the better tourist camps took away customers.[42]

More important, the fee system opened the door to private camp competition. Previously unable to compete directly with nearby subsidized public camps, private camps had flourished only where they were the only camp for miles, as in the townless desert; where the public camp idea was weak, as in New England; or where public camps were overcrowded, as in Los Angeles. In rural areas a farmer or gas station owner with a monopoly of camping opportunities could rent out his pasture or yard for as much as one dollar a night per car. Early tourists often resented being exploited by such entrepreneurs, especially when they received nothing but water and shade; they naturally preferred to receive the same thing, or more, free of charge at public camps.

Once the public became accustomed to the idea of paying for a public camp, however, the situation changed. For the same price the tourist could stay at a private camp better able to serve the touring habits of the mid-1920s. For example, road improvement favored camps on main highways: a farmer's yard converted to campsites, a gas station, or a roadside cafe's back lot. New through roads might bypass a town altogether, making the centrally-located public camp inconvenient. Ever concerned with making miles and saving time, campers could camp at a gas station offering overnight servicing, or at a farmer's camp offering fried chicken for dinner and fresh eggs for breakfast. Also, private operators were more selective in allowing only certain campers to stop, and such camps were likely to be smaller, less noisy, and less crowded. A resident proprietor could supervise his camp more actively than a paid caretaker, and by using members of his family for camp maintenance, he could save on overhead. In all, the profit incentive seemed to ensure better service—the ultimate market principle. As one analyst of the situation concluded, "Local patriotism may be a powerful force, but hope of personal profit is stronger. The tourist camp proprietor who has gone into the business on his own account is usually more considerate of his patrons, more concerned for their comfort than the man who is paid by a board of trade to run an auto park for the glory of the community.[43]

The mid-twenties were transitional years, when many towns imposed fees just as others began to abandon public camps altogether. As always, the West Coast took the lead, partly because year-around touring made roadside business there uniquely profitable, and partly because this region had the greatest difficulties with migrants and would-be settlers. In many cases, after charging a fee for a short period, town officials actively encouraged local entrepreneurs to take over the camp trade. Reserving the right to inspect and approve highway camps, local officials converted the town camp back into a daytime picnic area. A comparison of 1925 and 1928 AAA camp directories revealed a marked shift toward private camps. In 1925, only 9 of Colorado's 64 listed camps were privately run; by 1928, 65 were private, 20 public. In 1925, 9 of Ohio's 83 camps were private; in 1928, 57 of 102. Pennsylvania had 10 private camps in 1925 out of 32 listed; in 1928, 73 of 98.[44]

Meanwhile, some free camps lingered on, indifferently maintained, as muddy resting places for the lowest budget traveler. A 1926 Indiana health department survey of 101 camps indicated that 61 percent of the state's private camps deserved approval, against only 28 percent of the municipal camps. A 1930 poll of 59 cities found that 29 had abandoned their camps, the key variable being private competition. The remaining 30 successful camps existed where there were no commercial camps, and where there was still some civic spirit in support of the camp. But such spirit was hard to maintain if private competition did arise. Competition with private camps became even less justifiable when cottages began to appear. No public camp could make this adaptation, for it would be too brazen an encroachment on hotel and resort territory. By the mid-1930s, most remaining municipal camps had to be shut down as public nuisances by state health inspectors, and the low-income tourist had to turn to the cheapest private camps or to some secluded highway turnout where he would not get caught. Once the "roadside apartment" of the wealthy motor gypsy, the makeshift camp by the side of the road was now the illegal refuge of the unwanted auto tramp.[45]

Ultimately, municipal camps failed because their sponsors were torn between serving the public interests of outdoor recreation and serving the profit interests of local merchants. Idealism favored the free or low-fee camp; profit favored a more exclusive, expensive enterprise. The prevailing free-market ideology of the day complicated matters, for it worked against the wholly subsidized free camp, yet made it hard to justify a user's fee that placed public camps in direct competition with hotels. Private operators had no such qualms. They went right after the spending tourist, first with more attractive camping facilities, and then with cottages.

Early Motels
1925–1945

Despite the hopes of fee proponents, the pay camp was more a new stage in the commercialization of the roadside than a return to the original booster plan. Having evolved from squatter encampment to public institution, the autocamp was now a business. The focus of this narrative shifts, therefore, to roadside businessmen who paid close attention to the spending tourist's desire for accommodations that were economical yet comfortable, simple yet convenient, and intimate yet selective. Twenty years of experimentation with tourist camps, cabin camps, cottage camps, cottage courts, and motor courts would produce the motor hotel that came of age after World War II.

Although the motel of 1945 was a far cry from the municipal autocamp of 1920, history did repeat itself in at least one sense. Like their booster predecessors, private operators preferred "better-class" tourists to less affluent travelers. In pursuing this market they raised industry standards. Ironically, in making tourist camps respectable, they attracted a new group of investors whose large-scale motel building after the war would put most remaining tourist camp pioneers out of business.

From Camp to Cabin, 1925–1930

Who were these tourist camp pioneers, these not-so-distant forerunners of Holiday Inn's Kemmons Wilson and Travelodge's Scott King? Generally, they were from humble origins. While the shift to pay camps restricted camping opportunities for less affluent tourists, it expanded profit-making opportunities for small-scale entrepreneurs previously excluded from the autocamping trade. Just as the centrally located municipal camp had been designed to favor downtown merchants, the outlying private camp favored rural property owners. More important,

6

now there could be several camps within a given area, rather than just one per town. The private pay camp thus did for roadside entrepreneurs what the early roadside encampment had done for pioneer motor gypsies: both replaced monopolistic institutions, both extended individual options. Just as early autocampers had been able to squat virtually anywhere along the road, early tourist camp proprietors could lay out campsites on any land bordering a moderately busy highway. Gypsying had democratized camping; private camps democratized camp management.

Some tourist camp pioneers were owners of roadside food stands, grocery stores, boarding houses, or gasoline stations for whom a campground was originally a sideline. In the free camp days, some roadside vendors sought to compete with downtown merchants by encouraging free camping near their main business. But because such facilities were not self-supporting, they generally remained primitive. As the fee principle spread, however, campsites became profitable in themselves. Soon many others became infatuated with a camp business. Eyeing roadside property, they saw an opportunity to become independent operators in an industry that seemed destined to grow. To this was added the romance of the small innkeeper, the pleasure of serving the public. The prospect of meeting all kinds traveling along the open road was especially appealing to farmers' wives, daughters, and widows who longed for outside contact and income but were not ready to forsake country for city. Other pioneering proprietors were themselves autocamping migrants who looked to a roadside business as a way to settle down while keeping in touch with the liberated road lifestyle. The Bearl Sprotts, for example, went on a year-long autocamping trip in 1919 and, after motoring fifteen days from Memphis to Los Angeles, became enthralled by the easy living at Los Angeles's free Elysian Park campground. But the camp was too crowded and did not permit campers to stay more than a week. Sensing a ready market for a private camp with no time restrictions, they bought a cheap lot near Lincoln Park and rented tent space, with the aim of staying a season or two before hitting the road again.[1]

Similarly, in 1925 Clara and Will Keyton were rootless itinerants, working here and there in southwestern mining towns, living out of their car, saving money with the idea of buying a small business so they could "get off wages" for good. Driving through a small Arizona town, they decided, more or less on a whim, to buy a small plot on the outskirts and set up a filling station-grocery. When a tired tourist offered them twenty-five cents to camp out back, they decided to rent tent space, too. Since the town did not have its own public camp, there was much demand for this.[2]

Expansion generally followed a good season. Roadside peddlers learned early that it was best to sell a variety of products and services, for mileage-making tourists valued one-stop shopping. Gas stations added campsites, camp owners added gas stations. Diversification was also a hedge against seasonal fluctuations and bad weather, variables to which the tourist business was exceptionally vulnerable. Aiming to make autocamping a year-round business, Californians took the lead in building cabins to shelter tourists during rainy winter months. The Sprotts built their first simple cabins in 1922. The Keytons added cottages in 1926 to protect campers from Arizona dust storms. Through the traveler grapevine the idea spread. All regions experienced bad weather at the height of the touring season. It was easy to nail together a few heavy planks or to convert a chicken coop into a cabin to catch the extra autocamper who, during a thunderstorm, might otherwise speed ahead to a hotel.

Many cabins were little more than wooden tents with dirt floors. Autocampers still provided their own cots, chairs, and camp stoves. Other facilities differed little from regular camps: community toilets, showers, and, occasionally, a central kitchen. At fifty to seventy-cents a night, these shacks were intended for emergencies. Yet they proved popular in good weather as well, for they spared harried motorists the chore of setting up a tent each night and packing it each morning.

Still more popular were slightly more elaborate units that, at one dollar a night, furnished a simple iron bed with a straw-stuffed mattress, a few benches, a table, a water pitcher and bowl, and perhaps a coin-operated gas plate. Resort area camps had long rented such cabins to summer vacationists staying for a week or more, but after 1925 the idea caught on at through camps. Despite their Spartan furnishings, these cabins often filled up before dark. This was a real breakthrough, marking the end of autocamping and the beginning of the motel industry.

Cabins sold well because many tourists simply tired of tenting each night in a new place. Despite the expectation of promoters, camping was in fact a fad. After investing several hundred dollars in autocamping equipment, tourists discovered that they did not like gypsying after all. "We are not a knapsack, open-air people," one *Harper's* writer noted in explaining the rise of cabin camps. "We like nature, but we must have our roads straight and smooth, and we want to view the scenery through the windows (usually closed) of a two-door sedan." Deciding that they preferred "getting there" to lazing along, convenience and comfort to roughing it and self-reliance, many chose to save time and trouble by leaving their equipment at home. Reflecting the return of camping to its traditional wilderness form, tent sales fell from a peak in 1923–1924 to pre-1916 levels in 1929.[3]

The same infatuation with mileage making that had produced the shift from roadside encampment to organized campgrounds also favored cabin camps. Despite much editorial advice about slowing down and seeing things, tourists continued to drive longer and faster. "As a rule," one Arizona camp owner observed, "the motorist cares little for scenery. Nine times out of ten he is principally concerned with breaking his mileage record of the previous day."[4] To be sure, tourists did care about scenery, but at destination areas, not enroute. Better quality pavement, wider roads, the elimination of rail crossings, and more powerful engines, all facilitated longer trips over wider areas. Three hundred miles a day was a good day's drive in 1928; 450 a day was not uncommon, particularly in the West. By furnishing basic housing and equipment, cabin camps relieved travelers of the daily set-up/take-down routine. Motorists saved valuable minutes in the morning and could drive later at night. Nighttime driving was a novelty in the late 1920s. With safer roads and convenient cabins tourists could enjoy this latest automotive mastery over a once-impenetrable barrier: darkness.

Cabins also reduced tensions in family motoring. Intensive driving was very fatiguing, and vacationing families discovered that a long day's drive strained comradeship. Children became cranky, parents irritable. Rather than bringing everyone together, the evening set-up might be the last straw. This was especially true as the newness wore off by the second summer of autocamping. Moreover, very small children did not seem to appreciate roughing it the way their parents might. "It has always seemed to me that to take small children on these camping trips is the next thing to cruelty," wrote one former autocamper. "The little youngsters, being creatures of habit, are usually distressed by the very change of conditions which is so refreshing to grown-ups."[5]

The cabin seemed a happy compromise. There was still enough roughing it to reinvigorate family life. Beds and other domestic arrangements were cruder than home. Everyone lived in the same small space and huddled around a common old-fashioned stove. Since camps were generally located in the country, children could still play outdoors, and everyone could breathe healthy fresh air. Yet the cabin was more comfortable and secure than the tent. "Cottages camps are justly popular," camping advocate Frank Brimmer had to admit, "not only because of the time saved in pitching a tent and reloading the automobile—but also because they place over one's head a substantial roof, the windows and doors are closely screened against insect pests, and there is a clean floor underfoot." After a tiresome day on the road, parents, too, might appreciate peace and quiet. Frederic Van de Water, who experienced the whole evolution of roadside camps as he wandered westward in 1926, shared his wife's delight in a cabin in Oregon for one dollar a night: "The Commodore [the wife], who had looked with a certain suspicion upon our tent since its collapse in Omaha, slumbered soundly without regard for the force and direction of the winds, and the Engineer's [Van de Water's] lungs, untaxed by the ordeal of bed inflation, emitted normal sounds for the first time in five weeks."[6] Cabin comfort was not necessarily more expensive. For a dollar a night—just fifty cents more than the tent fee—a family saved one hundred dollars or more by not buying a good tent and camp furniture. By bringing their own bedding, food, and utensils, they still saved a good deal over hotels. Some camps also offered inexpensive meals, thus sparing road-weary mothers the evening chores. Tourists still saved money by eating breakfast in the cabin and picnicking on the road at noon.

To one father, the cabin camp better served the cause of family revitalization. Autocamping had been a good start, but it was too difficult. Cabins reduced work while strengthening intimacy and companionship. "The modern approved tourist camp is the answer to more problems than one. Now that the American family can all play together out of doors and go home rested and well, it will soon show up that they will work better together, stick closer to each other, and make better all-round citizens in every way."[7] The cabin camp thus inherited the autocamp's role as an important family-recreation institution.

The cabin camp also inherited the autocamp's communal appeal—with important qualifications. Strangers still swapped stories while waiting in line to use the shower or toilet, and commentators soon adopted the same superlatives in extolling this new democratic forum: "Informality is the pasword, snobbery is taboo, every man is your neighbor, and all are bound together by an almost unbelievably powerful tie—the dust of the open road. A tourist camp group often reminds one of a huge, old-fashioned family reunion."[8] At cabin camps, however, proprietor-hosts could ban black sheep, and cabin privacy was the ultimate protection. Once admitted, guests could keep to themselves, with no questions asked. Except for communal toilets and showers, public appearances were optional.

Perhaps most significant, the cabin resolved the autocamper's dilemma of how to go "light but right," to move freely yet to live comfortably. In autocamping, the motorist's freedom to come and go without constraint had been compromised by the camper's desire to be self-sufficient. The more equipment the autocamper took along to make himself at home, the harder it was to pick up and go at will. By patronizing the commercial cabin camp, the motor tourist now sacrificed romantic autarchy for the sake of easy mobility. Instead of carrying his own housing, he lived in someone else's house. In return for this freedom to travel effortlessly, he agreed to pay a fee. In effect he became a consumer again. This was a fateful decision, for it encouraged cabin owners to offer more conveniences at higher fees: sheets and blankets, soap and towels, dishes, hot showers, steam heat, radio, all-night cafe service. By 1930 one visionary predicted that within a few years every American of moderate means would be able to drive coast-to-coast with only a small suitcase. Able to depart each morning at a moment's notice, he would be assured of a comfortable, full-service "home away from home" each night. To *Fortune* magazine this seemed the ultimate in automobility: "motion with the least possible interruption."[9] The motel of the near future would thus fulfill the earliest motor gypsy's dream of a roadside hotel located everywhere along an unbounded open road, only now the vision would be pursued through consumption, not self-reliance.

In 1925, however, few cabin owners foresaw that they would soon be entering the hotel business. Most cabins were shacks. Indeed, fearing that tourists would steal anything not tied down, some proprietors at first hesitated to add such simple amenities as beds and tables. Sharing the autocamper's animus against the hotel, early pioneers valued the camp's unpretentiousness. In naming camps, entrepreneurs were ardent simplified spellers, preferring folksy phonetics to standard English, especially the certain *K* to the ambiguous *C*. "U-Smile Kamp," "Kamp Kozy Kabins," and "U Wanna Kum Back" were particular favorites. Roadside wits loved to call their humble establishments inns: "U Kum Inn," "Dew Drop Inn," "U Pop Inn," and "Tumble Inn." As if to mock the current fad for roadside tearooms called "Ye Ragged Robin" and "The Crumperie," one farmer called his crossroads filling station "Ye Olde Grease Shoppe." Another hung "Chez Quick Lunch" over her roadside hot dog stand. The non-camping tourist seeking some picturesque, "olde" hostelry could easily be tripped up by the country humorist's love of exaggeration. As one New England tourist found in 1925, some proprietors may have relished the confrontation:

When at last the [well-advertised] Mountain Inn bursts into view, you could burst into tears, you are so disillusioned. It is a blight on the landscape, a miserable little shack of logs that two boy scouts could put up in three days and a half. It is literally plastered with tin signs of the times advertising every vile concoction known to the service of substitution for real drink and food, and every tree and shrub surrounding the place has either been cut down or has given up the struggle voluntarily from too much buffeting from the world.
It is presided over by a slattern in a soiled bungalow apron and a breakfast cap. Her unkempt and equally soiled husband (he is

mentioned second because he is that kind of a man) attends to the gasoline and oil, and converses in nasal tones with a shifty-eyed truck driver about the unreasonable demands of the public, only this is how it sounds:

"Yeah. An' this bird had th' nerve to ast—'Is they a bathroom in connection with the room?' Bathroom! Huh, what does he think this is, the Waldorf-Astory? An' I says t'him, 'No, they ain't no bathroom, but they's a pitcher of good cold water in th' room, an' a cake of soap,' and he looked at me like I was a pizen snake, and got in his shiny sedan and drove off. I dunno what folks are comin' to these days."[10]

While overdrawn, the portrait accurately suggests the gulf between early cabin-style and genteel inn expectations. The fully literate, conscientious, ever-polite proprietor of a small Arizona cabin camp, Clara Keyton was no "slattern in a soiled bungalow apron and a breakfast cap," but she did greet arrivals in greasy overalls, for when not tending cabins, she helped pump gas and change oil. Keyton, for her part, had little interest in catering to noncompromisers, whose fussy pretentiousness offended her sense of practical propriety.

Yet the business shortly became much more complicated. Written in 1940–42, Clara Keyton's *Tourist Camp Pioneering Experiences* sentimentalized the easy early years precisely because they disappeared so soon. The Keyton camp opened in 1925. After adding simple cabins in 1926, the Keytons built twenty new cottages at a new site along U.S. 66 in 1928. By 1930 they had forty units and, by Clara's account, operated the most modern camp in the area, profitably serving the hotel-class customers she claimed to dislike. Similarly, the Bearl Sprotts, who had originally planned to return to Memphis after a year in the private camp business, expanded their camp yearly until, by 1933, their Lincoln Park Motor Cottage Camp had over two hundred units. Modest origins aside, these pioneers were alert to roadside entrepreneurial opportunities, and they quickly expanded operations far beyond original expectations.

Once a tourist camp began to fill up every night in the touring season, expansion was hard to resist. If a farmer had six cabins in 1925, he had ten in 1926. Structural improvements were financed by last year's profits. In the off-season he filled cracks, painted rough boards, screened windows, insulated walls, and ran a pipe from his kitchen to a communal shower stall so he could advertise hot showers. In the first season, campers slept on bare mattresses and threw a coat or skirt over the window for privacy; in expanding, owners sewed mattress covers and curtains.

Some went one step further. Sensing the motorist's interest in leaving as much camping equipment at home as possible, they furnished cabins more elaborately. If a Spartan cabin brought a dollar a night, a "cottage" might bring two. Such a unit would

Like most roadside businesses of the 1920s, the Peach Lake Tea-Garden, Brewster, New York, offered a variety of services: gasoline, meals, ice cream, artesian water, fishing tackle, bungalows, and tent sites. (Library of Congress)

have cotton-stuffed mattresses, a store-bought table and chairs, a bureau with mirror, coat hooks, possibly a throw rug, and a gas plate. For a quarter extra tourists might rent linen; another quarter would rent dishes as well.

While middle-class tourists wanted more comfort and efficiency, they did not necessarily want a modern hotel. Rather, they still desired the same sense of old-fashioned comradeship and informality they had sought as autocampers escaping trains and hotels. Now shrewd cabin owners sought to sell this image while also marketing convenience and comfort.

For example, it paid to cultivate the family reunion atmosphere that was so attractive to many tourists. In gypsying and at municipal camps, informal relationships had occurred among tourists themselves. Now the forum for comradeship shifted to owner-customer contacts. For literary critic Lewis Gannett, it was contact with the cabin owner—"a self-respecting individual"—that seemed to revive "something of the old intimacies" of stagecoach-inn travel. Mama-Papa proprietors greeted city people with a small-town manner that was polite yet colloquial. It paid to speak plainly, perhaps even a little gruffly when tourists complained or hesitated; customers seemed to like this no-nonsense, honest approach.

The woman's role was particularly important. While hotels were run by and for men, a camp virtually had to be run by a married couple for both practical and aesthetic reasons. While husbands built and improved cabins and screened "deadbeats," wives usually managed the daily business, much as farm women rented rooms to supplement egg money. Unlike the male atmosphere of commercial hotels, cabin camps displayed a distinctive woman's touch: chintz curtains, doilies on the dresser, rockers, flower boxes. Such homelike extras were said to put traveling women at ease, and this was essential in attracting the family trade. In explaining the rapid advance in camp plumbing and furniture from 1925 to 1940, operators generally cited the woman traveler as the key influence. "The auto courts have created a new travel etiquette," *Business Week* noted in 1940. "In hotels the husband and father registers for his party, which is assigned a room, sight unseen. In the auto court, it's more likely to be the woman who makes the arrangements, going from cabin to cabin, feeling mattresses and investigating plumbing." The woman operator was most responsive to these female interests.[11]

Although personality and conveniences were important in selling a camp, external appearance could be as important. In this high-speed transient business it was best if improvements could be seen from the road. Clean white paint, green shutters, front porches with rockers, window boxes with flowers, and playground equipment, all enhanced the homey cottage image. It also helped if the camp had a long driveway for easy turnoffs from the road; speeding tourists had little time for sudden exits. Clever signs every mile for thirty miles on either side informed tourists that an approaching camp had hot showers, flush toilets, cooking facilities, or home-cooked chicken dinners. A cute name might attract tourists seeking rural folksiness. Originally a private joke, "Kozy Korner Kabins" or "U Pop Inn" became a profitable asset. Although bungalow architecture predominated, some cabin designers tried other styles in line with premodern fantasies of automobile sightseers: log cabins, New England or Virginia colonial, Spanish Mission, English Tudor.[12]

Success spawned competition, which in turn prompted further improvements. By 1928 Clara Keyton wrote, "everyone wanted a camp, thinking those who had camps were getting rich. Those who already had camps wanted to expand to take care of the overflow of business that they were losing." Since each town

might have several private camps, competition was more intense than in the public camp era. As free camp boosters had already learned, tourists were indefatigable comparative-shoppers for whom the roadside was one elongated cut-rate bazaar. Now there was much more to compare. If the "Para-Dice" added mattress covers and gas stoves, then Wilson's across town had to do the same; otherwise customers complained or asked for a lower rate. Tourists swapped recommendations and were known to drive an extra twenty-five miles to find a particularly well-known place. "The motoring tourist is a great talker and nothing pleases him so much as to relate his experiences to any and all who will listen. He is not slow to express his appreciation of what he likes, nor is he slow to get out his little "hammer" and use it profusely regarding places and things which have displeased him." Road talk also forced whole regions to adapt. "Boise, Idaho, opened a camp and people talked about it from one end of the country to another," a camp proprietor recalled. "Paso Robles installed electric stoves in the community kitchen. Every tourist spread that news up and down the coast."[13] In this lucrative but uncertain business of serving the consumer, demand for the latest seemed insatiable. Having just built a new privy, a cabin owner next installed flush toilets. Innerspring mattresses replaced last year's cotton-stuffed.

Road changes could spur further modernization. Many roads were repaved and widened; other highways were rerouted under the numbered U.S. Highway system, which took shape in the late 1920s. Detours and bypasses forced some pioneers to relocate if they wanted to stay in business. Once at their new site, they were likely to invest in the most up-to-date facilities. When U.S. 66 was routed down a different street, the Keytons of Arizona leased out their old camp, bought a new site right on Route 66, and built twenty cottages. Since the new location was on a hill and was well-drained, the Keyton camp was the sole survivor in town when a nearby creek overflowed in torrential spring rains—a splendid irony, since their jealous competitors had lobbied successfully for the route change as a way to put the Keytons out of business.[14] The Keytons were lucky. The whims of nature or of some distant highway department could just as easily break a thriving business.

For those with a good location, the late 1920s were boom years. Despite growing competition, most camps filled up on summer nights. In particularly busy locations—a prime sightseeing area or a junction of two major highways—even backward camps could charge late-arriving tourists two dollars and get it. And with the arrival of a new group of tourists—former hotel patrons—the future looked even brighter.

Most of the original cabin improvements catered to autocampers who wanted to take less camping equipment. But autocampers had never comprised the total middle-class touring market. Although all motorists shared the dislike for railroads, not all of them rejected hotels. For most moderately well-to-do travelers autocamping was too difficult to be considered. "Cadillacs tour, too," *Nation* observed in a 1927 survey of autocamps, "but with suitcases, not tents. They pass on the road closed, with their small roomful of people conversing, whose memories are of good and bad hotels, who are ignorant of waking at sunrise and being out-of-doors. . . . The adventure of the random camp is not for them."[15] As some tourist camps approached hotel caliber, however, these motorists tried the roadside for the first time.

At the improved cabin camp, noncampers discovered advantages already familiar to autocampers: easy access, free parking, no reservations, no clerks, no tipping, informality, homelike ambience, fresh air—all in marked contrast with "suffocatingly hot" railroad hotels. The public showers and toilets were no hardship, since most small hotels lacked private baths. Cabin furniture was both more cheerful than the average small hotel's shabby Victorian remnants and less intimidating than the fancy furniture at better hotels. Tourists did not hesitate to hang wash over chairs, to picnic on the rug, or, to many owners' chagrin, to use towels as rags and mattresses as trampolines. For many, cabin privacy was the principal attraction. Privacy spared shy or inexperienced travelers the ordeal of the public lobby "gauntlet"; it allowed speeding motorists to come and go more freely; and it also attracted middle-class young people and well-dressed unmarried couples desiring to rendezvous in secrecy. Thus, the same informality endeared cabin camps to families, mileage fiends, and roadhouse patrons.

For some families, the cabin camp, rather than the autocamp, made possible their first joint touring vacation. More comfortable than autocamping, the cabin was also cheaper than the hotel. Cottages had lower overhead expenses. Generally located on outlying property with lower tax rates, these family-run businesses financed improvements with cash, not mortgages. A touring family of four could rent two "deluxe" double cabins for a dollar per person—half the hotel rate for comparable accommodations. If they brought towels and sheets, they could save another twenty-five cents a head. For a quarter extra they could rent dishes and kitchen privileges and save the three or four dollars that a hotel meal could cost. Commercial travelers also appreciated cheaper rates, especially after 1928, when many companies began to cut back on expense accounts—an advance warning of pending economic troubles. Some salesmen now took wives along, both for companionship and for economy; while he visited clients in town, she cooked meals in the cabin. The drummer's conversion from train to car, hotel to cabin, was a severe blow to small-town commercial houses; in many cases it was fatal. The cabin industry, however, entered yet another stage of growth.

Impressed by hotel types flocking to tourist camps, still more entrepreneurs entered the field between 1928 and 1931. At a time of agricultural depression, hard-pressed farmers with highway frontage found tourists a better summer crop than corn or wheat. As housing starts declined from a peak of 937,000 in 1925, to 509,000 in 1929, lumber and plumbing suppliers extended attractive credit terms to those wanting to build or upgrade facilities, much as seed companies had advanced farm supplies in anticipation of a bumper harvest. National lumber processors discovered a lucrative sideline in prefabricated cottages. Oil companies urged jobbers and retailers to build up-to-date units in conjunction with highway service stations.[16]

The broadened market also caught the eye of manufacturers of brand-name mattresses, soap, towels, soft drinks, kitchen appliances, and linoleum floors. Engaged in massive advertising campaigns to develop national brand consciousness, these companies saw the roadside camp as a new mass medium potentially as powerful as billboards and magazine advertisements. Affluent tourists looked for familar brand names, for they had learned to distrust local eccentricities. A suspicious traveler, out of his own region, felt more secure sleeping on a Simmons Beautyrest mattress, or drinking a Coca Cola. Assuming that a brand-name product was superior, many consumers were willing to pay a premium for such insurance. Cabin owners learned that advertising a Simmons mattress or Congoleum floor attracted additional guests. Also, stocking brand names helped camps communicate with long-distance travelers. Camp ownership and management were strictly individualistic at this point—no chains, no group advertising. As historian Daniel Boorstin puts it, a brand name joined consumers in a "consumption community" that crossed regional lines, making them feel at home wherever they happened to be. Manufacturers also hoped that tourists would encounter new brands, which they would then purchase at home.[17]

Anxious to cash in on this new market, owners who had not improved their cabins since 1925 slapped on fresh paint, installed running water, and landscaped driveways. A community building with flush toilets and separate compartments for men and women became minimum equipment. Unable to afford the investment, some backward camps went out of business or subsisted by renting tent plots to the diminishing flow of autocampers. More ambitious and prosperous camp owners added innerspring mattresses, linoleum floors, hot and cold running water, throw rugs, and colonial-style furniture. To attract more hotel customers, some constructed new units with private showers and garages. The well-paying patron, they reasoned, would not want to stand in line or to leave his shiny sedan unprotected from bad weather and thieves.

A few entrepreneurs, struck more by Packards than by Chevrolets in camp driveways, envisioned ultradeluxe establishments catering exclusively to the most affluent. Convenience, not price, was said to be the main concern of these travelers. They liked camp informality, privacy, and accessibility, but they also valued hotel comforts and service and were willing to pay $3.00 to $5.00 a night for two. Journalists heralding the arrival of the "motor hotel" generally took their examples from California, Florida, and Texas. With a year-round touring season and a disproportionate percentage of affluent, long-range tourists, these "courts" could afford the heavier investment in hotel-class equipment: indoor plumbing, sturdier brick or stucco construction, overstuffed sofas, separate kitchenettes with gas ranges, refrigerators, and dinette sets. Unlike the standard $150 to $300 cabin, such units could cost over $1,000 to build; yet they were still cheaper than a centrally located, multi-story hotel that could run $5,000 a unit. James Vail is credited with the first use of "mo-tel" at his San Luis Obispo, California, Motel Inn, but this was more a hotel with automobile facilities than a modernized tourist camp. Some of the motor hotel establishments were in fact run by hotel men who reasoned that the professional hotelkeeper could best serve the hotel class. As far as they were concerned, the days of the conventional small hotel were numbered, but so were those of "flimsy" cabin camps with their "amateur," Mama-Papa management.[18]

Several oil companies took the vision a step further and planned coast-to-coast chains of "auto-havens," "motor inns," and "highway hotels," with full hotel service, professional staffs, centralized research, and national advertising. They also incorporated such known camp attractions as homey decor, coaching imagery, pleasing hostesses, no tipping, and curbside parking.[19] By 1930 the Holiday Inn style was already outlined: yet such chain schemes proved premature. Touring was still too seasonal in most of the country to support a heavily capitalized motor hotel that required year-round patronage to break even. Also, the tourist camp was not sufficiently standardized to warrant mass production; much experimentation remained to be done. Did tourists prefer cooking in their rooms to eating out? Did they prefer a bath to a shower? Did they prefer the bungalow style to the more pretentious "historic"? On-site entrepreneurs were more attentive to changing tourist tastes than were central research departments. And with their small investments and diversified services, they were better able to absorb the costs of being wrong about a particular innovation; as a hedge, most still offered a wide variety of accomodations, from tent plots to simple cabins to deluxe cottages with private bathrooms. Finally, expensive motor hotels needed very affluent customers, yet wealthier non-campers were only beginning to come to the roadside. An AAA survey found that 75 percent of its members still frequented hotels in 1929.[20] The depression brought many more to courts, but it also bankrupted potential chain investors. Big capital would have to await the return of prosperity after 1945, by which time the motor hotel concept would be well defined and nationally feasible. In the meantime, the profits and liabilities of this expanding but perilously insecure service industry would be left to Mama-Papa "amateurs."

Depression Dilemmas, 1930–1935

The depression made the motel industry, but the operators of the 1930s did not necessarily benefit from "having arrived." Hard times converted more tourists to economical tourist camps. By forcing camp owners to provide better service and conveniences for these more finicky travelers, depression competition raised standards and thereby solidified public support for camps; many converts would stick with roadside lodging once better times returned. At the same time, however, increased costs and low prices kept profits small until after the war. By then many pioneers had dropped out and the rewards of victory would be reaped by a new generation of entrants.

Middle-class Americans continued to take automobile vacations in the early 1930s. While railroad coach and Pullman fares dropped from $201 million in 1929 to $80 million in 1933, Americans spent almost as much on gas, oil, and other vacation car operating expenses in 1933 as in 1929, $1,102 million and $1,040 million, respectively. By 1935, with the slight economic upturn, these expenditures reached an all-time high of $1,331 million. Compared to other recreational industries—movies, radios, sporting goods—automobile travel fared spectacularly well. According to economist Julius Weinberger, 1935 vacation travel—85 percent of it by car—accounted for over half of the total estimated expenditures for all recreational purposes, $1,788 million out of $3,316 million.[21]

For hotels, however, the depression was disastrous. Tourists economized on operating expenses, mainly room and board, in order to keep cars running. Expenditures for hotels, restaurants, vacation clothing, and travel supplies fell from $872 million in 1929 to $444 million in 1933. Hotel occupancy rates fell from 70 percent in 1929 to 51 percent in 1932. Taking 1929 as 100, the room sales index fell to 52 in 1933.[22]

To a large extent lower hotel receipts reflected fierce competition within the industry as hotels cut prices drastically, but lower sales also reflected loss of trade to camps. The AAA estimated that the portion of its members staying at hotels fell from 75 percent in 1929 to 60 percent in 1936. Some hotel customers who had resisted the camp because of its residual association with tin can tourists found that the economy-forced discovery could be a pleasant surprise. "If by chance you have the idea that tourists patronizing tourist cabin camps are in general an undesirable class looking for the cheapest accommodations, it might be well to revise that opinion," advised one writer for *National Petroleum News*, an oil industry journal. At first the author had thought camp guests to be "Cheap Johns," but after noting the surprising number of expensive cars parked alongside the cabins he felt positively "bullish." Another tourist wrote that he had always thought tourist camps were for " 'tin can tourists,' who wander over the country in Model T Fords, loaded down with six children and the bird cage." He assumed that for comfort it was necessary to stop at a hotel. Pulling into a filling station on U.S. 90 in Texas, however, he was delighted to find cottages with as much privacy and as many conveniences as any hotel. "No hotel room could have been more comfortable. The bed and mattress was a standard, nationally advertised product. Needless to say, I stopped there that night, and have been a booster ever since." A hotelman noted sadly that camp guests "were not tin-canners, but well-to-do people in high-priced cars who are evidently induced to stop at cabins by their proximity to the highways, the convenience of parking, the car actually at the door of the cabin, the lure of the 'open air.' "[23]

For every wealthy tourist who liked the convenience alone and did not care about price, there were many others who needed to scrimp during the depression: traveling salesmen, unemployed white collar workers looking for new opportunities, and vacation-ing families with reduced budgets. Tourists accustomed to pri-vate baths tried community showers. Families who had eaten meals out ate in their rooms. Businessmen accustomed to good steaks at fancy chophouses ate at roadside cafes or took wives along to cook in cabins. Although the depression simply acceler-ated an established movement, many viewed the tourist camp as a depression-built business. "One of the few oases of the depres-sion," went one typical report, "this business has thrived on hard times and limited purchasing power."[24]

In aggregate terms the industry doubtlessly did well. At a time of general retraction, most camp operators managed to survive and make modest improvements. With memories of the late 1920s boom leading them on, more farmers and women who were forced to support families thought about entering the cot-tage business. Hotelmen opened court annexes. Reasoning that tourists who spent less on rooms would spend more on gas and oil, more gas stations opened camps. Reliable statistics do not exist, but most accounts agreed that the number of establish-ments increased from around 5,000 in 1927 to between 15,000 and 20,000 in 1935. Lumber, plumbing, and heating suppliers reported that cabin building and upgrading was one of the few bright spots in an otherwise disastrous period for construction men. Advertising journals outlined recovery plans based on sell-ing brand-name supplies to cash-paying camp owners.[25] And by September 1932, during the very worst of times, the industry had its own journal, *Tourist Trade,* whose opening editorial ex-pressed the proud owner's sense of success:

We are sorry we have no blare of trumpets, as they do on the radio, to precede this announcement, so that we might say with great gusto—"TOURIST TRADE is now on the air!" However, this is what we are trying to do with mere white paper and black type, and the feeling, sincerity, and enthusiasm could be no more if we had a battery of French horns to announce our arrival into your industry—yes, industry, for that is just the proportions it is gaining, and if you haven't given it that much importance, just glance through the pages of our first issue and you will be sure to find some figures and facts that will cause you to swell your chest with importance that you are the owner of an establishment ca-tering to the tourists' needs.[26]

By 1934 this publication had a respectable circulation of 12,000—almost twice that of the progressive hotel journal *Hotel Management.*

Thriving tourist camps attracted considerable attention from journalists anxious to prove that the business system still worked. Here was a business where the small-timer could still get in on the ground floor and make it. That the business was connected to the automobile made the success even sweeter. Overcoming the doubts of the late 1920s, the automobile's place at the center of American life seemed confirmed by the continued growth of touring at the worst of all times. Millions of people might be out of work, but Americans still knew how to hit the road and play. Things could not be *that* bad.

Furthermore, at camp Americans seemed to play *together*.

All America, in course of time, rolls up their little concrete drive and goes to bed in their cabins. Something of the old fellowship of the road is being reborn in these places. The travelers, as well as the owners, enjoy the casual friendships, the brief contacts, the sudden intimacies at these cottages—anybody, and all kinds of people.[27]

The "all kinds" rhetoric was familiar to autocampers, but hard times made old imagery newly reassuring. "The touring world is democratic, especially in, or shortly after, a major depression . . . Friendship at first sight the rule, outside the cities, they are all thoroughly acquainted by 7." At a time of class unrest, the road seemed to bind people as playground and symbol. According to a widely read 1934 *Fortune* essay, the familiar roadside was a unifying "organism" and the tourist camp was a central cell, "a racial institution and a rich study in anthropology and folk ways." While other capitalist institutions crumbled or proved ineffective, the tourist camp, having come to stay, could now be pronounced "an American institution, patronized generously by millions of all types and classes of people." To be sure, as in the heyday of the free municipal autocamp, the "all kinds" were predominantly middle class, for few poor people could afford a dollar a night for the most primitive cabin. And as in autocamping ideology, the patronage of the wealthy signaled camp success. "There Packards rub shoulders with Fords, and cars that date back to the early post-war days become neighbors with the free wheelers of 1932."[28] In the long run, this depression image of democratic congeniality and remarkable business success won still more middle-class converts to tourist camps and served as a useful public relations theme for the automobile industry.

In the short run, however, the benefits of publicity were more ambiguous. Having encroached on hotel territory, tourist camps had to fend off a hotel-sponsored counterattack that accused them of being unsafe, immoral, and uncomfortable. To bolster the image of camp respectability, *Tourist Trade* advocated further upgrading. At the same time, however, the increased competition from new tourist camps and widespread comparison shopping by budget-minded tourists encouraged price slashing, or chiseling. The industry was thus caught in a squeeze: Pressures from above favored modernization, but depressed prices inhibited it.

Hotelmen could not be expected to accept quietly the loss of established trade. Speculatively financed overbuilding of new hotels, combined with a tightening of commercial travelers' expense accounts, contributed to a fall in occupancy rates beginning in 1928. By 1932, 80 percent of hotel mortgages were in default, 32 percent of all hotels did not earn enough to pay taxes, and 15 percent could not meet their greatly reduced payrolls. Three-quarters reported deficits to the American Hotel Association.[29] Although most industry leaders saw the main problems to be overbuilding and price-cutting by hotels themselves, automobile camps also cut into their trade. In the language of the day, the cabin camp seemed an obvious case of overproduction of rooms. Beginning in 1929 hotel journals began to take a greater interest in what they called the "tourist camp menace." Their discussion of how to deal with this troublesome usurper typified debate in the wider business community over the roles that private competition and public regulation should play in aiding depressed industries.

Two schools of thought divided hotelmen. One side favored market co-optation, the other legal suppression. To more progressive leaders, generally the less threatened, large city hotels, camps had to be accepted as de facto legitimate competition. Since the public obviously wanted camps, hotels could not claim unfair competition. "Does the traveler exist for the hotel or the hotel for the traveler?" asked one opponent of legislative suppression.[30] According to this view, the small drummers' hotels most threatened by camps had their own backwardness to blame and should be written off; the better hotels, however, could try to win back lost automobile trade. Even before the stock market crash, progressives had urged hotels to adapt to motorist needs by relaxing dress codes; by providing free parking and special automobile entrances so that dusty motorists would not have to parade through the main lobby; by hiring more female staff and redecorating rooms in a more homelike atmosphere; by redesigning menus to appeal to women and children's special tastes; by eliminating tips; and by advertising hotel features on huge highway billboards.

But these reforms had limits. Adjacent land for a hotel garage was hard to acquire, except in low-density cities like Los Angeles. A conservative pride in hotel traditions kept many managers from changing established dress codes or tinkering with venerable menus. Low wages made tipping mandatory. And billboard advertising was still considered vulgar—worthy only of cheap wayside camps and "hot dog kennels." Many hotels did hire more women, however—mainly as housekeepers and dietitians. Some hotelmen went one step further and opened highway camp annexes as a way to co-opt the court trade before even more outsiders stepped in.[31]

But no one condoned cutting prices to camp levels. That seemed financially disastrous. "Competition of wayside camps and lodging houses may be even more keen than usual during the coming summer [1931]," *Hotel World-Review* predicted. "No hotel man should, however, on this account cut the price of his rooms and meals below cost of production. He hasn't the well-known 'China Man's chance' of surviving if he ignores this business principle, as against the usual chance if he adheres to it."[32] There was a large group of affluent tourists who could be attracted with better, auto-oriented services, and price-cutting would make it impossible to finance such needed improvements. Like many business leaders in the early depression, these hotelmen earnestly believed that the crisis was a relatively minor economic adjustment that could be weathered by better marketing rather than by reliance on government action.

The other school of thought, representing hard-hit smaller hotels, called for legal harrassment of tourist camps. Cabins had unfair advantages, they argued, because hotels inevitably had larger staffs and higher overhead, paid more taxes, and were subject to more health and housing regulations. Editorial sermons against price-cutting failed to deal with harsh realities: these camps *forced* small hotels to cut prices below cost, for even the better camps had lower fixed costs and could charge less for equivalent accommodations. Given the oversupply of rooms, travelers could compare rates and haggle. A hotel manager preferred filling a $3.00 room for $1.50 than leaving it vacant for the sake of principle. Such chiseling made modernizing impossible. Camps thus forced marginal hotels into a vicious cycle of lower rates and further deterioration. As unemployment grew, small-hotel spokesmen also argued that camp competition cost jobs. Noting that most camps were run by families, they claimed that camps could charge low rates because they did not hire outside workers but could "sweat" children and women. Moreover, many camps were merely sidelines to gas stations, cafes, and produce stands. Thus hotel employees with families to support were being put out of work by "frivolous" concerns run by housewives for whom a little extra "pin money" seemed like big earnings.[33]

Understandably reluctant to accept their own demise as inevitable, these hotelmen looked for legislative relief, mainly at the state level, for local aid was deemed insufficient. Restrictive zoning and higher property tax assessments did not deal with camps situated beyond municipal boundaries. Local authorities were in any case reluctant to regulate or restrict camps within their jurisdictions, partly because private camps had bailed out troublesome public camps, and partly because camps were often run by influential local citizens. Proposals for highway beautification—as a way to harrass "unsightly" camp architecture and advertising—went nowhere because beautification threatened large corporate billboards. Therefore state health and housing licensing requirements seemed the best solution: since camps competed with hotels, hotel lawyers argued, they should be subject to the same regulations.

Outnumbering larger city hotels, the sentimental, small hotels—where many successful hotel executives got their start—had considerable clout with state hotel associations, which lobbied aggressively in state legislatures. Starting in 1929, numerous state bodies drafted hostile camp licensing laws. Advocates hoped that costly sanitary requirements would put most camps out of business and would force the remaining few to raise prices to hotel levels.

But hotels underestimated their competition. As farmers and rising small businessmen, camp owners had political leverage, too. Tourist camps had a good press because they provided cheap lodging for budget-minded families. In California, with more camps than any other state, camp allies managed to get code enforcement switched from the State Board of Public Health, known to be hotel-biased, to the Division of Housing, whose officers appreciated the vital role of camps in a state with a housing shortage. Moreover, the rules were seldom sufficiently repressive, for the camp industry was rapidly improving on its own. Most state codes imposed minimal health requirements that might have had some effect in 1925 but not in 1930: flush toilets, screens, separate facilities for men and women, safe water supply, and more space between cabins. Indeed, from the point of view of better camps the laws were a boon. They drove out the cheapest competition, allowed the better camps to charge higher rates, and, best of all, legitimized the business. Camps meeting the law were often required to post a state certificate, which, as advertising, attracted new tourists who earlier had shunned camps for fear of inadequate sanitation. Now the state itself certified that a camp posting the "Approved" emblem was a good place to stay. Similarly, beautification laws improved camp appearance, and zoning ordinances sanctioned camps within the zone. From the hotels' point of view, therefore, legislation was counterproductive.[34]

Unable to secure legislative redress, hotelmen then mounted a vicious public relations campaign against camp safety and morality. In effect, they sought to link cabin camps with discredited municipal autocamps. Recalling the image of dangerous public campsites, state hotel associations sponsored billboards and magazine advertisements with the theme of "Wayside or Safeside?" These advertisements contrasted the tourist camp—a supposedly unsupervised, unsanitary, unpoliced firetrap—with the fireproof, well-maintained hotel, whose clerk screened guests. Some hotelmen called for police investigation of highway camps, which they claimed were replacing roadhouses as centers of debauchery. In a well-reported speech, the president of the American Hotel Association charged that 75 percent of the sixty-two camps in New Jersey were just "an assortment of dime dance halls, beer joints, disorderly houses, and criminal hangouts." In some attacks the camp was portrayed as harboring lower-class tin can tourists; in other cases the camp was said to threaten middle-class family life, for its "no questions asked" management policy attracted partying young people and unmarried couples. Either way, here was an assault on the image of the tourist camp as a respectable family institution.[35]

To reassure hotel customers bothered by tin can tourist associations, many camp owners began to substitute such terms as cottage, court, lodge, and apartment, for camp. Instead of tourists, clients were called motorists, touring public, and motoring public. To further emphasize the distance between their present orientation and ancient camping origins, most stopped renting tent space.

Middle-class vice was more difficult to screen, however, for most customers did come from this class, and cabin privacy was a major selling point to all tourists. Moreover, the couple trade was quite profitable, since single cabins could be rented several times a day. Some camps began to require registration—name, address, license plate—and they refused rooms to local people and travelers without bags. But many revelers were hard to screen out, for they frequently were well-dressed tourists in new cars. Like hotels, camps inevitably catered to travelers for whom being away from home was what sociologist Norman Hayner has called a moral holiday.[36]

In the view of many camp leaders the best defense against hotel charges was a good offense: to go even more aggressively after the hotel trade by providing still more hotel-like facilities. If the new all-brick unit with its heavy armchairs was homelike, it was more like the suburban home of a hotel customer than like a farmer's bungalow. Figuring that hotel-class customers wanted private baths but ate out, some owners converted kitchenettes to bathrooms. Newer establishments advertised the privacy and security of individual, locked garages and well-insulated apartments, but dropped such community features as the central kitchen and shower room. *Tourist Trade* urged camp owners to hire maids, to institute room service, and to be more ingratiating—in all, to practice more "salesmanship." "These ultra-fastidious people are quite sure to be your best boosters and future patrons after you have pleased them by your superior service and hospitality."[37] In effect owners hoped that a tourist's consumerism outweighed his moralism.

Yet individual improvement had boundaries. To upgrade meant raising prices to cover increased costs, but by the summer of 1933, the depression had caught up with the roadside. Based on optimistic extrapolations from precrash prosperity, many new entrepreneurs had entered the field in 1930 and 1931, and this was when older camps made their most ambitious improvements. Since automobile tourism declined only slightly during those years, few worried about increased competition. But the decline continued, and by 1933 recreational travel expenses had fallen 36 percent from 1929.[38] People still drove, but they wanted to save money on food and rooms—including cabins. Budget-minded tourists far outnumbered those for whom price was no object.

At the same time, tourists expected ever more elaborate facilities. Camp owners found themselves trapped by their own modernization rationale. Motorists had come to see the roadside as an extension of the annual automobile model change. Even eastern camps, traditionally more backward, found that higher western standards were trickling eastward.

While there still are a few "hard shell" operators who maintain that "easterners don't expect anything, the westerners want everything, but they all will take what they can get," the men who have studied the field and who are certain to become the successful camp owners of the future, realize that they must give their customers real accomodations.[39]

Increasingly sophisticated and road-wise tourists might be forced to stop at a sub-par camp one night, but they would not return on the way back or on the next trip. In a business that relied heavily on repeat trade and word-of-mouth recommendations, this could be fatal. "The dirty camp, the unattractive camp, the camp without modern equipment may get the tourist for a night, but they will not get him a second time." Not only were the old-time cabin campers growing more discriminating but the latest hotel converts expected such standard equipment as good mattresses, hot showers, and free soap and linen. "Remember they all are used to other conveniences supplied by the hotels, and if you are going to build your business to appeal to them, you must remember that the expense will warrant your *keeping* them on your guest register."[40]

Exploiting the increased competition, financially-pressed tourists haggled for lower rates. Pitting one camp against another down the road, they sought 1932 cottages at 1925 shack rates. Clara Keyton, owner of the Arizona camp, thought that the depression brought out the worst in people: "How many camp operators in those days heard the old tiresome phrase, 'You just ought to see what we had last night. The loveliest cottage with a toilet, bath, hot and cold water, etc., all for one dollar. Why we've been getting them all along the line like that for a dollar.' You can't tell them to their faces that they are prevaricators." More than before, tourists stole blankets, towels, even mattresses and stoves. Instead of renting linen, they demanded it free. Instead of taking whatever cottage was available—as they had to do in the old seller's market—they would insist on seeing all the units and would bounce on all the beds. After getting a lower price by insisting that they did not want to cook, they would use all the dishes and leave a mess. After telling the owner that two were in the party, a man might sneak his large family into the cottage. Arriving after midnight, they would ask to be charged for only half a night or would insist on getting a full twenty-four hours for one day's rent.[41]

The wealthy liked to haggle too. Clara Keyton thought that many affluent tourists took advantage of the hard times, while the legitimately indigent camped by the roadside or stayed home. "Some managers thought that with the Depression there came a cleaner, better class of tourists. I grant the cleaner, but I doubt the better part. There was less of drunken parties and riff-raff. I felt that I could stand a little more dirt and less of grouching and miserliness." Some of the wealthy tourists bargained for sport. Indeed, this opportunity to negotiate endeared the roadside to some travelers. The camp seemed so democratic partly because it was so cheap. Here was a chance to obtain decent accommodations at ridiculously low prices. Thus Lewis Gannett devoted several pages of *Sweet Land* to the subtleties of "beating down" the price. For a few tourists this may also have been sweet revenge for earlier years when farmers had asked two dollars for chicken coops.[42]

With so many camps in operation tourists could get their price. Since units no longer filled up early in the afternoon, owners were forced to lower rates. "Chiseling was going on all along the line," Keyton recalled. "Our competitors tried to get a customer at one price, and if he saw that he was going to lose him, he rushed out and cut his price twenty-five cents, and sometimes fifty cents." Gas stations in gasoline price wars frequently cut cabin rates below cost in order to boost gallonage. Cafe owners with a few cabins out back lowered charges to attract more dinner and breakfast trade. Camp owners with a wide variety of accommodations, from 1925-era shacks at seventy-five cents to a few deluxe cottages at $2.00, could afford to take a slight loss on the most expensive units, since they could make it up on the less elaborate cabins whose income was pure profit. Cutting prices on the best cottages soon spread through the grapevine. If a camp cut prices in Phoenix, a Pasadena proprietor might hear about it two days later. Worst hit were progressive camps with modern units only. Rather than leave a deluxe cabin empty, they were forced to rent it at $1.00 or $1.50 for two.[43]

Accustomed to good profits and visions of an unlimited future, the most advanced camp owners were most embittered by such price-cutting. Faced with rising costs and declining revenues, they now turned not against haggling tourists—and certainly not against wealthier tourists who seemed to ensure their future—but against smaller operators with lower overheads and modest ambitions. These marginal camps, they argued, could undersell their cabins because they did not know how to figure true costs. For example, they did not account for laundering expenses because they included camp laundry with family wash, or they did not account for labor costs because family members did the work. Ignorant of business methods, and content with netting a few extra dollars a week, they "sweated" their labor and endangered public saftey with inadequately maintained facilities. The larger camp, on the other hand, built new cabins, helping the construction industry, paid taxes, and hired workers. In short, this seemed like a classic case of the depression-causing cycle of price-cutting, lower revenues, and increased unemployment. There was thus a certain symmetry to depression-era claims of unfair competition. Large hotels complained of substandard, backward small hotels; small hotels complained of the overproduction of tourist camps; and the better camps complained of chiseling by inferior camps.

Moreover, everyone complained of the "tourist home menace"—private homes renting out a few extra bedrooms for one dollar a night. Quite often accommodations could be as comfortable and as convenient as good camps and small hotels. Their role increased markedly in the 1930s as hard-pressed families sought new income opportunities. With so many clustered along highways and main streets, tourists could simply drive in and park outside. Most rooms had free linen and a hot shower down the hall. Sounding the standard premodern theme, writers likened these homes to coaching inns where one met all kinds in a congenial atmosphere. Usually run by women, the homey decor and easy informality attracted families and salesmen. After a good seventy-five-cent meal, tourists could listen to the radio in the parlor or chat with host and fellow boarders on the front porch.

To hotels and camps alike, tourist homes were a threat, since they competed for the most desirable class of traveler. On the East Coast these places outnumbered all other accommodations and were directly responsible for the relative scarcity of first-class camps in the region. A Maryland tourist home association claimed 2,800 members in 1933; Virginia issued five-dollar licenses to 1,000 homes in the Richmond area alone. More than one camp owner whose own business had begun as a sideline now joined hotelmen in attacking "bored housewives" out to earn extra "pin money." The better camps also sided with hotels in supporting beautification laws and state health licenses, but they wanted these to apply only to the competition below. Mild beautification laws might force the fly-by-night down the road with only a few ugly shacks to close or to raise prices. Health regulations might suppress tourist homes that lacked separate male/female restrooms and restaurant-quality kitchens. By limiting supply through legislative restrictions they hoped to bring the market back to more favorable, pre-1930 conditions.[44]

To further stabilize competition advanced courts in such year-round states as California, Texas, and Florida formed trade associations to fix prices. With names like Motor Court Trade Association, United Motor Courts, Tourist Cottage Owners Association, they avoided unfavorable tourist camp connotations. Only the most elaborate establishments were admitted, their facilities being scrupulously inspected. Upon admission camps displayed special insignia guaranteeing superior accommodations. Through billboards and mutual recommendations, they urged tourists to patronize member camps; with time, perhaps their colorful emblems would serve as nationally recognized name brands. Members also agreed on rate schedules to prevent chiseling. At the state level, groups lobbied to head off further hotel harrassment. Through newsletters and journals, they urged other camps to modernize and set prices.[45]

Signifying a more sophisticated way to organize roadside selling, these local associations foreshadowed the cooperative marketing and franchising that would standardize the roadside after 1945. But in 1932 four factors limited the success of such voluntary cooperation. First, camp owners were still highly individualistic; in fact, their proud independence was a major selling point with tourists who valued premodern imagery. Furthermore, even if the best camps could agree on prices, nonmembers down the road could chisel and set off a destructive chain reaction. Third, even if owners could agree on prices within a region, tourism was an interstate business. Finally, the touring public was becoming skeptical of road advertising, which was often so hyperbolic that tourists had little reason to trust a particular local group's claims.

Frustrated by these problems, organizers seized on an opportunity presented by the National Industrial Recovery Act of June 1933. According to the act, representatives of each trade or industry could draw up codes of fair competition that would apply throughout the country and have the force of law. Here was an opportunity for camp leaders to impose their vision not only on nearby chiselers, but also on backward camps in the distant East. In December 1933, 150 members of a dozen western and southern trade associations met in Texas to form the National Tourist Lodge and Motor Court Trade Association (NTL-MCTA), which they hoped would be recognized as the responsible code negotiator for the industry. Its leadership represented the most ambitious operators who, with their heavy investments, were most vulnerable to price-cutting. For president the convention chose John C. Stevens, of Jacksonville, Florida, whose Phoenix Park Cottages comprised a dozen three-room cabins, all with baths, toilets, kitchens, and dining rooms, and all renting in 1933 for a bargain $1.50 a night. For secretary they chose a Houston man, Robert C. Stuart, whose "modern apartments" rented for as low as $1.00.

Citing President Roosevelt's goal of eliminating the "predatory five or ten percent" who slashed prices and prolonged the depression, their code proposal called for a schedule of prices fixed 50 percent above prevailing rates; a uniform health code; an end to the couple trade that gave camps a bad name; a single, nationwide cost accounting system that would include family labor costs; and cooperative advertising by the NTL-MCTA. Minimum standards and rates were to be enforced by a code authority dominated by association representatives—that is, the most advanced camps. Since unions did not seem a threat, owners routinely agreed to collective bargaining guarantees as required by the National Recovery Administration (NRA). However, on the grounds that they were struggling working men providing economical lodging for vacationing laborers, they requested wage and hour provisions more lenient than desired by Washington. Camps that complied to code provisions could display the coveted Blue Eagle—"We Do Our Part." In effect leaders hoped to use the Blue Eagle as a federally sanctioned brand with far more name recognition than United Motor Courts or Simmons Beautyrest.

After considering the proposal for several months, NRA officials rejected it in June 1934. In part, public opinion would not tolerate such blatant price-fixing, especially at the consumer level. Also, labor advisers objected to the wage and hour proposal. Noting camp leaders' claims of spectacular growth and national importance, the NRA officials doubted that higher wages and shorter hours would bankrupt the business. Furthermore, they argued that because camps took away hotel jobs, they should be included in the hotel industry's code. This was anathema to camp leaders. Knowing that such inclusion was favored by the American Hotel Association, operators rightly feared that it would amount to suppression; having been unsuccessful at statewide suppression, hotels might now win at the national level. Unfortunately, the NTL-MCTA leaders' case for a separate code was damaged by internal divisions within the camp industry. While NTL-MCTA leaders claimed to represent "99 percent" of the industry, many small-scale and eastern camp operators complained of being left out. Given rising public criticism of trivial, unenforceable codes, the NRA was not ready to recognize a national association that was not fully accepted by the trade.[46] National standardization seemed premature.

In all, the same factors that inhibited national chain development precluded a single national code. In the North and East business remained seasonal. Although the "better class" was arriving in greater numbers, most tourists could not afford higher prices. And it was still unclear what tourists wanted: private or community baths, cafes or kitchenettes? Yet the NRA episode showed how sophisticated the business had become in just a few short years. In a sense, camp organizers were more sensitive to the car's implications than were NRA officials. Aware that car touring was a truly interregional pastime, camp leaders logically looked to national institutions to rationalize the industry. Although the NTL-MCTA dissolved in late 1934, the leaders' organizational experience eventually paid off. The local associations survived, and later in the decade, with the business upturn, the trade was ready for a more solidly based national organization. Moreover, after further experimentation, the troublesome questions of tourist preference would be closer to resolution.

Back in Gear, 1935–1940

From a low point in 1932–33, travel expenditures began to rise in 1934, increasing steadily until the 1938 recession, then reaching new heights in the 1940–41 boom. The AAA reported that 1934 was the best touring year since 1929, with a 25 percent gain in expenditures over 1933. Total vehicle mileage rose, breaking the 1931 record in 1935. Gasoline sales also picked up—after a slight decline—and more people bought new cars in 1935 than in 1930. For the travel industry as a whole, people had more money to spend on room and board in 1935 than in any year since 1929.[47]

For hotels, the upturn signified that the worst was over. From a 1932–33 low of 51 percent, the percentage of total rooms occupied rose to 56 percent in 1934 and 66 percent in 1937. Although the legalization of liquor helped city hotels, many small houses never recovered from the depths of the depression. While Repeal received more attention in the trade press than did motor camps, hotelmen continued to advertise camp crudeness and hotel safety, thus keeping up the pressure to modernize camp facilities. Some urged a wait-and-see attitude; since tourists seemed to be asking for more service and comfort, they might yet come back to hotels. A 1938–39 American Hotel Association campaign thus reiterated hotel advantages: prestige, service, comfort, central location, and professionalism.[48]

For camps, the 1934 upturn relieved some of the chiseling. Units again began to fill up earlier in the day, but the total number of camps probably did not increase markedly until after 1940. The pre-1929 boom years had meant such easy profits with minimum investiment that the troubles of 1932–33, combined with the rising costs of operating a good camp, may have convinced some potential new entrants to look elsewhere—perhaps to the roadside food business. But those already in the camp business tended to hang on—there were few buyers anyway—and increased spending meant more income to reinvest in better facilities.

As before, the South and West set the pace. In 1937, out of the defunct NTL-MCTA sprang the International Motor Court Association, whose *Tourist Court Journal* of Temple, Texas, preached the familiar virtues of modernization: better facilities would attract more hotel customers who would pay higher rates. Chastened by the price wars of 1932–33, writers urged owners to stress luxury not economy. Preferring "court" to "camp," the journal advocated tiled baths, thick bedspreads, carpeting, twin beds, air conditioning, and swimming pools.

Typical of the most advanced southwestern courts of 1937 was Robert Stuart's newly refurbished Bluebonnet Courts in Houston. Each of the NRA code leader's forty-nine "air-cooled sleeping rooms" had a private bath, telephone, and electric refrigerator. Believing that a hotel-motel merger was imminent, Stuart wrote an article in *Hotel Management* advocating an alliance of better courts and hotels to work for the elimination of ugly, backward shacks. Former NTL-MCTA president J. C. Stevens called for the replacement of the industry's "individualistic drifters" by businessmen whose accommodations were of a "reasonably high class."[49]

Although the most spectacular innovations came in warm regions, in the mid-1930s many northern and eastern camps did begin to exploit a growing stream of winter travelers, especially salesmen and affluent tourists heading to Florida or ski resorts. By adding heating and insulation, they lengthened their season and could then finance further improvements. The NRA code leaders had failed in 1934 mainly because their standards had not yet represented the national norm. By 1940, however, the better year-round northern camps approached California levels, especially on improving main highways near larger cities and resort areas. As more regional associations developed, the International

Tourist cabins near Antigo, Wisconsin, 1941. These units typified the basic cabins of the 1928–1932 era. The larger building at the far right is a community toilet and shower. (Library of Congress)

Cottage Court near Phoenix, Arizona, 1940. As in auto-camping, early court patrons valued the easy accessibility and natural setting of highway camps. Advanced for 1930, these cottages were out-of-date by 1940. (Library of Congress)

Mission Courts, near Dallas, Texas, 1942. Built in the mid-1930s, this motor hotel combined appropriately pre-modern imagery and hotel-quality service. With a year-round touring market, southwestern courts were the most advanced. (Library of Congress)

Another mission-style court of the 1930s, also near Dallas. (Bureau of Public Roads, National Archives)

Wigwam Village, near
Bardstown, Kentucky, 1940.
Wandering tourists emulated
plains nomads in these tepee
huts of the late 1930s. A bit
too extreme for most tastes,
this would-be national chain
was mildly successful in the
Border South. (Library of
Congress)

Roadsigns detailed the latest conveniences and testified to the diversity of products offered along the highway bazaar. In 1940 the American Automobile Association's *Directory of Motor Courts and Camps* rated the Grandview Cabins of Holyoke, Massachusetts, very highly. All of its seventeen cabins had hot and cold running water and private toilets; eight had showers. Rates were two to three dollars a day for two persons. Breakfast was 20 to 49 cents; lunch, 35 to 60 cents. (Library of Congress)

Colonial Cottages, Louisville, Kentucky, 1940. Flower boxes, shrubs, shutters, and lawn chairs enhanced the homey feel of these up-to-date bungalows. The "no locals" policy reduced the notorious "bounce-on-the-bed trade." (Library of Congress)

Deluxe Cottages, Roanoke, Virginia, 1940s. By the 1940s, premodern associations were reduced to faint symbolic suggestion. Here high-pitched roofs and fake beams recall Tudor coaching inns. (Bureau of Public Roads, National Archives)

Howard Johnson's, Baltimore, Maryland, 1942. Food stands evolved in the same direction as motels. Howard Johnson joined early American motif with franchising, ample parking, and standardized products. His specially designed steeple and orange roof caught motorists' attention for miles around. (Bureau of Public Roads, National Archives)

Berkshire Hills, Massachusetts. At home on the road—1941 style. (Library of Congress)

Motor Court Association claimed members from all over the country.

Guidebooks and trade journals recorded the steady elaboration of camp furnishings and operation. *National Petroleum News* noted in 1937 that it was hard to tell which improvements came in response to specific tourist demand and which improvements created new demand. "The question as to whether these [deluxe] camps are the result of a demand for such conveniences on the part of the motorist, or whether the camps developed in the motorists a taste for such accommodations—it is a lot like which comes first, the chicken or the egg, controversy.[50] As far as *Tourist Court Journal* was concerned, camps simply responded to the tastes of well-heeled travelers; yet in catering to these clients they raised the expectations of the rest. More than one frustrated operator complained that some tourists seemed to want more on the the road than they had at home. Cheap depression prices introduced some travelers to innnerspring mattresses, flush toilets, hot showers, and steam heat, none of which were universally domestic equipment in the early 1930s. Similarly, in the 1950s many motel guests would receive their first exposure to wall-to-wall carpets, vinyl upholstery, sliding glass doors, television, Scandinavian furniture, and air conditioning. Serving a similar advertising function in the nineteenth century, hotels had introduced Americans to indoor plumbing, elevators, and single beds. In effect, motels joined hotels as a promotional arm of the construction and home decorating industries. Younger operators familiar with the demand-creation role of modern marketing were pleased with this trend. Camp pioneers with more utilitarian standards of comfort accused tourists of living beyond their means and grew tired of the treadmill-like process of product elaboration.

To be sure, even the progressives were not quite in control of the market. For example, an important debate raged in *Tourist Court Journal* in the late 1930s over whether court owners should run gas stations. One side upheld the traditional diversification rationale for a filling station: speeding, road-weary tourists valued one-stop service because they preferred to have cars serviced while they ate or slept. Moreover, a gas station-grocery provided a profitable sideline, especially in the off-season. The other side dissented on the basis of new experience. Because gas station owners down the road resented the competition of a camp filling station, they would not recommend the camp to inquiring tourists. It was better, they felt, to cultivate a live-and-let-live relationship with fellow roadside businessmen. "I have always taken the position that the other fellow has his living to make as well as myself," wrote one Muskogee, Oklahoma, operator. "The service man sends all of his inquiries to my camp, and I believe I make more by being fair to him than if I had the station."[51] Anxious to de-emphasize price competition, progressives sought symbiotic arrangements that would allow all within a region to make a decent profit.

Also, many tourists suspected that a camp station was likely to charge higher prices than a campless station down the road. Others did not like having a noisy, ugly repair station in the court. "Guests who are patronizing the better courts do not want a cottage shown to them by a service station attendant who is greasy and dirty . . . and who obviously knows a great deal more about the gas pump than he does about the cottage, which is really the concern."[52] In this view courts had to become more specialized, for guests demanded more service. Since most camps remained Mama-Papa operations through the 1930s, few owners could run both a gas station and a full-service court. The days of the self-service cabin, where the owner collected a fee and returned to his porch, were over. Tourists had to be greeted around the clock, cabins had to be cleaned daily, and owners had to cultivate salesmanship. By the late 1940s most court owners chose to drop their gas stations, but in the late thirties a good case was still being made for the other side.

Whether to have private garages was another troublesome issue. Here the convenience clearly met a tourist demand that owners preferred to ignore. A private garage adjoining each unit took away space for additional rooms. Architects predicted that future motor hotels would be multilevel buildings with all units connected and with parking at some distance, perhaps in a central garage or lot. This would be a more efficient use of space. Yet tourists in the thirties still wanted some sort of shelter for their cars. In the earliest autocamping days, tourists slept in and under their cars, carefully draping the whole vehicle in special tents. In some early cabins, tourists might drive right into a unit that was little more than a garage with cots. Proud of their new acquisition and jealous of its delicate finish, tourists of the 1920s would walk a hundred yards through the rain to a pit toilet, but they would not let their cars get wet. This supersensitivity to the car's finish appears to have continued throughout the 1930s.

There were other reasons for insisting on private garages. In northern states, a heated garage was as much a necessity in extending the season as heating the cabin itself. In Texas and California an open shelter offered sufficient protection from the weather, but near cities motorists valued locked garages for security. And all tourists liked the convenience of having a car at the doorstep for easy loading. *Tourist Court Journal* advised prospective builders to provide adjoining garages even if they were wasteful. "If it were not for them there would be more room for rentable rooms, . . . but if it were not for garages, there would be no reason for motor courts."[53] This insistence on separate garages delayed acceptance of the now-familiar court pattern—adjoining units in a line, or an *L*- or *U*-shape—until after the war, when higher construction and land costs forced builders to eliminate garages.

Garages also inhibited courts from imitating the more flamboyant architecture of the roadside food industry, where hot dog-shaped buildings sold hot dogs and two-story ice cream buckets sold ice cream. A few courts experimented with the streamlined, cream-enameled or glazed-tile look associated with gas stations of the 1930s. The historic style remained popular, but only if it was low-keyed. One Portland, Maine, experiment in roadside picturesqueness—a meticulously recreated "Danish Village," complete with narrow, crooked streets, overhanging lamps, weather vanes, stucco and beam walls, and a high-steepled town hall housing a cafeteria and souvenir stand—was a notorious flop. Teepee villages were popular in the South, Spanish Colonial in the Southwest. Sensing the more conservative mood of the times, ice cream vendor Howard Johnson designed simpler blue and orange New England/Virginia colonial churchstyle restaurants that would become motor lodges in the 1950s. Most camps remained bungalows, however. Tourists still liked the privacy and homey feel of separate cabins, and proprietors concentrated on internal improvements, where the greatest changes occurred.[54]

Free linen and towels became mandatory, for few tourists now carried camping equipment. Market surveys found that the primary tourist demand was for private baths. In 1933 a respectable camp might have flush toilets and hot showers in a central building; in 1939 the issue was not whether to have private baths, but whether they should be tiled. At the same time, surveys determined that an increasing number of tourists preferred to eat out. Tired of cooking every night, and more able to afford a commercially-prepared meal, more tourists frequented roadside cafes. Modernizing campowners generally converted some or all kitchenettes to private bathrooms. Whereas well over half of all cabins had housekeeping facilities in the early 1930s, by 1940 perhaps only 10 percent provided individual kitchenettes—mostly in resort areas.[55]

The decline of cooking at through camps showed that novice travelers were becoming well at ease in the larger world of commercially rendered services. In the early 1920s tourists carried virtually everything, as if afraid to trust anyone to provide for their needs. By the mid-1920s many were willing to accept a strange roof—a cabin—in lieu of their tent. The next substitution was a strange bed for their own cot. As anthropologists have noted, food habits are generally the last idiosyncratic traits immigrants give up as they assimilate into a new culture; in a sense, all tourists were immigrants in this new world of the road. Although economy had always been a major rationale for cooking, many had also distrusted fancy hotels and uncertain roadside stands. Several years of experience changed this. By the late 1930s tourists felt more secure about roadside food, in part because sharp vendors like Howard Johnson met them halfway by eliminating local variants. Roadside cafes now served simple, predictable food in an informal atmosphere. By 1939, almost half of the better camps featured cafes.[56]

The growing demand for private showers and toilets was the other side of the coin. Earlier, few had minded outdoor baths and toilets because indoor plumbing was still a novelty. The earliest facilities were single shacks used by either sex. The first step toward greater privacy came with the provision of separate facilities for men and women at the end of the 1920s. By the mid-1930s most middle-class Americans took indoor showers and flush toilets for granted. At the cabin they wanted a private shower so they could clean up fast and go out to eat. Tourists were no longer willing to line up with strangers for a shower.

Since the new tourist court was strictly a business venture catering to private tastes and interests, writers no longer extolled the communal values of the cabin camp—except as distant heritage. Those seeking a road community or the latest in unfettered automobility now turned to the trailer camp. After 1935 trailers received much more attention than did tourist courts. The 1935-37 volume of *Reader's Guide* listed eleven articles under "tourists' camps," five of which dealt with trailer camps. Under "automobile trailers" it listed sixty-four articles, with titles like "Back to the Covered Wagon," "Nation of Nomads," "Tin-Canners: Nomads of the Road," "Home of the Free," and "Gospel by Gas: Priest Uses Modern Trailer Spreading Faith in Southern Alabama." As several hundred thousand Americans invested up to a thousand dollars each in streamlined caravans, gypsying and tin can tourists became respectable again. Enthusiastic trailerites proclaimed the virtues of motor vagabonding in a home on wheels. Futurists predicted that every American would soon live permanently in a cheap trailer. Businessmen envisioned a new billion-dollar trailer market. Sporting goods manufacturers forecast a revival of motor camping and an end to outdated hotels and dangerous tourist courts. Sociologists pondered the mores of trailer camp denizens. Bothered by the affluence of many trailerites, hotels decried the "Trailer camp menace." Middle-class moralists worried about migrants with whom they shared many camps. State health departments investigated public camps and formulated minimum sanitation requirements. State and municipal trailer camps soon gave way to private trailer courts and travel parks with better restrooms serving the "better class." It was autocamping all over again. Bothered by the new competition, some cabin owners rented trailer space; a few older camps gave up on cabins and served trailers exclusively. But because most had been through this before, they stoically endured the hyperbole, glad perhaps that tourist courts were no longer a fad.[57]

The progressive court owner of the late 1930s could feel reasonably confident. The traveling middle class now accepted the court as a viable alternative to hotels, which continued to lose their share of the automobile travel market. A 1939 AAA survey found that only 32 percent of its members stayed at hotels en route, versus 75 percent in 1929.[58] Yet the same privatism that endeared courts to hotel types could also be a public relations liability. Numerous articles and movies continued to portray camps as vice-ridden and dangerous. Although hotel men led the campaign, the most famous attack came from J. Edgar Hoover, whose 1940 "Camps of Crime" article in the *American Magazine* received national notice. With little evidence, the FBI Director charged that all but a few hundred camps were "dens of vice and corruption," haunted by nomadic prostitutes, hardened criminals, white slavers, and promiscuous college students.[59] Hoover's charges were long familiar to camp owners, but they could do little except tighten registration and screening. Noting that all public accommodations, from medieval inns to skyscraper hotels, had problems with undesirables, *Tourist Court Journal* advised owners to maintain a respectable public front and otherwise be patient:

The truth "sin is where you find it" applies equally to every branch of the tourist trade, and constant vigil by the wise tourist courter will weigh heavily on the side of truth. Eventually even casual observers will see the obvious difference between flop houses and established businesses, whether it be hotel or tourist court. Story writers are constantly in search of the new locale for an old plot . . . and it is flattering to the tourist court that even the best writers are aware of this tremendous industry still in its teens.[60]

Even as tourist camps became still more respectable after the war, the "no-tell motel" image remained, mostly because the couple trade *was* profitable. As long as it was handled discretely, however, it did not necessarily deter other trade. As before, the best defense was to emphasize modern comforts and gracious hospitality.

More serious were the problems common to all hotel management: theft, messy tourists, noisy children, staff problems, taxes, and endless complaining. *Tourist Court Journal* ran numerous articles counseling courters to be kinder to customers, to be more "entertaining." "Look before you leap in this modern industry," advised one successful Florida owner. "The cottage court as a hobby cannot be considered, and it behooves you to expel such ideas if you ever had them." Running a court was not a casual affair. The modern court had become "a variation of the hotel business;" overhead was much higher. A 1939 article estimated that the average investment in a new twenty-unit court was $1,000 a unit against $100 a unit in 1925 and $450 for a deluxe cabin in 1929. On top of this, owners faced trailer camp competition and highway rerouting. The proposed limited access interstate highway system was particularly troublesome. *Tourist Court Journal* lamented that such superhighways "will render out-of-date and obsolete many roads at present in service; their construction will destroy the value of many tourist courts in their present locations, thereby wiping out millions of dollars." The editor urged courters to write Congress opposing "this scheme for raiding the treasury."[61]

Furthermore, the depression had left its legacy. Camp owners and tourists no longer trusted each other. Although owners wished to rent rooms sight unseen from the office—like hotels—tourists still insisted on inspecting every bed. Owners suspected every tourist of trying to get something for nothing. Tourists still bargained and competitors still chiseled. Although times were better than in 1932–33, good units still sold for under $1.50 in many areas, with profits comming from increased volume rather than from higher rates. Some tourists haggled for tradition's sake, but for others times were still hard, budgets still tight. Claiming that "Mr. Average Citizen" could not yet afford the more advanced accommodations, an angry proprietor called on *Tourist Court Journal* to "lay off the 'Palais Royale' stuff." Even if every camp could raise prices to meet the progressives' high standards, he wanted to know what would happen to the "bulk of the tourist business." The moderate traveler "would have two choices, put up at a 'Love Nest' or carry a tent." Although many owners continued to make improvements, others did let things slide. The AAA motor court guides listed many camps that were rated deluxe in 1931, but—with the same accommodations—were only fair in 1939. Indeed, one suspects that many of Hoover's "dens of vice" may once have been decent places that, unable to keep up, turned to the "hot-pillow trade" as a last resort. For veteran Clara Keyton, the fun of being an independent entrepreneur had long gone out of the business, and she finally sold her camp in 1940. Other operators hung on, still awaiting the return of pre-1929 prosperity.[62]

On to Mass Production

For some, prosperity came in 1940. The war-related boom put more Americans than ever on the road, both for business and for pleasure, and with more to spend. Many camps experienced the old seller's market, with tourists forced to pay inflated prices. Yet no sooner had the next wave of modernization begun than gasoline rationing curtailed touring in 1942. Rail passenger service revived, and city hotels reported unprecedented occupancy ratios of close to 90 percent. While the housing shortage filled courts located near large coastal cities, bases, and war plants, many midwestern and southwestern camps on major touring routes were wiped out. For the well-situated, however, these were good times. Price controls kept costs constant, and 100 percent occupancy meant net earnings of 30 to 40 percent on room sales. [63]

Postwar affluence, coupled with a housing shortage, brought record numbers of people into courts. For many returning veterans, the highway hospitality business seemed an ideal place to get started; the old romance of the independent roadside inn seemed especially welcome after fifteen years of depression and war. The abolition of rent control in 1947 encouraged widespread upgrading and new construction. By 1948 there were over 26,000 courts— twice the 1939 census. Another 15,000 were built between 1949 and 1952.[64] Most were small-scale and individually owned, for conventional wisdom held that large units or chains with paid employees could not succeed in a business requiring homey service and close monitoring of ever-changing tourist tastes.

Within a few years, however, it was clear that this old maxim was more appropriate to the earliest, high-risk stage of an industry and to a period of scarce investment capital than to the booming 1950s. Massive highway and suburban development seemed to guarantee an unlimited future for automobile-oriented trade. More important, since the court's appeal to the wealthier traveler was now well-established, daily procedures could be systematized and centrally supervised. It was no longer necessary for nervous owners to oversee everything; salaried employees could be trained according to prescribed rules.

Having won the hotel-class customer, Mama-Papa courts could give way to larger "motor hotels." There were definite economies of scale in motel construction. A motel with fifty or more units could break even at 50 percent occupancy, whereas the average court of twenty units required 70 percent or more. The trade would now be dominated by the larger establishments. In 1953 *Hotel Management* estimated that although only 10 percent of the country's courts had twenty-five or more rooms, these leaders did 40 percent of the business, especially along the lucrative main routes.[65] In resort areas, however, business remained seasonal, small-scale, and backward—a lot like the old country hotels of the turn-of-the-century.

Large-scale development was further encouraged by the limited-access highway building of the 1950s. The fervent opposition by established court groups was of little avail. As *Tourist Court Journal* had predicted in 1938, many court pioneers were bypassed completely or were forced to sell their property to state highway departments. Those refusing to sell were often left without access to the six-lane road running through their backyards. Only the more heavily capitalized could afford to locate on prime land near highway interchanges. Expressways also brought more motorists to high-rise motor hotels built on expensive downtown real estate. Many of the new ventures of fifty or more rooms were in fact operated by hotel corporations—Hilton, Sheraton, Albert Pick. Others were modeled on hotel operations— Holiday Inn, Ramada Inn, Marriott. With their banquet and meeting rooms, these large motels succeeded regular hotels as community centers. With the growth of the car rental industry, large motels also sprang up around airports. Businessmen could fly in, take a nearby room, and then rent a car to visit clients in town. These motels thus inherited the commercial-house function once filled by the drummers' hotel down by the rail depot.

Along with hotel methods, the new motels blended the camp pioneers' discoveries: free parking, family orientation, easy check-in, informal dining, self-service, female hostesses, and homey decor. Anxious to capture the harried motorist's eye, the newcomers used architecture as advertising, and many exploited the crucial antimodernist themes that still motivated vacation travel. Northern resort area motels looked like log cabins, southwestern motels remained loyal to Spanish models. Ramada Inn capitalized on the familiar Williamsburg motif, Howard Johnson the New England church. Marriott's Hot Shoppes recalled the old tearoom and "grille," while the neon palm of Holiday Inn's "Great Sign" suggested tropical primitivism. In the 1960s, English pubs reminiscent of Elizabethan coaching houses would be popular; in the 1970s, neo-Victorian.

And these carefully designed packages of quasi nostalgia could be nationally mass-produced. The secret was franchising. Only a few motel chains were wholly owned by a single company. In most cases, each motel was owned separately by a local resident who paid a fee for the right to operate a Holiday Inn or a Howard Johnson's. The national office furnished the logo, supplies, market analysis, architectural plans, financing, management advice, and extensive advertising. Centralized public relations were particularly helpful in neutralizing the lingering aura of motel immorality. Howard Johnson and Conrad Hilton projected scrupulously clean-cut Americanism. The Marriotts made no secret of their Mormon decency. Holiday Inn's Kemmons Wilson displayed the ten commandments as well as photographs of Pat

Boone, Billy Graham, and the pope in his Memphis office. Many Holiday Inns had chaplains on call, and chambermaids were directed to open each room's Bible to a new page every day—a quiet but forceful rebuke to the "bounce-on-the-bed trade."

Franchising thus combined the romance of independent entrepreneurship with the security of the national brand name that had eluded prewar camp organizers. The synthesis revolutionized roadside selling, for it allowed a national corporation to spread its name and influence for a relatively small cost. Each investor assumed the liabilities of his particular venture, and the national office could revoke his franchise if his service deteriorated due to poor business. The voluntary cooperative associations—Quality Courts, Best Western, Master Hosts— similarly blended on-site ownership with group referral, national advertising, and quality control. Tourists welcomed this formula, for they were assured both personal attention from resident owners—the homey touch—and the comfort of knowing that Tourinns in California and Pennsylvania met the same standards. To be sure, this security cost more, but the more desirable guest seemed willing to pay the premium.

Although an occasional observer might urge motelmen to pay more attention to travel needs of the economy-minded, trade publications generally congratulated owners on their prosperous clientele and luxurious accommodations, and they dismissed pre-1945 tourist courts as relics of distant "dog-house days." Having pursued the hotel class for almost forty years, the industry enjoyed a sweet victory in 1962, when the American Hotel Association became the American Hotel and Motel Association. Yet, as hotels had already learned, there were liabilities in being so successful. Some analysts worried that motels were overbuilt, much as hotels had overexpanded in the 1920s. There were also dangers in being tied to one form of transportation. Just as automobiles had threatened rail-oriented commercial hotels, motels were vulnerable to overseas air travel, rail revival, telecommunications, and gasoline shortages.

Perhaps most unsettling, the auto-motel complex was now the all-too-familiar beaten path. This was especially harmful in the vacation market, which depended so heavily on the sale of contrast to people tired of everyday ruts. The same dreams that had brought tourists to the roadside in 1910 could take them away from motels in the 1960s. Preferring more simplicity, some travelers turned to no-frill motor inns and private campgrounds. Seeking democratic intimacies, neovagabonds grouped their motor caravans at rock festivals. In search of lost cultures, some flew to Greece or Morocco. In search of lost landscapes, families toured national forests in self-sufficient recreational vehicles.

More ascetic explorers rediscovered the most individualized pre-railroad mode, walking.

Each new vacation alternative promised personal liberation from business world constraints, and, in a recreational market much larger than that of 1910, each invited mass participation and commercial elaboration. The success of each innovation thus tended to undermine its original attractions. Private campgrounds grew too luxurious, rock festivals too institutionalized, Greece too mercenary. Backpackers had to make reservations for popular park trails. But such frustrations spawned new ventures: gliders, the Galapagos Islands, jogging, four-wheel drive. The business prospects were as bright as the search was self-defeating.

Notes

Gypsying
1910–1920

1. For a list of such literature, see the bibliography.

2. Historian James J. Flink credits John C. Burnham with the first analytical use of the term "automobility." "The term conveniently sums up the combined impact of the motor vehicle, the automobile industry, and the highway plus the emotional connotations of this impact for Americans." James J. Flink, *The Car Culture* (Cambridge, Mass.: MIT Press, 1975), note, p. 1.

3. "Vacation Times Enhanced by the Motor Car," *Motor Car,* June 1912, p. 17; "Two weeks' Vagabonds," *New York Times,* July 20, 1922, sec. VII, p. 7; Elon Jessup, *The Motor Camping Book* (New York: G. P. Putnam's Sons, 1921), p. 4.

4. "Vacation Times," *Motor Car,* p. 17.

5. Lloyd Osbourne, "Motoring Through California," *Sunset,* April 1911, p. 376.

6. F. E. Brimmer, *Autocamping* (Cincinnati: Stewart Kidd, 1923), pp. 19–20; *Motor Campcraft* (New York: Macmillan, 1923), pp. 3–4.

7. "Practical Hints for the Motor Camper," *Sunset,* June 1916, p. 74. On England's "gentleman gypsies," see William M. Whiteman, *The History of the Caravan* (London: Blandford Press, 1973), pp. 17–32.

8. "The Gypsy in Modern America," *Touring Topics,* March 1929, pp. 28–29.

9. *Touring Topics,* April 1928, p. 30.

10. "James the Chauffeur," *Jokes of the Automobile* (Baltimore: I. & M. Ottenheimer, 1913), p. 27.

11. Stephen Leacock, "On the Art of Taking a Vacation," *Outlook,* May 25, 1921, pp. 161–162.

12. *Touring Topics,* July 1929, p. 11.

13. Elizabeth W. Spurge, "Life, Liberty, and the Pursuit of Happiness," *Motor Camper and Tourist,* February 1925, p. 563.

14. Rafford Pyke, "Summer Types of Men and Women," *Cosmopolitan,* September 1903, pp. 484–485; Ruth Aughiltree, "Stokes State Forest," *Motor Camper and Tourist,* July 1924, p. 106; "Why a Vacation?" *New York Times,* July 22, 1922, p. 4.

15. J. C. Long and John D. Long, *Motor Camping* (New York: Dodd, Mead, and Co., 1923), p. 1; Charles G. Percival, "The Tin Can Tourist Tribe," *Motor Camper and Tourist,* August 1925, p. 187.

16. *American Motorist,* May 1929, pp. 20–21.

17. "The Call of the Wild," *Building Age,* April 1928, pp. 460–461; E. C. MacMecken, "A Home for the Migratory Motorist," *Outing,* June 1918, p. 161; Long and Long, *Motor Camping,* p. 16.

18. *Touring Topics,* May 1926, p. 13.

19. Peter Schmitt, *Back to Nature: The Arcadian Myth in America* (New York: Oxford University Press, 1969).

20. Melville Ferguson, *Motor Camping on Western Trails* (New York: Century, 1925), p. 4.

21. Dick Wood, "Go Light Motor Camping," *Motor Camper and Tourist,* September 1924, p. 204; Frank J. Taylor, "This Looks Like a Good Place," *Collier's,* August 4, 1928, p. 20.

22. Helen Lukens Gaut, "Motoring Up the Pacific Coast," *Motor Life,* September 1913, p. 7.

Cars versus Trains
Back to Stagecoach Days

1. Dean MacCannell, *The Tourist* (New York: Schocken, 1976), pp. 8–9.

2. Dallas Lore Sharp, *The Better Country* (Boston: Houghton Mifflin, 1928); Robert Sloss, "Camping in an Automobile," *Outing,* May 1910, p. 236; Theodore Dreiser, *A Hoosier Holiday* (New York: John Lane, 1916), p. 92.

3. Henry Norman, "The Coming of the Automobile," *World's Work,* April 1903, p. 3308; "Gregarious and Individual Transportation," *American Motorist,* May 1910, p. 68; Norman, p. 3304.

4. Henry B. Joy, "The Traveller and the Automobile," *Outlook,* April 25, 1917, p. 739; "Automobile Topics," *New York Times,* March 22, 1903, p. 14.

5. In 1900 there were 507,421,000 passengers; 1910: 971,683,000; 1920: 1,269,413,000; 1930: 707,987,000. *Statistical History of the United States* (Stamford, Conn.: Fairfield Publishers, 1965), p. 430.

6. "Gregarious and Individual Transportation," *American Motorist,* p. 68.

7. On wartime and postwar rail troubles see *Railway Age,* July 20, 1917, p. 93; August 19, 1917, p. 219; Dec. 31, 1920, pp. 1140, 1161–1162.

8. "Gregarious and Individual Transportation," p. 68.

9. On the positive virtues of nature's intervention, see *The Club Journal,* April 17, 1909, p. 9; Emily Post, *By Motor to the Golden Gate* (New York: D. Appleton & Co., 1916), pp. 10, 82–84.

10. Elon Jessup, *The Motor Camping Book* (New York: G. P. Putnam's Sons, 1921), p. 3.

11. Sharp, *Better Country,* pp. 30–32.

12. Cleveland Moffett, "Automobiles for the Average Man," *Review of Reviews,* American ed., June 1900, p. 710.

13. Sharp, *Better Country,* p. 32.

14. Elon Jessup, "Motor Camping Comfort," *Outing,* June 1918, p. 196; Hamilton Laing, "The Transcontinental Game," *Sunset,* February 1917, p. 80; James P. Holland, "The Future of the Automobile," *Munsey's Magazine,* May 1903, p. 174; Dreiser, *Hoosier Holiday,* p. 93.

15. Helen Lukens Gaut, "Motoring Up the Pacific Coast," *Motor Life,* Sept. 1913, p. 7; Sharp, *Better Country,* p. 130.

16. Effie Price Gladding, *Across the Continent by the Lincoln Highway* (New York: Brentano's, 1915), p. ix; Laing, "Transcontinental Game," p. 80.

17. Earl Pomeroy, *In Search of the Golden West: the Tourist in Search of America* (New York: Alfred A. Knopf, 1957), p. 32. Much of the discussion of rail tourism is based on this important book.

18. *New York Times* quoted in Richard S. Lambert, *The Fortunate Traveler* (London: Andrew Melrose, 1950), p. 201; *American Motorist,* March 1, 1915, p. 150; John R. Eustis, "The Banner Year of Tours Begins," *Independent,* April 5, 1919, p. 36; Albert Bushnell Hart, "See America First," *Outlook,* December 27, 1916, pp. 933–938.

19. Post, *By Motor to the Golden Gate,* p. 88.

20. Gladding, *Across the Continent,* p. 203.

21. Frederic F. Van de Water, *The Family Flivvers to Frisco* (New York: D. Appleton, 1926), p. 47.

22. Post, *Motor to the Golden Gate,* pp. 198–199, 213, 237–240.

23. Gladding, *Across the Continent,* p. 58; Melville F. Ferguson, *Motor Camping on Western Trails* (New York: Century, 1925), p. 183. For a history of southern California motoring see Ashleigh E. Brilliant, "Social Effects of the Automobile in Southern California During the 1920s," (Ph.D. dissertation, University of California, Berkeley, 1964).

24. Malcolm M. Willey and Stuart A. Rice, *Communication Agencies and Social Life* (New York: McGraw-Hill, 1933), pp. 77–78.

25. For examples see "Motoring Near Home," *American Motorist,* June 1909, pp. 85–89; A. H. Van Voris, "Waysiding in Your Own County," *Motor Camper and Tourist,* April 1925, pp. 666–667.

26. Julian Street, *Abroad at Home* (New York: Century, 1914), pp. 513–514.

27. James Fullerton Muirhead, *America, The Land of Contrasts,* 3rd ed. (London: John Lane, 1902), p. 38.

28. "A 'Resort' Requirement," *Scribner's,* August 1908, p. 252; Edith Wharton quoted in Foster Rhea Dulles, *Americans Abroad: Two Centuries of European Travel* (Ann Arbor: University of Michigan Press, 1964), p. 144.

29. Post, *Motor to the Golden Gate,* pp. 23–24; Dreiser, *Hoosier Holiday,* pp. 92–93.

30. "Gasoline: Its Dispensing Stations Can Be Made Sightly," *Building Age,* January 1928, pp. 116–117; "Roadside Signs for Town Betterment," *House and Garden,* August 1925, pp. 76–77; Felix I. Koch, "Road Signs and Mile Posts," *Motor Camper and Tourist,* August 1924, pp. 164–165; "Selling Tips from the Broad Highway," *Printer's Ink,* August 20, 1925, p. 150; "Motorists' Caravansary is New Industry," *Popular Mechanics,* October 1922, pp. 522–523; "Stage Coach Days are Back, with Luxuries," *Literary Digest,* December 12, 1924, p. 56; "Broad Highways and Modern Inns," *Building Age,* August 1928, pp. 69–71.

31. Kathryn Hulme, *How's the Road?* (San Francisco: n.p., 1928), p. 18; F. E. Brimmer, *Motor Campcraft* (New York: Macmillan, 1923), p. 16.

32. *Complete Official Guide* (Detroit: 1915), pp. 11, 25.

33. Post, *Motor to the Golden Gate,* pp. 140, 250.

34. Jessie Rockefeller, "When Friend Wife Goes Camping," *Motor Camper and Tourist,* September 1925, p. 257.

35. Post, *Motor to the Golden Gate,* p. 44; John Burroughs, "A Strenuous Holiday," in *Under the Maples* (Boston: Houghton Mifflin, 1921), p. 122; Ferguson, *Motor Camping,* p. 297.

36. Laing, "Transcontinental Game," p. 74.

37. Post, *Motor to the Golden Gate,* p. 44.

38. Hulme, *How's the Road?,* p. 2.

39. "Spectator," *Outlook,* July 21, 1906, pp. 646–647; Edward Hungerford, "Sleeping Cars and Microbes," *Harper's Weekly,* Feb. 7, 1914, pp. 20–22; "Sanitary Dining Car," *Literary Digest,* October 10, 1914, p. 683; Harvey Wiley, "The Peril of the Peripatetic," *Good Housekeeping,* April 1915, pp. 449–452; Orin C. Baker, *Traveler's Aid Society in America* (New York: Funk and Wagnalls, 1917), pp. 74–75, 138–141; *Railway Age Gazette,* July 20, 1917, editorial, p. 93.

40. George H. Dacy, "Touring the Land of Our Last Frontier," *Motor Camper and Tourist,* December 1925, pp. 521–523.

41. Hulme, *How's the Road?,* p. 78; Laing, "Transcontinental Game," p. 78.

42. Laing, "Transcontinental Game," p. 78.

43. Ferguson, *Motor Camping,* pp. 66–67; *Official Guide* (1918 edition), pp. 46–47.

44. Daniel J. Boorstin, "From Traveler to Tourist: the Lost Art of Travel," *The Image* (New York: Atheneum, 1962), pp. 77–117.

45. Beatrice Massey, *It Might Have Been Worse* (San Francisco: Harr, Wagner, 1920), p. 143; Post, *Motor to the Golden Gate,* p. 281.

46. Massey, *It Might Have Been Worse,* p. 143; Van de Water, *Family Flivvers,* p. 6; Mary Crehore Bedell, *Modern Gypsies* (New York: Brentano's, 1924), p. 262.

47. Thomas W. Wilby, "By Motor to the Pacific Coast and Back," *Travel,* June 1912, p. 28.

48. Van de Water, *Family Flivvers,* pp. 246–247.

49. Ferguson, *Motor Camping,* pp. 111–112; Bedell, *Modern Gypsies,*

pp. 262–263; John Randolph Stidman, "The Road," *AAA Travel,* March 1931, p. 1.

Autocamping versus Hotels
Back to the Family Homestead

1. Zoe A. Tilghman, "An Automobile Camping Trip," *Woman's Home Companion,* June 1917, p. 31.

2. See James J. Flink, *America Adopts the Automobile, 1895–1910* (Cambridge: MIT Press, 1970), pp. 88–100.

3. William Copeman Kitchin, *A Wonderland of the East* (Boston: Page, 1920), p. 292; Mary Crehore Bedell, *Modern Gypsies* (New York: Brentano's, 1924), p. 261; Harry Irving Shumway, "Take Up Your Bed and Trail," *Field and Stream,* June 1920, p. 223.

4. J. J. Rout, "My Transcontinental Automobile Tour," *American Motorist,* April 1920, pp. 18–19; Lincoln Highway Association, *Official Road Guide* (Detroit: 1915), p. 138.

5. Charles G. Percival, "The Call of the Road," *Motor Camper and Tourist,* October 1924, p. 284; "Rebel Vacationists," *New York Times,* July 9, 1922, VII, p. 3.

6. For income figures see *Statistical History of the United States* (Stamford: Fairfield Publishing Co., 1965), pp. 180, 184; George Soule, *Prosperity Decade* (New York: Harper Torchbooks, 1968), p. 221.

7. F. E. Brimmer, *Motor Campcraft* (New York: Macmillan, 1923), p. 22.

8. Elon Jessup, "Motor Camping Comfort," *Outing,* June 1918, p. 196.

9. "Vacation Times Enhanced by the Motor Car," *Motor Car,* June 1912, p. 17; Elon Jessup, *The Motor Camping Book* (New York: G. P. Putnam's Sons, 1921), p. 5; Adelaide Andrews, "Signs of the Times," *Motor Camper and Tourist,* April 1925, p. 650.

10. Sinclair Lewis, *Free Air* (New York: Grosset and Dunlap, 1919), p. 36; Jessup, "Motor Camping Comfort," p. 196.

11. Quoted in Jefferson Williamson, *The American Hotel* (New York: Alfred A. Knopf, 1930), p. 190.

12. Robert Sloss, "Camping in an Automobile," *Outing,* May 1910, p. 236; "Hotel Travel Number," *Christian Science Monitor,* April 30, 1910, p. 1.

13. Ralph D. Paine, "Discovering America by Motor," *Scribner's,* February 1913, p. 142; Mary Harrod Northend, *We Visit Old Inns* (Boston: Small, Maynard, 1925).

14. James F. Muirhead, *The Land of Contrasts* (Boston: Lamson, Wolffe, & Co., 1898), p. 255; "The Hotel Problem," *Nation,* July 11, 1901, p. 26.

15. Lewis, *Free Air,* p. 259.

16. Muirhead, *Land of Contrasts,* pp. 30–31. For the sleeping porch fad, see Russell Lynes, *The Domesticated Americans* (New York: Harper & Row, 1957), p. 277; "Why Not a Sleeping Porch for Everyone?" *House Beautiful,* May 1919, p. 284.

17. Emily Post, *By Motor to the Golden Gate* (New York: D. Appleton,

1915), p. 87; James Montgomery Flagg, *Boulevards All the Way–Maybe* (New York: George H. Doran, 1925), p. 84.

18. Norman Hayner, *Hotel Life* (Chapel Hill: University of North Carolina Press, 1936), pp. 38–39, 96; "The Drummer Passed with the Horse Age," *Hotel Management,* November 1938, p. 425; Lewis Atherton, *Main Street on the Middle Border* (Bloomington: Indiana University Press, 1954), pp. 59–60, 230–233, 237–240.

19. Martha H. Clark, "Saving the Country Hotel," *Country Life,* August 1916, p. 52; *Independent,* November 12, 1912, p. 453; editorial, *American Motorist,* June 1909, pp. 121–122.

20. James David Henderson, *Meals by Fred Harvey* (Forth Worth: Texas Christian University Press, 1969), pp. 29, 51–52.

21. Beatrice Massey, *It Might Have Been Worse* (San Francisco: Harr, Wagner, 1920), p. 16.

22. Melville F. Ferguson, *Motor Camping on Western Trails* (New York: Century, 1925), pp. 271–272.

23. For Goffman's applicability to camping, see Gregory P. Stone and Marvin J. Taves, "Camping in the Wilderness," in Eric Larrabbee and Rolf Meyersohn, eds., *Mass Leisure* (Glencoe, Ill.: Free Press, 1958), pp. 300–301; Dallas Lore Sharp, *The Better Country* (Boston: Houghton Mifflin, 1928), p. 113; Earl Pomeroy, *In Search of the Golden West* (New York: Alfred A. Knopf, 1957), pp. 178–179.

24. Williamson, *The American Hotel,* pp. 169–191; Kathryn Busbey, *Home Life in America* (New York: Macmillan, 1910), p. 268.

25. F. E. Brimmer, *Autocamping* (Cincinnati: Stewart Kidd, 1923, pp. 16–17.

26. Quoted in Floyd Miller, *America's Extraordinary Hotelman Statler* (New York: Statler Foundation, 1968), p. 139.

27. Soule, *Prosperity Decade,* p. 37; "Tips are Smaller but Tipping Persists," *New York Times,* December 31, 1933, sec. VI, p. 6. On Prohibition and illegal liquor, see Hayner, *Hotel Life,* pp. 168–169; Rufus Jarman, *A Bed for the Night* (New York: Harper & Row, 1952), pp. 87–92.

28. Miller, *Statler,* p. 164; Jarman, *Bed for the Night,* pp. 256–257.

29. Editorial, "Help Yourself," *Independent,* October 30, 1913, pp. 192–193.

30. Advertisement, "Motor Rambling," *Field and Stream,* July 1920, p. 289.

31. See Brimmer, *Autocamping*, pp. 24–182; Jessup, *Motor Camping*, pp. 18–163.

32. Post, *Motor to the Golden Gate,* p. 100; *Hotel Monthly,* February 1900, p. 21; advertisement, *Field and Stream,* July 1920, p. 289.

33. Hayner, *Hotel Life,* pp. 168–169; "When You Eat in Hotels This Summer," *Ladies' Home Journal,* July 1918, p. 67; J. O. Dahl, "How Eating Habits Are Changing," *Hotel Management-Food Service,* February 1925, pp. 17–21.

34. Post, *By Motor to the Golden Gate,* p. 87; Lewis, *Free Air,* p. 44;

Flagg, *Boulevards*, p. 81; Anna May Nichols, "Lunching by the Wayside," *Motor Camper and Tourist*, October 1924, p. 275.

35. On tearooms see Charlotte B. Jordan, "The Tea-Room by the Wayside," *Ladies' Home Journal*, May 15, 1911, p. 15; "At the Sign of the Tea-Room," *Good Housekeeping*, July 1917, pp. 56–57; "She Teaches People How to Run Wayside Eating Places," *American Magazine*, April 1924, pp. 69–70.

36. *Official Manual of Motor Car Camping*, AAA (Washington, D.C.: 1920), p. 39; Shumway, "Take Up Your Bed and Trail," p. 222.

37. "Let's Eat," *Motor Camper and Tourist*, July 1924, p. 77; Shumway, "Take Up Your Bed and Trail," p. 222.

38. J. O. Dahl, *Selling Public Hospitality* (New York: Harper, 1929), p. 315.

39. Muirhead, *Land of Contrasts*, p. 17.

40. "The Hotel Martha Washington," *Independent*, June 25, 1903, p. 1492; "Tales of Feminine Travelers," *Good Housekeeping*, June 1906, p. 587; "Comfort While You Travel," *Outing*, October 1909, p. 85; Gerald Carson, *The Polite Americans* (New York: Morrow, 1966), pp. 228–229.

41. Earl Barnes, "Women's Place in the New Civilization," in *Women in Public Life, The Annals* 56(November 1914), pp. 16–17.

42. Allison Gray, "How the Hotel Clerk Sizes You Up," *American Magazine*, November 1922, p. 103; Ruth Dunbar, "Adventures of a Small-Town Hotel Keeper," *American Magazine*, March 1925, p. 195; "The Forgotten Guest," *Hotel Management*, November 1953, p. 47.

43. Thorstein Veblen, *The Theory of the Leisure Class* (New York: Modern Library, 1934), pp. 81–85.

44. Busbey, *Home Life*, pp. 346–347.

45. William M. Varrell, *Summer by-the-Sea: the Golden Era of Victorian Beach Resorts* (Portsmouth, N.H.: Strawberry Bank Print Shop, 1972), pp. 15–16; Busbey, *Home Life*, p. 347; "Spectator," *Outlook*, October 5, 1912, p. 273; "Reflections of Old Age on Life at Summer Hotels," *Nation*, September 2, 1915, p. 287.

46. Carl Van Vechten, "On Visiting Fashionable Places Out of Season," in *Excavations* (New York: Alfred A. Knopf, 1926), p. 8; "Alone in New York" *New York Times*, July 10, 1921, sec. VIII, p. 15.

47. "Summer on the Sands," *Munsey's Magazine*, August 1897, pp. 654–655; "North Woods," *World's Work*, August 1902, p. 2393.

48. Anna Page Scott, "Berkshire Barnacles," *Good Housekeeping*, June 1906, p. 595.

49. Rafford Pyke, "Summer Types of Men and Women," *Cosmopolitan*, September 1903, p. 487; William Dean Howells, "Confessions of a Summer Colonist," *Atlantic*, December 1898, p. 745.

50. "The Tour of the Rolling Tin," *Motor Camper and Tourist*, October 1924, p. 277. On the Jewish "invasion" see "The Summer Problem Need Not Trouble You," *American Hebrew*, July 6, 1928, p. 2371; Joseph E. Voss, *Summer Resort* (Philadelphia: University of Pennsylvania Press,

1941), pp. 39–41; "East Siders in 'the Mountains,'" *Survey,* July 15, 1923, pp. 443–444.

51. Harrison Rhodes, "American Holidays: Fresh Water and Inland Valleys," *Harper's,* July 1915, pp. 220–221; Marion Harland and Virginia Van de Water, *Everyday Etiquette* (Indianapolis: Bobbs-Merrill, 1905), p. 294.

52. Edward Bok, "Summers of Our Discontent," *Ladies Home Journal,* May 1901, p. 16; "Which of These Is Best for Children?" *Ladies' Home Journal,* July 1912, p. 49.

53. Bok, "Summers of Our Discontent," p. 16; editorial, *Ladies' Home Journal,* April 1902, p. 16.

54. "Concerning Summer Hotel Life," *Good Housekeeping,* August 1910, p. 141.

55. Theodore Dreiser, *A Hoosier Holiday* (New York: John Lane, 1916), pp. 40–42; Bok, "Concerning Summer Hotel Life," p. 487; William A. McKeever, "The Choice of Social Companionship for the Young," *Good Housekeeping,* April 1912, p. 449. On summer camps for children see Peter Schmitt, *Back to Nature* (New York: Oxford, 1969), pp. 96–105.

56. For examples, see "Is the Game Worth the Candle?" *Ladies' Home Journal,* April 1902, p. 16; Dorothy Dix, "How a Husband Likes to be Treated," *Good Housekeeping,* December 1914, pp. 742–743.

57. "Preserving a Husband in Summer," *Ladies' Home Journal,* May 1901, p. 18.

58. Martha Bensley Bruere, "Equal Rights of Parent and Child," *Good Housekeeping,* July 1914, pp. 74–75.

59. Brimmer, *Motor Campcraft,* pp. 2–3; "The Tour of the Rolling Tin," p. 277. For the switch to farm board, see "Summer Board as Business," *Nation,* August 29, 1889, pp. 163–64; "Keeping Summer Boarders with Success," *Ladies' Home Journal,* May 1901, p. 20.

60. W. C. Rucker, "Sanitary Advice for Summer Tourists and Sanitary Advice for Keepers of Summer Resorts," *Public Health Reports* 17, no. 21 (May 24, 1912), p. 3; "Sewage Disposal Problem of a Coast Summer Resort," *American Journal of Public Health* 7(November 1917), p. 944.

61. Brimmer, *Motor Campcraft,* p. 2.

62. Elon Jessup, "The Flight of the Tin Can Tourists," *Outlook,* May 25, 1921, p. 166.

63. *Official Manual,* AAA, p. 31.

64. Norine H. Morton, "Motor Camping, My First Real Vacation," *Motor Camper and Tourist,* February 1925, p. 533; Shumway, "Take Up Your Bed and Trail," p. 133.

65. Ferguson, *Motor Camping,* pp. 23–26; *Official Manual,* AAA, p. 31.

66. E. P. Powell, "A Simple Vacation," *Independent,* June 4, 1903, p. 1324.

67. Rebecca N. Porter, "The New Hospitality," *Scribner's,* June 1921, pp. 738–739.

68. Joseph W. Stray, "We Go A-Motor Hoboing," *Motor Camper and Tourist,* December 1924, p. 412; Powell, "A Simple Vacation," p. 1324.

From Fad to Institution
Municipal Camps, 1920–1924

1. Erik Cohen, "Nomads from Affluence: Notes on the Phenomenon of Drifter-Tourism," *International Journal of Comparative Sociology,* 14(1973): 89–103; Michael A. Smith and Louis Turner, "Some Aspects of the Sociology of Tourism," *Society and Leisure,* 5(1973): 55–69.

2. "Our Sanitary Obligation to Tourists," *Minnesota Municipalities,* February 1923, p. 17; "Tourist Camps," *American Municipalities,* October 1924, p. 15; *American City,* May 1927, p. 661; *Texas Municipalities,* September 1924, p. 107; *City Manager Magazine,* April 1926, p. 13.

3. Rebecca N. Porter, "The New Hospitality," *Scribner's,* June 1921, p. 735; Roland S. Wallis, "Tourist Camps," *Engineering Extension Service Bulletin,* Iowa State College, Ames, Iowa, vol. 21, no. 36(February 7, 1923), p. 40; S. R. Boer, "Denver's Automobile Camp," *Parks and Recreation,* April 1919, pp. 45–51.

4. "Motor Car Camping Grows More Popular Each Year," *American Motorist,* March 1920, pp. 5–8; Harry Shumway, "Pretty Soft Rough Stuff," *Field and Stream,* March 1921, p. 983; F. E. Brimmer, *Motor Campcraft* (New York: Macmillan, 1923), pp. 3, 7; Charles G. Percival, "The Wonderful Motor Camping Movement," *Motor Camper and Tourist (MCT),* July 1925, p. 85; Dick Wood, "Go LIGHT Motor Camping," *MCT,* September 1924, p. 204.

5. Elon Jessup, *The Motor Camping Book* (New York: Putnam, 1921), p. 179; Harriet Geithman, "Our Camping Neighbors; A Cosmopolitan Group," *MCT,* November 1925, p. 432.

6. Elon Jessup, "The Flight of the Tin Can Tourists," *Outlook,* May 25, 1921, p. 166; quoted in J. C. Long and John D. Long, *Motor Camping* (New York: Dodd, Mead, 1923), p. 2; *MCT,* June 1924, p. 5.

7. Earl Chapin May, "The Argonauts of the Automobile," *Saturday Evening Post,* August 9, 1924, p. 89; Frederic F. Van de Water, "The Education of the Tin Can Tourist," *World's Work,* December 1926, pp. 175–190; *Statistical History of the United States* (Stamford, Conn.: Fairfield Publishers, 1965), p. 462.

8. Xena W. Putnam, "The Law of the Road," *MCT,* November 1924, p. 362; Elizabeth Frazer, "The Destruction of Rural America," *Saturday Evening Post,* May 9, 1925, p. 39; "Trippers and Trespassers," *Saturday Evening Post,* July 18, 1925, p. 8.

9. Cornelia James Cannon, "The Untidy Tourist," *Outing,* December 1922, p. 113; A. D. Mueller, "Common Sense Camping," *MCT,* July 1924, p. 71; Brimmer, *Motor Campcraft,* p. 200.

10. "The Motorists League for Countryside Protection," *Field and Stream,* June 1923, p. 239; F. V. Coville, "Courtesy of the Camp," *Proceedings, National Conference on Outdoor Recreation* (Washington, D.C.: 1924), pp. 27–28; Brimmer, *Autocamping,* pp. 240–243; Richard K. Wood, "Northward Trek," *MCT,* July 1925, p. 102.

11. Joseph W. Stray, "Reflections of a Motor Camper When Not Motor Camping," *Field and Stream,* May 1923, p. 81; "Unusual Signs," *MCT,*

October 1924, p. 291; Clifford C. Leck, "Tourist Camps," *Minnesota Municipalities*, October 1924, pp. 170–171.

12. For examples, see "Carry Your Own Water," *MCT*, November 1924, p. 359; A. J. Clark, "The Automobile as a Public Health Hazard," *Literary Digest*, December 13, 1924, p. 26.

13. Boer, "Denver's Automobile Camp," pp. 47–51.

14. Wallis, "Tourist Camps," p. 7; John R. Eustis, "Gypsying De Luxe," *Independent*, May 3, 1919, pp. 184–185; "What the Hotel Man Stands to Gain from the Legitimate Tourist Camp," *Hotel Management*, June 1926, pp. 439–442.

15. "An Auto Camp De Luxe," *American Motorist*, December 1915, p. 739.

16. Marguerite A. Salomon, "Automobile Campsites and the 'Gypsy' Motorist," *Review of Reviews*, May 1921, pp. 529–532; *New York Times*, February 6, 1921, p. 6; Jessup, "Flight," p. 166.

17. Quoted in Long and Long, *Motor Camping*, p. 3.

18. C. P. Halligan, "Tourist Camps," *Michigan Agricultural College, Special Bulletin*, no. 139, Rural Landscape Series no. 2(June 1925), p. 3; S. C. Pier, "The Tourist Camp—Asset or Liability?" *American City*, April 1923, p. 365.

19. A. G. Vestal, "Camp Sites Along Western Highways," *Illustrated World*, July 1921, p. 801; William Charles Bettis, *A Trip to the Pacific Coast by Automobile* (author, 1922), p. 19; L. Bauchle, "Gateway to Vacation Land," *MCT*, March 1925, pp. 606–607; Melville F. Ferguson, *Motor Camping on Western Trails* (New York: Century, 1925), pp. 606–607.

20. Ferguson, *Motor Camping*, pp. 118–132; Salomon, "Automobile Campsites," p. 530; "A Wayside Inn," *Sunset*, May 1923, p. 62; Walter Prichard Eaton, "Tenting on the New Camp Ground," *Nation*, September 14, 1921, p. 287.

21. George Mansfield, "Hints from the Handy Man on Auto Camping," *MCT*, January 1925, p. 485.

22. Beatrice Massey, *It Might Have Been Worse* (San Francisco: Harr, Wagner, 1920), pp. 3–4; Maurice H. Decker, "Unburdened, Yet We Camp Comfortably," *MCT*, February 1925, pp. 517–519; Eric Howard, "Camping Along the Redwood Highway," *MCT*, August 1924, p. 154.

23. O. J. Gidney, "Pointers for Transcontinentalists," *Motor Life*, August 1919, p. 14; Vernon McGill, *Diary of a Motor Trip* (Los Angeles: Grafton, 1922), p. 5.

24. Wood, "Go LIGHT," p. 204.

25. Massey, *It Might Have Been Worse*, pp. 11–12.

26. Mary Roberts Rinehart, "The Family Goes A-Gypsying," *Outlook*, June 12, 1918, p. 263.

27. Emilie B. Snow, "Motor Hoboing De Luxe," *MCT*, December 1924, p. 395; Lloyd Osbourne, "Motoring Through California," *Sunset*, April 1911, p. 376; Mary Crehore Bedell, *Modern Gypsies* (New York: Brentano's, 1924), p. 130; Brimmer, *Autocamping*, p. 20; "Home Comforts in Outdoor Life," *Craftsman*, June 1913, pp. 340–341.

28. Shumway, "Pretty Soft Rough Stuff," p. 981; Adelaide Ovington, "Camping and the Motor Car," *Outlook,* June 12, 1918, p. 276.

29. Arthur O. Lovejoy and George Boas, *Primitivism and Related Ideas in Antiquity* (Baltimore: Johns Hopkins, 1935), pp. 10–11.

30. Jessie Call, "Casual Campers," *MCT,* October 1925, p. 330.

31. George W. Sutton, "The Camper on Tour," *Field and Stream,* May 1923, p. 64; Sutton, "Roshanara Goes Camping," ibid., June 1923, p. 195; Frank Brimmer, "Nomadic America's $3,300,000,000 Market," *Magazine of Business,* July 1927, pp. 18–21.

32. Brimmer, *Motor Campcraft,* pp. 12, 92–93; Ruth and Jim Aughiltree, "For Your Stomach's Sake," *MCT,* June 1925, p. 59.

33. Rinehart, "Family Goes A-Gypsying," p. 127; Bedell, *Modern Gypsies,* p. 130.

34. Jean Cunningham, "A Woman's Advice on Motor Camping," *MCT,* April 1924, pp. 654–656; Fred Smith, "Camping Is What You Make It," ibid., March 1925, p. 593.

35. Jessie Rockefeller, "When Friend Wife Goes Camping," *MCT,* September 1925, p. 257.

36. Post, *Motor to the Golden Gate,* pp. 31–32.

37. Mueller, "Common Sense Camping," p. 71; editorial, *Des Moines Register,* July 7, 1925, p. 6; Claude M. Kreisler, "On Discarding Needless Burdens," *MCT,* October 1924, p. 263.

38. Osbourne, "Motoring Through California," pp. 364–366; T. W. Wilby, "Along European By-Ways," *The Club Journal,* Automobile Club of America, April 17, 1909, p. 23; Charles Merz, "The Once Open Road," *Harper's,* November 1925, p. 698; James Montgomery Flagg, *Boulevards All the Way—Maybe* (New York: George H. Doran, 1925), p. 29.

39. Ferguson, *Motor Camping,* p. 110; Post, *Motor to the Golden Gate,* p. 111.

40. For example, see Effie Price Gladding, "To the Woman Tourist," in *The Complete Official Road Guide of the Lincoln Highway* (Detroit: 1915), pp. 7–8.

41. Frederic F. Van de Water, *The Family Flivvers to Frisco* (New York: D. Appleton, 1927), p. 57; George H. Dacy, "Touring the Land of Our Last Frontier," *MCT*, December 1925, p. 558.

42. For a survey of the overall progress in mileage and speed, see Myron M. Stearns, "Notes on Changes in Motoring," *Harper's,* September 1936, pp. 441–444.

43. For examples, see "Shooting the Market on the Wing," *Printer's Ink Monthly,* October 1922, p. 101; "Intensive Flivving," *Atlantic,* August 1923, pp. 278–280; Merz, "The Once Open Road," p. 698; Irvin S. Cobb, *Some United States* (New York: George H. Doran, 1926), pp. 276–299.

44. John Dollard, "The Changing Functions of the American Family," (Ph.D. dissertation, University of Chicago, 1931), p. 20; Margaret Mead, "Outdoor Recreation in the Context of Emerging American Values:

Background Considerations," in *Trends in American Living and Outdoor Recreation* (Washington, D.C.: 1962), p. 12; Eugene Litwack, "Geographic Mobility and Extended Family Cohesion," *American Sociological Review*, 25(June 1960): 385–394.

45. *Hotel Monthly*, September 1925, p. 30; "Railroads Trying to Beat the Autos," *Literary Digest*, June 19, 1926, p. 19; "Why We Should *Not* Lower the Cost of Tourist Travel," *Hotel Management*, May 1925, pp. 295–299.

46. Rebecca N. Porter, "The New Hospitality," *Scribner's*, June 1921, p. 735.

47. Porter, "The New Hospitality," p. 738.

48. Brimmer, *Autocamping*, p. 23; Harry B. Ansted, "The Autocamp Community," *Journal of Applied Sociology*, November 1924, p. 139; Earl Chapin May, "The Argonauts of the Automobile," *Saturday Evening Post*, August 9, 1924, p. 89.

49. Leslie Bray, "The Trail of the Tampans," *MCT*, July 1924, p. 74; Van de Water, *Family Flivvers*, p. 179; Dallas Lore Sharp, *The Better Country* (Boston: Houghton Mifflin, 1928), p. 95.

50. Calvin Coolidge, "Address," *Proceedings, National Conference on Outdoor Recreation* (Washington, D.C., 1924), p. 13.

51. Van de Water, *Family Flivvers*, p. 176.

52. Geithmann, "Our Camping Neighbors," p. 433; Mrs. C. G. Elmore, "Omaha Tourist Camp," *MCT*, August 1924, p. 183.

53. "Neighbors for a Night in Yellowstone Park," *Literary Digest*, August 30, 1924, p. 44; Charles Moreau Harger, "Free Tourist Camp, One Mile," *Outlook*, August 15, 1923, p. 592; Richard K. Wood, "Northward Trek," *MCT*, July 1925, p. 102; Charles G. Percival, "The Tin Can Tourist Tribe," *MCT*, August 1925, p. 185.

54. *American Motorist*, February 1920, p. 15; Boer, "Denver's Automobile Camp," p. 518; Malcolm A. Willey and Stuart A. Rice, *Communication Agencies and Social Life* (New York: McGraw-Hill, 1933), pp. 62–64.

55. Porter, "The New Hospitality," p. 735; May, "Argonauts of the Automobile," p. 89.

56. Wood, "Go LIGHT," p. 204.

57. Frazer, "Destruction of Rural America," p. 197; Salomon, "Automobile Camp Sites," p. 529.

58. Geithmann, "Our Camping Neighbors," p. 433; Jessup, "Flight of the Tin Can Tourists," p. 168; Wood, "Go LIGHT," p. 204.

59. Percival, "Tin Can Tourist Tribe," p. 187; Geithmann, "Camping Neigbors," p. 432.

60. Anne O'Hare McCormick, "Main Street, too, Winters in Florida," *New York Times Magazine*, February 22, 1925, p. 3; "Neighbors for the Night in Yellowstone," p. 46.

61. Van de Water, "Education," p. 175.

62. Ferguson, *Motor Camping*, pp. 179–180; Van de Water, *Family Flivvers*, p. 124.

63. McCormick, "Main Street," p. 3; Bedell, *Modern Gypsies,* p. 145; Brimmer, *Autocamping*, pp. 23, 234; Van de Water, "Education," pp. 179–180.

64. Ferguson, *Motor Camping,* p. 179; Nels Anderson, *The Hobo* (Chicago: University of Chicago Press, 1923), p. 16.

65. Ferguson, *Motor Camping,* pp. 179–180.

66. Harger, "Free Tourist Camp," p. 592; Flagg, *Boulevards,* p. 47; "Neighbors for the Night in Yellowstone," p. 44; John J. McCarthy and Richard Littell, "Three Hundred Thousand Shacks," *Harper's,* July 1933, p. 187.

67. Ferguson, *Motor Camping,* pp. 179–180; Van de Water, *Family Flivvers,* p. 34.

68. Gula Sabin, *California by Motor* (Milwaukee: author, 1926), n.p.

69. Van de Water, *Family Flivvers,* p. 15; Lawrence S. Clark, "Six Weeks in a Ford," *Outing,* July 1922, p. 164.

70. Siegfried Giedion, *Mechanization Takes Command* (New York: Norton, 1969), pp. 469, 389–481.

71. "A Vacation in a Portable Lodging House," *Independent,* June 3, 1909, pp. 1222–1223; "California Combination Car," *Motor Car,* December 1909, p. 13.

72. *Popular Mechanics Auto Tourist's Handbook No. 1* (Chicago: 1924), p. 4; Jessup, *Motor Camping,* p. 14.

73. Irwin, "Safeguarding Health," p. 634; "A Folding Family for Motor Camping," *MCT,* December 1924, p. 401; "The Tour of the Rolling Tin," *MCT,* October 1924, p. 277.

74. May, "Argonauts of the Automobile," p. 92.

75. Wallis, "Tourist Camps," p. 65.

76. Cohen, "Nomads from Affluence."

Limiting Access
Pay Camps, 1923–1928

1. "Is a Tourist Camp a Paying Investment?" *Texas Municipalities,* November 1924, pp. 154–156.

2. Harriet Geithmann, "Our Camping Neighbors: A Cosmopolitan Group," *MCT,* November 1925, p. 474.

3. Rebecca N. Porter, "The New Hospitality," *Scribner's,* June 1921, p. 735.

4. Ibid., p. 736.

5. Ibid., p. 740.

6. Kathryn Hulme, *How's the Road?* (San Francisco: n.p., 1928), pp. 49–50; Melville Ferguson, *Motor Camping on Western Trails* (New York: Century, 1925), pp. 295–296.

7. Fred E. Trainer, "Tourist Camps," *American Municipalities,* October 1924, p. 11.

8. Frederic F. Van de Water, *The Family Flivvers to Frisco* (New York: D. Appleton, 1926), p. 109; Frances Scarborough, "Texas Tourist Camp

Problems and Their Solutions," *Texas Municipalities,* September 1924, p. 107.

9. Reynold M. Wik, *Henry Ford and Grass-Roots America* (Ann Arbor: University of Michigan, 1972), p. 30.

10. Van de Water, *Family Flivvers,* p. 40.

11. Ibid., p. 100. See also, "The Hobo Hits the Highroad," *American Mercury,* July 1926, pp. 334–338.

12. *Popular Mechanics Auto Tourist's Handbook No. 1* (Chicago: 1924), p. 69; Frank J. Taylor, "This Looks Like a Good Place," *Collier's,* August 4, 1928, p. 47.

13. "Vacations for Factory Workers," *Monthly Labor Review,* August 1921, pp. 474–475; Charles M. Mills, *Vacations for Industrial Workers* (New York: Ronald Press, 1927), pp. 5, 14, 128. On local use of autocamps see Robert L. Thayer, "Camp-Siting," *MCT,* June 1925, p. 17; John D. Long, "Week-Ending East and West," *MCT,* August 1924, pp. 144–145.

14. *Literary Digest,* October 20, 1923, pp. 68–69.

15. Mildred Adams, "Now We Are Discovering America Again," *New York Times,* July 13, 1930, quoted in Earl Pomeroy, *In Search of the Golden West* (New York: Alfred A. Knopf, 1957), pp. 203–204; "Survey of Business Trends," *Sporting Goods Illustrated,* July 1928, p. 129; "Extra Gold Profits from the Summer Resorters," *Sporting Goods Journal,* July 1928, pp. 42–44.

16. Mrs. C. G. Elmore, "Tin Can Tourists of the World," *MCT,* July 1924, p. 91; William G. Irwin, "Tin Canners Annual Convention," *MCT,* July 1925, pp. 116–117; Van de Water, *Family Flivvers,* p. 178; Mrs. A. Sherman Hitchcock, "Style and Comfort for Women Campers," *MCT,* August 1924, p. 141.

17. Charles G. Percival, "The Trailer Folks," *MCT,* August 1924, p. 149; "Convertible Carry-all and Auto Step,"*MCT,* December 1924, p. 435.

18. F. W. Leuning, *Motor Camping* (Milwaukee: Milwaukee Journal Tour Club, 1926), p. 1; Fred Smith, "Camping is What You Make It," *MCT,* March 1925, p. 583.

19. Smith, "Camping Is What You Make It," p. 593.

20. James J. Flink, *The Car Culture* (Cambridge: MIT Press, 1975), pp. 143, 140–167; "Motors and Morality," *Survey,* October 15, 1925, pp. 102–105; William Ashdown, "Confessions of an Automobilist," *Atlantic,* June 1925, pp. 786–792; Lawrence F. Abbott, "The Vices and Virtues of the Automobile," *Outlook,* December 15, 1926, pp. 491–492.

21. "Toll of the Automobile: Animal Casualties," *Science,* February 16, 1925, pp. 56–57; "Stepping on the Gas—and Results," *Literary Digest,* October 4, 1925, pp. 35–36; "Health Perils from Motor Travel," *Literary Digest,* December 13, 1924, p. 26; editorial, *Outlook,* November 10, 1926, p. 327; *Planning for City Traffic, The Annals,* Austin F. Mac-Donald, ed., 133(September 1927), pp. 156–185.

22. B. F. Clark, "Hunting a Good Place to Camp," *MCT,* October 1925, p. 329; Frank E. Brimmer, "How to Camp Successfully," *Catalog of Sporting Goods Manufacturers, 1929* (New York: Sporting Goods Journal, 1929), p. 84.

23. For examples, see "Intensive Flivving," *Atlantic*, August 1923, pp. 278–280; Lewis L. Thomas, "Touring Amid Beauties with Unseeing Eyes, *MCT*, November 1924, pp. 340–341; Frances Warfield, "America on Wheels," *Outlook*, August 14, 1929, pp. 603–605.

24. "Radio for the Camper on Tour," *Field and Steam*, August 1923, pp. 491, 508; advertisement, *MCT*, November 1925, p. 401; "Radio in Camp," *MCT*, June 1924, p. 35.

25. Richard Dakin, The Lure of the Far West," *MCT*, August 1924, pp. 159–160; Charles G. Percival, "The Tin Can Tourist Tribe," *MCT*, August 1925, p. 185.

26. Bertha Streeter, "Hygiene of the Tourists' Camps," *The Forecast*, June 1927, pp. 370–372; "Our Sanitary Obligations to Tourists," *Minnesota Municipalities*, February 1923, pp. 17–18; Harry N. Burhans, "Standardization of Auto Tourist Camps," *Municipal and County Engineering*, August 1924, p. 82; W. G. Turnbull, "The Purity of Roadside Drinking Water," *The Automobile: Its Province and Problems, The Annals*, 116(November 1924), pp. 60–62; Scarborough, "Texas Tourist Camp Problems," pp. 109–110.

27. Streeter, "Hygiene of the Tourists' Camps," p. 371.

28. J. P. Soderstrum, "Rapid City's Successful Tourist Park," *Public Management*, July 1927, pp. 582–586.

29. *New York Times*, March 22, 1925, sec. IX, p. 11; Earl C. Elliott, "The Case Against the Tourist Camp," *American City*, January 1923, p. 77; "Campsite Management," *MCT*, September 1924, p. 240.

30. Streeter, "Hygiene of the Tourists' Camps," p. 372; A. D. Mueller, "Common Sense Camping," *MCT*, July 1924, p. 71; F. E. Brimmer, *Motor Campcraft* (New York: Macmillan, 1923), p. 195; Elliott, "Case Against," p. 79.

31. Clifford C. Leck, "Tourist Camps," *Minnesota Municipalities*, October 1924, p. 172; Chester Cohen, "Making the Tourist Camp Safe for Your Own Town," ibid., May 1925, pp. 88–89.

32. Charles Moreau Harger, "Free Tourist Camp, One Mile," *Outlook*, August 15, 1923, p. 591; Frank E. Brimmer, "Fundamentals of Motor Camping," *Official AAA Camp Directory* (Washington, D.C.: 1928), p. 5; Burhans, "Standardization," pp. 82–84.

33. "Tourists Spending Billions of Gold," *MCT*, June 1925, p. 5; Frank E. Brimmer, "Nomadic America's $3,300,000,000 Market," *Magazine of Business*, July 1927, pp. 18–21; *American Motorist*, January 1929, p. 33.

34. Oscar Lewis, "Free Auto Camp Ground," *Essays of Today (1926–27)* Odell Shepard and Robert Hillyer, eds. (New York: Century, 1928), pp. 117–123.

35. Harry B. Ansted, "The Auto-Camp Community," *Journal of Applied Sociology* 9(1924), pp. 138–139; "A Wayside Auto Inn," *Sunset*, May 1923, p. 67.

36. *New York Times*, March 22, 1925, sec. IX, p. 11.

37. See Jefferson Williamson, *The American Hotel* (New York: Alfred A. Knopf, 1930), pp. 180–190.

38. Scarborough, "Texas Tourist Camp Problems," p. 108.

39. Theodore Wirth, address, *Proceedings, National Conference on Outdoor Recreation* (Washington, D.C.: 1924), p. 137; Trainer, "Tourist Camps," p. 13; Burhans, "Standardization," p. 84.

40. S. C. Pier, "The Tourist Camp—Asset or Liability?" *American City,* April 1923, p. 385; Barney L. Allis, "What the Hotel Man Stands to Lose from the Poorly Operated Camp," *Hotel Management,* July 1926, p. 11; Soderstrum, "Rapid City," p. 582.

41. Earl Brown, "The Modern Auto Camp," *MCT,* December 1924, p. 401.

42. Elliott, "Case Against," p. 79; W. I. Hamilton, *Promoting New Hotels: When Does It Pay?* (New York: Harper Bros., 1930), pp. 1–49.

43. Van de Water, *Family Flivvers,* p. 145.

44. *Official Camping and Campsite Manual* (Washington, D.C.: AAA, 1925); *Official AAA Camp Directory* (Washington, D.C.: 1928).

45. *American City,* March 1927, p. 661; Howard K. Menhinick, "Municipal Tourist Camps," ibid., March 1930, pp. 98–99; Marion Hathway, *The Migratory Worker and Family Life* (Chicago: University of Illinois, 1934), pp. 105–114; *New York Times,* June 16, 1935, sec. XI, p. 15; *Hotel Monthly,* October 1935, p. 50.

Early Motels
1925–1945

1. A. E. Holden, "Cottage Pioneer Looks Ahead," *Tourist Trade,* May 1933, pp. 20–22.

2. Clara Keyton, *Tourist Camp Pioneering Experiences* (Chicago: Adams Press, 1960), pp. 5–37. For similar experiences, see Gilbert S. Chandler, "Starting from Scratch and Building a Deluxe Motor Court," *Tourist Court Journal,* November 1937, p. 5; Myron M. Stearns, "That Bungalow Camp," *Saturday Evening Post,* August 27, 1927, pp. 35–37.

3. John J. McCarthy and Robert Littell, "Three Hundred Thousand Shacks," *Harper's,* July 1933, p. 184; "Changing Trends in Camp Goods Obsolete Old Equipment," *Sporting Goods Illustrated,* January 1929, pp. 56–58; "Camp Goods Volume Shrinks 50% During 1929," *Sporting Goods Illustrated,* January 1930, pp. 67, 76–77.

4. "They Built a Paying Camp Site on an Abandoned Ranch," *American Magazine,* June 1927, p. 68.

5. Frank J. Taylor, "Tips for Two-Week Vacationists," *Better Homes and Gardens,* June 1931, p. 94.

6. Frank E. Brimmer, "Outdoor Hotels," *Woman's Home Companion,* July 1928, p. 42; Frederic F. Van de Water, *The Family Flivvers to Frisco* (New York: D. Appleton, 1927), pp. 233–234.

7. Gusse T. Smith, "Arizona's Approved Tourist Camps," *Arizona Highways,* April 1929, pp. 13, 15.

8. Frank E. Brimmer, "The 'Nickel and Dime' Stores of Nomadic America," *Magazine of Business,* August 1927, p. 152.

9. "The Great American Roadside," *Fortune,* September, 1934, p. 56.

10. Adelaide A. Andrews, "Signs of the Times," *MCT,* April 1925, p. 689;

for further examples, see "The Traveling Smile Bringer," *MCT*, February 1925, p. 556.

11. Lewis Gannett, *Sweet Land* (Garden City: Sun Dial, 1937), p. 5; "America Takes to the Motor Court," *Business Week,* June 15, 1940, pp. 19–20; "Cleanliness, Quiet, Attractiveness," *National Petroleum News,* August 12, 1931, p. 61.

12. "Do Your Signs Sell?" *Tourist Trade,* October 1932, pp. 8–9; "Putting Ideas into Signs," ibid., February 1933, pp. 9–11; "Broad Highways and Modern Inns," *Building Age,* August 1928, pp. 69–71; "Dutch Mill Stations," *National Petroleum News,* April 30, 1930, pp. 105–106.

13. Keyton, *Tourist Camp,* pp. 20, 37; A. E. Holden, "How Three Hotel Men are Operating Successful Tourist Courts," *Hotel Management,* June 1930, pp. 543–549; "Cottage Pioneer Looks Ahead," p. 21.

14. Keyton, *Tourist Camp,* pp. 38–53.

15. Lois E. B. Brown, "Modern Gypsies," *Nation,* May 4, 1927, p. 500.

16. *Statistical History of the United States* (Stamford, Conn.: Fairfield Publishing Co., 1965), p. 393; "Broad Highways and Modern Inns," pp. 69–71; "Oil Company Tourist Camp is a Good Advertisement," *National Petroleum News,* April 24, 1929, pp. 93–94.

17. Daniel J. Boorstin, *The Americans: The Democratic Experience* (New York: Vintage, 1974), pp. 146–148, 445–446; Stuart Ewen, *Captains of Consciousness: Advertising and the Social Roots of the Consumer Culture* (New York: McGraw-Hill, 1976).

18. For examples, see "Vagabonds-de luxe and Plain of the Tourist Trails," *Literary Digest,* June 27, 1931, pp. 36–38; Holden, "Three Hotel Men," p. 533; "Tourist Camps 'Deluxe' in the Southwest," *Forbes,* August 1, 1928, pp. 25–26. On James Vail's Mo-Tel, see Arthur S. White, *Palaces of the People* (London: Rapp and Whiting, 1968), p. 168; Ashleigh E. Brilliant, "Social Effects of the Automobile in Southern California During the 1920s," (Ph.D. dissertation, University of California, Berkeley, 1964), p. 218.

19. "Pierce Undertakes New Experiment in Caring for Motor Tourists," *National Petroleum News,* February 13, 1929, pp. 90–92; "Standard, Swift, National Dairy to Aid Chain of 1000 Wayside Inns," *Sales Management,* May 23, 1931, p. 313; "National Motor Inns Will Establish Chain of 'Super-Camps,' " *Sales Management,* October 3, 1931, p. 30.

20. *American Motorist,* January 1929, p. 33.

21. Julius Weinberger, "Economic Aspects of Recreation," *Harvard Business Review* 15(Summer 1937), pp. 448–463, especially 456.

22. Ibid., p. 456; *Statistical History,* p. 528.

23. "Cleanliness, Quiet, Attractiveness," p. 60; "Gas Stations Sell Cottages," *Tourist Trade,* January 1933, p. 8; "Among the Hotel Associations," ibid., December 1932, p. 27.

24. John J. McCarthy, "Pay Dirt in Tourist Camps," *Advertising and Selling,* May 25, 1933, p. 26; Henry Schmidt, Jr., "Overnight Rest-Cabins Spreading," *Literary Digest,* June 9, 1934, p. 40.

25. For examples, see "Good Profits Building Tourist Camps," *American Builder,* April 1931, pp. 88–89; "The Tourist Camp Market," *Print-

er's Ink, December 8, 1932, p. 56; John J. McCarthy, "The Market Business Forgets," Nation's Business, August 1933, pp. 38–40.

26. "Across Our Desk," Tourist Trade, September 1932, p. 3.

27. McCarthy and Littell, "Three Hundred Thousand Shacks," p. 187.

28. L. H. Robbins, "America Hobnobs at the Tourist Camp," New York Times Magazine, August 12, 1934, p. 9; "The Great American Road-side," p. 55; McCarthy, "Pay Dirt," p. 26; Tourist Trade, December 1932, p. 11.

29. "Boom-Time Financing Explains Sad Plight of Hotel Business," Business Week, July 1, 1931, pp. 18–19; James S. Warren, "Hotels are Seeking a Way Out," Nation's Business, January 1933, p. 45; "Economic Status of the Hotel Business," Hotel Monthly, October 1933, pp. 45–46.

30. Clarence Madden, "How Many Sides Are There to This Question of Unfair Competition?" Hotel Management, September 1933, p. 175.

31. Ruel McDaniel, "How to Profit from the Waning Popularity of Tourist Camps," Hotel Management, May 1926, pp. 337–340; J. O. Dahl, "Tourists Accommodated—No Questions Asked," ibid., October 1929, pp. 299–304; "Hotel Men Should Render Better Service to Guests with Cars," ibid., April 1930, pp. 331–332; Holden, "Three Hotel Men," pp. 543–549; "Will a Cottage Court Solve Your Cabin Competition?" Hotel Monthly, March 1934, pp. 17–19.

32. Editorial, Hotel World-Review, May 16, 1931, p. 4.

33. "Among the Hotel Associations," Tourist Trade, December 1932, pp. 14–15; "Unfair Competition Issue," Hotel Management, December 1933, pp. 460–461.

34. Hotel World-Review, November 19, 1932, pp. 13, 16; "Licensing and Regulation of Tourist Inns, Cabins, and Camps," Hotel Management, November 1932, p. 233; "State Legislation Helps Cottage Establishments," Tourist Trade, March 1933, pp. 5–7.

35. New York Times, November 14, 1935, p. 19; "Wayside or Safeside?" Hotel Management, January 1934, p. 8; "More Thoughts on the Tourist Camps," Hotel World-Review, November 19, 1932, p. 16.

36. Norman Hayner, Hotel Life (Chapel Hill: University of North Carolina, 1936), p. 6.

37. "Hospitality Opens Purse Strings," Tourist Trade, August 1933, p. 16.

38. Weinberger, "Economic Aspects," p. 455; Jesse Steiner, Research Memorandum on Recreation in the Depression (New York: Arno, 1972), pp. 95–96.

39. "Where To—Cottage Owners?" Tourist Trade, September 1932, p. 7.

40. John Emery, "Your Business—Today and Tomorrow," Tourist Trade, February 1933, p. 6.

41. Keyton, Tourist Camp, pp. 85–86, 104–148.

42. Ibid., p. 108; Gannett, Sweet Land, pp. 209–210.

43. Keyton, Tourist Camp, pp. 119, 120.

44. Vera Connolly, "Tourists Accommodated," Delineator, March

1925, p. 15; *Journal of Home Economics* 23 (January 1931), pp. 41–42; "Tourists Accommodated," *Saturday Evening Post*, May 14, 1932, p. 32; "Maryland Tourist Homes to Organize," *Hotel World-Review*, October 21, 1933, p. 6; Tourist Trade, January 1933, p. 3; "Roadside Shacks," *Highway Host*, June 1934, p. 5.

45. "Association Notes," *Tourist Trade*, May 1933, pp. 14–15; "Associated Camps and Resorts," ibid., September 1933, pp. 9–10.

46. This account is taken from letters, working drafts, internal memoranda, and reports in 3 ½ boxes, labeled "Tourist Code and Motor Court Trade," located in the National Recovery Administration's Consolidated Unapproved Industry Code File, boxes 6595–6598, at the Washington Records Center, Suitland, Maryland; and from the "History of the Code of the Tourist Lodge and Motor Court Trade," March 4, 1936, National Archives, Washington, D.C., Box 7318.

47. Steiner, *Research Memorandum*, pp. 95–96; *New York Times*, September 16, 1934, sec. VIII, p. 8; *Business Week*, May 9, 1936, p. 14; *Statistical History*, pp. 462–463; Weinberger, "Economic Aspects," pp. 455–457.

48. *Statistical History*, p. 529; "Hotel Hopes Rise," *Business Week*, June 8, 1940, pp. 21–22; "Industry Gets Set for a Half Million Dollar Campaign in Fight for Business," *Tourist Court Journal*, February 1939, pp. 9–10.

49. *Directory of Motor Courts and Camps* (Washington, D.C.: AAA, 1937), p. 82; Robert C. Stuart, "Do Quality Motor Inns Belong as Part of the Hotel Business?" *Hotel Management*, May 1935, pp. 366–367; J. C. Stevens, "Tourist Court Organization," *Tourist Court Journal*, August 1938, p. 25.

50. Allen S. James, " 'Travel' Camps in the Ozarks," *National Petroleum News*, August 4, 1937, p. 37.

51. Letter, "Service Stations," *Tourist Court Journal*, August 1939, p. 18.

52. "The Tourist Wants Special Attention. . . . Give It to Him!" *Tourist Court Journal*, February 1938, pp. 23–24.

53. C. E. McCullough, "Simple, Home-Like Arrangement of Court Cottages is Most Desirable," *Tourist Court Journal*, August 1938, p. 9; "El Patio," ibid., July 1938, p. 17.

54. "Glazed Tile and Its Practical Use in a Motor Camp," *Tourist Court Journal*, November 1937, pp. 9–10. On the Danish Village, see Mary Lee, "America Goes Gypsying for a Vacation," *New York Times*, September 1, 1935, p. 13; "English Village," *National Petroleum News*, December 15, 1937, p. 30.

55. *Tourist Trade*, December 1932, pp. 12–13; "Bathroom Renovation," *Tourist Court Journal*, June 1939, p. 13; "El Patio," *Tourist Court Journal*, August 1938, pp. 17–18.

56. Helen H. Gifft, et al., *Nutrition, Behavior, and Change* (Englewood Cliffs: Prentice-Hall, 1972), pp. 25–53; Miriam E. Lowenberg, et al., *Food and Men* (New York: John Wiley, 1968), pp. 65–124; "The Great American Roadside," *Fortune*, September 1934, pp. 61–63, 172–174; "Food Along the Highroad," *New York Times*, July 14, 1935, sec. VII, p.

14; "Cafes Operated by 47% of Courters," *Tourist Court Journal,* June 1939, pp. 5–6. For food trends in the 1930s, see Warren Belasco, "Toward a Culinary Common Denominator: Origins of Howard Johnson's," *Journal of American Culture* II (Fall 1979).

57. See *Trailer Travel,* 1936–1937; *Trailer Caravan,* 1936–1937; Wally Byam, *Trailer Travel Here and Abroad* (New York: David McKay, 1960); "What About This New Interest in Auto-Travel Coaches?" *Sporting Goods Journal,* March 1933, pp. 80–81; "New Modes in Auto Touring," *Sporting Goods Journal,* June 1936, pp. 30–34; "Labor and Social Effects of Migration by Trailer," *Monthly Labor Review,* May 1937, pp. 1189–1191; Donald O. Cowgill, *Mobile Homes: A Study of Trailer Life* (Washington, D.C.: American Council on Public Affairs, 1941); and Michael A. Rockland's forthcoming study of recreational vehicles and mobile homes.

58. *Tourist Court Journal,* February 1939, pp. 9–10.

59. J. Edgar Hoover, "Camps of Crime," *American Magazine,* February 1940, pp. 14–15; "America Takes to the Motor Court," *Business Week,* June 15, 1940, pp. 19–20.

60. "Publicity," *Tourist Court Journal,* August 1939, p. 18; editorial, "It's High Time to Change Tactics," ibid., February 1946, p. 17.

61. Gustavus Basch, "Look Before You Leap in this Modern Industry," *Tourist Court Journal,* October 1938, p. 11; front cover, ibid., April 1939; "Oil Company Tourist Camp," *National Petroleum News,* April 24, 1929, pp. 93–94; "Watch the Super-Highway Idea," *Tourist Court Journal,* March 1938, p. 16.

62. Letter from E. S. Tweedale, *Tourist Court Journal,* March 1939, p. 23; prices in AAA *Directory of Motor Courts and Cottages* (1939). For chiseling and haggling, see "Price Cutters," *Tourist Court Journal,* December 1937, p. 28.

63. "American Tourism Heads for the Top," *Business Week,* May 18, 1940, p. 20; "Hotel Hopes Rise," ibid., June 8, 1940, pp. 21–22; "America Takes to the Tourist Court," pp. 19–20; "Touristless Courts," ibid., April 5, 1942; "1945 Tourist Court Earnings Remain Steady," *Tourist Court Journal,* August 1945, pp. 5–7.

64. Automobile Manufacturers Association, *Automobile Facts and Figures* (Detroit, 1950), pp. 40–41; *American Motel Magazine, Market Analysis of the Motel Industry* (Chicago: 1952), p. 1.

65. Editorial, *Hotel Management,* November 1953, p. 5.

Bibliographical Guide

General Automobile Literature

Considering the car's major role in American life, the scholarly historical literature is remarkably sparse. The most important introductory surveys are John B. Rae, *The American Automobile: A Brief History* (Chicago: University of Chicago Press, 1965); and James J. Flink, *The Car Culture* (Cambridge: The MIT Press, 1975). Flink's *America Adopts the Automobile, 1895–1910* (Cambridge: The MIT Press, 1970), covers initial views of the car, early manufacturing, and the development of auto clubs, licensing, roads, and servicing. For the interaction between the automobile industry and the broader culture, one might also look at the ever-fascinating Henry Ford, particularly Reynold M. Wik, *Henry Ford and Grass-Roots America* (Ann Arbor: University of Michigan Press, 1973); David L. Lewis, *The Public Image of Henry Ford* (Detroit: Wayne State University Press, 1976); and the encyclopedic volumes by Allan Nevins and Frank Ernest Hill, *Ford: The Times, The Man, The Company, 1865–1915* (New York: Charles Scribner's Sons, 1954); *Ford: Expansion and Challenge, 1915–1933* (New York: Charles Scribner's Sons, 1957); and *Ford: Decline and Rebirth, 1933–1962* (New York: Charles Scribner's Sons, 1963).

The auto buff literature tends to be long on nostalgia and short on analysis. Two notable exceptions are Stephen W. Sears, *The American Heritage History of the Automobile in America* (New York: American Heritage, 1977); and Ant Farm, *Automerica: A Trip Down U.S. Highways from World War II to the Future* (New York: E. P. Dutton, 1976).

Recent controversy over the car's effects has spawned a good deal of polemical material. The most effective attacks are Kenneth R. Schneider, *Autokind vs. Mankind* (New York: W. W. Norton, 1971); and Emma Rothschild, *Paradise Lost: The Decline of the Auto-Industrial Age* (New York: Random House, 1973). John B. Rae's *The Road and the Car in American Life* (Cambridge: The MIT Press, 1971) is the most informed defense, while B. Bruce-Briggs, *The War Against the Automobile* (New York: E. P. Dutton, 1977), is a challenging counterattack. For a thoughtful analysis of how this debate has been treated in American fiction, see Cynthia Golomb Dettelbach, *In the Driver's Seat: The Automobile in American Literature and Popular Culture* (Westwood, Conn.: Greenwood, 1976).

There are a number of works in progress which should add appreciably to our understanding of the car culture. Mark Foster is undertaking a comprehensive study of the role of urban planners in paving the way for cars between the wars. Mark Rose's *Interstate: Express Highway Politics, 1941*–1956 (Lawrence, Kansas: Regents Press of Kansas, 1979), is the first full-length study of the politics of limited-access roadbuilding. Michael A. Rockland's forthcoming book on mobile homes and trailer life should complement my own work on motels, for both motels and trailer camps had roots in the autocamps of the 1920s—before splitting into separate subcultures in the 1930s.

Gypsying
1910–1920

To capture the novelty, enthusiasm, and innocence of early motoring, the best place to begin is with the general touring accounts written between 1910 and 1930. After 1930 the sense of newness began to pale and, with only a few exceptions, travel writers tended toward cliches. The most comprehensive bibliography of such accounts, many of which are to be found on copyright deposit in the Library of Congress, is Carey S. Bliss, *Autos Across America: A Bibliography of Transcontinental Automobile Travel* (Los Angeles: Dawson's Book Shop, 1972). Typical of the privately published accounts are: Hugo Alois Taussig, *Retracing the Pioneers from West to East in an Automobile* (San Francisco: n.p., 1910); Paul H. Marley, *Story of an Automobile Trip from Lincoln, Nebraska, to Los Angeles* (n.p., 1911); and Vernon McGill, *Diary of a Motor Journey from Chicago to Los Angeles* (Los Angeles: Grafton Publishing Co., 1922).

Motoring also captured the more mainstream literary imagination. Strangely, when established writers took to publishing their motor memoirs, they were often as naive and boosterish as the raw amateurs. Apparently that first automobile tour reduced everyone to the same state of adolescent excitement. See: Theodore Dreiser, *A Hoosier Holiday* (New York: John Lane, 1916); Kathryn Hulme, *How's the Road?* (San Francisco: n.p., 1928); Dallas Lore Sharp, *The Better Country* (Boston: Houghton Mifflin, 1928); and Lewis Gannett, *Sweet Land* (Garden City: Sun Dial, 1937).

As a burgeoning fad, touring spawned a number of diaries and guides written primarily for profit by free-lance adventurers. The most informative are: Effie Price Gladding, *Across the Continent by the Lincoln Highway* (New York: Brentano's, 1915); Emily Post, *By Motor to the Golden Gate* (New York: D. Appleton, 1916); Beatrice Massey, *It Might Have Been Worse* (San Francisco: Harr, Wagner, 1920); and, in a more humorous vein, James Montgomery Flagg, *Boulevards All the Way* (New York: George H. Doran, 1925). For early motor camping trips, see Melville Ferguson, *Motor Camping on Western Trails* (New York: The Century Co., 1925); Mary Crehore Bedell, *Modern Gypsies* (New York: Brentano's, 1924); and Frederic F. Van de Water, *The Family Flivvers to Frisco* (New York: D. Appleton, 1927). Van de Water's account is especially useful because he experienced virtually every variety of roadside accommodation, from simple gypsy encampment to private campground to early cabin.

Guides published by camping editors, road associations, and auto clubs contain a wealth of information about tourists' problems and the commercial potential of touring. See: Lincoln Highway Association, *Complete Official Road Guide of the Lincoln Highway* (Detroit: 1915); American Automobile Association, *Official Manual of Motor Car Camping* (Washington, D.C.: 1920); *Popular Mechanics' Auto Tourists' Handbook* (Chicago: 1924). The most useful autocamping guidebooks are Frank E. Brimmer, *Autocamping* (Cincinnati: Stewart Kidd, 1923); Brimmer, *Motor Campcraft* (New York: Macmillan, 1923); Elon Jessup, *The Motor Camping Book* (New York: G. P. Putnam's Sons, 1921); and J. C. Long and John D. Long, *Motor Camping* (New York: Dodd, Mead, 1923).

Another major source is the travel magazine, especially *American Motorist, Motor Travel,* and *Motor Camper and Tourist.* For treatment in the more popular magazines, consult *Reader's Guide* under "Automobile Touring." Typical discussions of motor gypsying include John R. Eustis, "Nomadic Motoring," *Independent,* June 1, 1918, p. 374; A Gordon Vestal, "On the Trail of the Motor Gypsies," *Illustrated World,* August 1918, pp. 840–843; and "Two Weeks' Vagabonds," *New York Times,* July 20, 1922, sec. VII, p. 7. Those wishing to compare with more recent gypsying might see John Steinbeck, *Travels with Charley: In Search of America* (New York: Viking Press, 1961); and Ken Ringle, "The Season of the Gypsy Soul," *Washington Post,* June 5, 1975, p. D9. The most famous literary exploration of the automobile-bohemian connection is, of course, Jack Kerouac, *On the Road* (New York: Viking, 1957).

On American bohemianism between 1910 and 1930, see Malcolm Cowley, *Exile's Return* (New York: Viking, 1951), pp. 58–66; Henry F. May, *The End of American Innocence* (Chicago: Quadrangle, 1964), pp. 283–285; and Albert Parry, *Garrets and Pretenders: A History of Bohemianism in America* (New York: Covici-Friede, 1933). There is very little on real gypsies, but one might start with Konrad Bercovici, *The Story of the Gypsies* (New York: Cosmopolitan, 1928), chapter nine. For concern with hoboes during this period, see James Gilbert, "Vagabondage, The Symbol of Industrial Malaise," in *Work Without Salvation* (Baltimore: Johns Hopkins, 1977), pp. 23–30. The definitive work on real tramps is Nels Anderson, *The Hobo* (Chicago: University of Chicago Press, 1923). See also "Tramps" in *Reader's Guide, 1910–1914.* For the "discovery" of the free-spirited Negro in the 1920s, see Gilbert Osofsky, *Harlem: The Making of a Ghetto* (New York: Harper Torchbook, 1971), pp. 179–187. An excellent introduction to our western fascination with primitivism is Arthur O. Lovejoy and George Boas, *Primitivism and Related Ideas in Antiquity* (Baltimore: Johns Hopkins, 1935), especially pp. 1–22.

For rigorous treatment of the regenerative qualities of the wilderness experience, see Peter Schmitt, *Back to Nature: Arcadian Myth in America* (New York: Oxford University Press, 1969); and Roderick

Nash, *Wilderness and the American Mind* (New Haven: Yale University Press, 1973). Nash's *The Call of the Wild, 1900–1916* (New York: George Braziller, 1970), is a compilation of documents relating to the wilderness theme of this period. The related concept of the "middle landscape"—the happy compromise between nature and civilization—is best developed by Leo Marx in *The Machine in the Garden: Technology and the Pastoral Ideal* (New York: Oxford University Press, 1964).

Cars versus Trains
Back to Stagecoach Days

Noting the recurrent strain of nostalgia in American politics and culture, most writers have followed Richard Hofstadter in classifying this ache for a lost past as a reactionary force. Yet perhaps nostalgia may be viewed as a weapon of "progress"—that is, technological, capitalistic development. For hints of this, see Lawrence W. Levine, "Progress and Nostalgia: The Self Image of the Nineteen Twenties," in *The American Novel and the Nineteen Twenties,* Malcolm Bradbury and David Palmer, eds. (London: Edward Arnold, 1971), pp. 37–58; and John William Ward, "The Meaning of Lindbergh's Flight," in *Studies in American Culture,* Joseph J. Kwiat and Mary C. Turpie, eds. (Minneapolis: University of Minnesota, 1960), pp. 27–40. A more full-scale, albeit elusive treatment is Raymond Williams, *The Country and the City* (New York: Oxford University Press, 1973). Dean MacCannell discusses the disorienting, modernizing function of historical sightseeing in *The Tourist: A New Theory of the Leisure Class* (New York: Schocken, 1976). In selling cars and the car culture, Henry Ford was the preeminent master of coupling modern technology with premodern imagery. See David L. Lewis, *The Public Image of Henry Ford,* especially pp. 211–234; and Reynold M. Wik, *Henry Ford and Grass-Roots America.*

Much has been written about the importance of railroads to nineteenth-century economic development. John Stover's *American Railroads* (Chicago: University of Chicago Press, 1961), is a handy introduction. Also George Rogers Taylor, *The Transportation Revolution, 1815*–1860 (New York: Harper Torchbooks, 1968); and Edward Chase Kirkland, *Industry Comes of Age* (Chicago: Quadrangle, 1967). In *The Machine in the Garden,* Leo Marx discusses mid-century qualms about the railroad's clash with traditional ideals. For one novelist's portrait of the railroad's seemingly monopolistic hold on turn-of-the-century America, see Frank Norris, *The Octopus* (Boston: Houghton Mifflin, 1958).

For the joys and perils of rail travel, the best place to begin is Earl Pomeroy, *In Search of the Golden West: The Tourist in Western America* (New York: Alfred A. Knopf, 1957). Pomeroy's superb study is the major background source for much of this chapter. Further information on train travel may be found in Burt C. Blanton, *400,000 Miles by Railroad* (Berkeley: Howell-North Books, 1972); August Mencken, *The Railroad Passenger Car* (Baltimore: Johns Hopkins University Press, 1957); and Daniel J. Boorstin, *The Americans: The Democratic Experience* (New York: Vintage, 1974). With the golden years of the train now long gone, the railroad is a major object of nostalgia. For an analysis of America's foremost rail buff, see George H. Douglas, "Lucius Beebe: Popular Railroad History as Social Nostalgia," *Journal of Popular Culture,* 4(1971), pp. 893–910. For good detail and train lore, see Beebe and Charles Clegg, *Hear the Train Blow* (New York: E. P. Dutton, 1952).

Bicyclists articulated many of the arguments against the train in the 1890s. See Gary Allan Tobin, "The Bicycle Boom of the 1890s: The Development of Private Transportation and the Birth of the Modern Tourist," *Journal of Popular Culture,* 8(Spring 1974), pp. 838–849. On the grievances against streetcars and commuter railroads, see Glen E. Holt, "The Changing Perception of Urban Pathology; An Essay on the Development of Mass Transit in the United States," in *Cities in American History,* Kenneth T. Jackson and Stanley K. Schultz, eds. (New York: Alfred A. Knopf, 1972), pp. 324–342; and Clay McShane, "American Cities and the Coming of the Automobile, 1870–1910," (Ph.D. Dissertation, University of Wisconsin, 1975). Other problems with trains, especially during wartime, may be found in the editorial pages of *Railway Age,* 1917–1920. For concern about poor coach sanitation, see William W. Sanford, "To Protect the Health of Railway Travelers," *Harper's Weekly,* November 25, 1905, pp. 1702–1704; and Edward Hungerford, "Sleeping Cars and Microbes," *Harper's Weekly,* Feb. 7, 1914, pp. 20–22. Norman T. Moline's *Mobility and the Small Town, 1900–1930* (University of Chicago, Dept. of Geography Research Paper No. 132, 1971), is a detailed account of how automobiles revolutionized transportation options in Oregon, Illinois.

Earl Pomeroy delineates the railroad tourist's search for "Europe in the Wilderness" in *In Search of the Golden West,* pp. 31–72. The best overall introduction to nineteenth-century American travel remains Foster Rhea Dulles, *Americans Abroad: Two Centuries of European Travel* (Ann Arbor: University of Michigan Press, 1964). Also worth a glance is Richard S. Lambert, *The Fortunate Traveler* (London: Andrew Melrose, 1950). See the bibliographical notes for the chapter on municipal camps for further discussion of travel literature.

For the effects of motoring on local vacation opportunities, see "The Summer Question," *American Motorist,* September 1909, p. 250; Harrison Rhodes, *In Vacation America* (New York: Harper and Bros., 1915); and Edward Hungerford, "America Awheel," *Everybody's Magazine,* June 1917, pp. 678–680. See also the summer vacation sections of the *New York Times,* 1910–1930.

Examples of the historic motif in sightseeing: Louise Closser Hale, *We Discover the Old Dominion* (New York: Dodd, Mead, 1916); and Mary Harrod Northend, *We Visit Old Inns* (Boston: Small, Maynard, 1925). Roderick Nash discusses this period's concern with colonial history in *The Nervous Generation: American Thought, 1917–1930* (Chicago: Rand McNally & Co., 1970), pp. 76–77; as does John Higham in *History: Professional Scholarship in America* (New York: Harper & Row, 1973), pp. 74–78. Laurence G. Henderson's *With Heritage So Rich* (New York: Random House, 1966) and Charles B. Hosmer, Jr.'s *Presence of the Past* (New York: G. P. Putnam's Sons, 1965) are good introductions to the historic preservation movement.

Autocamping versus Hotels
Back to the Family Homestead

There are a number of popular histories of American hotels. Still fresh and informative is Jefferson Williamson, *The American Hotel: An Anecdotal History* (New York: Alfred A. Knopf, 1930). Also anecdotal are Arthur S. White, *Palaces of the People: A Social History of Commercial Hospitality* (New York: Taplinger, 1970); Christopher Matthew, *A Different World: Stories of Great Hotels* (New York: Paddington Press, 1976); and Lesley Dorsey and Janice Devine, *Fare Thee Well: A Backward Look at Two Centuries of American Hostelries* (New York: Crown, 1964). Although they tend to be too adulatory, biographies of famous hotelmen contain useful details. James D. Henderson, *Meals by Fred Harvey: A Phenomenon of the American West* (Fort Worth: Texas Christian University Press, 1969); Floyd Miller, *America's Extraordinary Hotelman, Statler* (New York: Statler Foundation, 1968); Rufus Jarman, *A Bed for the Night* (New York: Harper, 1952); and Conrad Hilton, *Be My Guest* (Englewood Cliffs: Prentice-Hall, 1957). More analytical are Earl Pomeroy, *In Search of the Golden West,* and Daniel Boorstin's excellent chapter on small-town hotels in *The Americans: The National Experience* (New York: Vintage, 1965), pp. 134–147. The best sociological study of the hotel remains Norman Hayner's pioneering *Hotel Life* (Chapel Hill: University of North Carolina, 1936). For a sense of small town hotel problems after 1900, see Sherwood Anderson's *Winesburg, Ohio* (New York: Viking, 1958); and W. I. Hamilton, *Promoting New Hotels: When Does It Pay?* (New York: Harper & Bros., 1930).

Hotel trade literature provides helpful insights into problems and trends in the hospitality business. *Hotel Management* and *Hotel Monthly* are the most important journals for this period. J. O. Dahl's *Selling Public Hospitality* (New York: Harper & Bros., 1930) is a valuable textbook written by a prominent hotel reformer of the 1920s. For more recent instruction see Donald E. Lundberg, *Inside Innkeeping* (Dubuque: W. C. Brown, 1956), and Gerald W. Lattin, *Modern Hotel and Motel Management* (San Francisco: W. H. Freeman, 1968).

For problems with clerks, waiters, porters, and tipping, see J. O. Dahl, *The Efficient Bellman and Elevator Operator* (New York: J. O. Dahl, 1937); William R. Scott, *The Itching Palm: A Study of the Habit of Tipping in America* (Philadelphia: Penn Publishing Co., 1916); E. S. Turner, *What the Butler Saw* (New York: St. Martin's Press, 1963). Make sure to consider the employee's perspective in Robert E. Turner, *Memories of a Retired Pullman Porter* (New York: Exposition Press, 1954); Allison Gray, "How the Hotel Clerk Sizes You Up," *American Magazine,* November 1922, p. 49; Margaret A. Barner, "How We Behave Away from Home," *American Magazine,* March 1931, pp. 22–23. James F. Muirhead's *Land of Contrasts* (Boston: Lamson, Wolffe, and Co., 1898) is a good all-around portrait of hotel and rail problems—from an Englishman's point of view.

Etiquette manuals are an excellent source of social data, particularly about middle-class travel customs and complaints, the servant problem, and trends in food, housing, and clothing. For a guide to such literature, see Gerald Carson, *The Polite Americans* (New York: Morrow, 1966);

Russell Lynes, *The Domesticated Americans* (New York: Harper & Row, 1957); Esther B. Aresty, *The Best Behavior* (New York: Simon and Schuster, 1970); and Arthur M. Schlesinger, *Learning How to Behave: A Historical Study of American Etiquette Books* (New York: Macmillan, 1946).

For changing attitudes toward public dress, see George Van Ness Dearborn, *The Psychology of Clothing*, in *Psychological Monographs*, 26(1918); Claudia B. Kidwell and Margaret C. Christman, *Suiting Everyone: The Democratization of Clothing in America* (Washington, D.C.: Smithsonian Institution Press, 1974); and William Dean Howells, "Dressing for Dinner," in *Imaginary Interviews* (New York: Harper and Bros., 1910), pp. 274–282. On food trends, see *Ladies' Home Journal*, *Good Housekeeping*, and *Woman's Home Companion*. Waverly Root's *Eating in America* (New York: Morrow, 1976) is an encyclopedic history. Miriam E. Lowenberg, et al., *Food and Man* (New York: John Wiley and Sons, 1968) views food habits from the standpoint of nutritional and anthropological theory. For hotel perspectives on changing tastes in the 1920s, see J. O. Dahl, *Restaurant Management* (New York: Harper & Bros., 1927), and Dahl, "Fashions in Food," *Hotel Management-Food Service*, October 1926, pp. 68–71.

The clearest introduction to the Victorian separate spheres is Barbara Welter's seminal article, "The Cult of True Womanhood, 1820–1860." *American Quarterly*, 16(Summer 1966): 151–174. Also, Aileen Kraditor, ed., *Up from the Pedestal* (Chicago: Quadrangle, 1968). Charles Frederick Goss, *Husband, Wife and Home* (Philadelphia: The Vir Publishing Co., 1905) illustrates the transition from "lady" to "pal". For the ideology of the companionate family, with special reference to the role of leisure, see John Dollard, *The Changing Functions of the American Family, 1900–1930* (Chicago: University of Chicago Press, 1931); James H. S. Bossard, *Social Change and Social Problems* (New York: Harper & Bros., 1938); Bossard and Eleanor S. Boll, *Ritual in Family Living* (Philadelphia: University of Pennsylvania Press, 1950); John Sirjamaki, *The American Family in the Twentieth Century* (Cambridge: Harvard University Press, 1953). A useful summary of changing ideology may be found in Paul S. Fass, *The Damned and the Beautiful: American Youth in the 1920s* (New York: Oxford University Press, 1977), pp. 53–118. For a curiously sympathetic treatment of the separate spheres, accompanied by a scathing attack on the companionate ideal, see Christopher Lasch, *Haven in a Heartless World: The Family Besieged* (New York: Basic Books, 1977). Gilman Ostrander's *American Civilization in the First Machine Age, 1890–1940* (New York: Harper Torchbooks, 1972) is especially good on the changing role of children within the companionate scheme. Finally, for a first-hand view, one should consult the women's magazines, such as Washington Gladden, "Marriage as Friendship," *Good Housekeeping*, April 1912, pp. 488–491; Jesse Lynch Williams, "The New Marriage," *Good Housekeeping*, February 1914, pp. 181–185; Sarah Comstock, "Mother-craft," *Good Housekeeping*, May 1915, pp. 497–502.

Like the train and city hotel, the Victorian resort is now the object of considerable nostalgia. Typical of such treatment are William M. Varrell,

Summer by-the-Sea: the Golden Era of Victorian Beach Resorts (Portsmouth, New Hampshire: Strawberry Bank Print Shop, 1972); Richmond Barrett, *Good Old Summer Days* (Boston: Houghton Mifflin, 1952); and Cleveland Amory, *The Last Resorts* (Westport, Conn.: Greenwood, 1973). The forthcoming volume by Richard Oliver and Jeffrey Limerick, promises to be both analytical and pictorially evocative. To understand the turn-of-the-century case against the resort, investigators should turn to the summer vacation issues of *Harper's, Good Housekeeping, Scribner's,* and other upper-middle-class journals. William Dean Howells was an exceptionally sensitive recorder of such dissatisfaction. See "The Problem of Summer," in Howells' *Literature and Life* (New York: Harper, 1902), and "Leaving Town in Summer," *Harper's,* September 1903, p. 642. Also, "Concerning Summer Hotel Life," *Good Housekeeping,* August 1916, pp. 138–140; Helen B. Lowry, "Two Weeks with Full Pay—Obligatory," *New York Times,* July 18, 1920, sec. III, p. 18; Frank Moore Colby, "The Summer Experiment," in *Imaginary Obligations* (New York: Dodd, Mead, 1904).

From Fad to Institution
Municipal Camps, 1920–1924

Historians have virtually ignored the tourist industry. Earl Pomeroy, *In Search of the Golden West,* and Daniel J. Boorstin, "From Traveler to Tourist: The Lost Art of Travel," in *The Image: A Guide to Pseudo-Events in America* (New York: Harper & Row, 1961) make valuable contributions to the study of infrastructure, but both tend to let their high-culture bias get in the way of objective analysis. Hugh De Santis takes a more even-handed approach in "The Democratization of Travel: The Travel Agent in American History," *Journal of American Culture* 1(Spring 1978), pp. 1–17. The main work has been done by sociologists and has focused primarily on Europe, where tourism is a high priority industry. See Erik Cohen, "Toward a Sociology of International Tourism," *Social Research* 39(1972), pp. 164–182; Erik Cohen, "Nomads from Affluence: Notes on the Phenomenon of Drifter-Tourism," *International Journal of Comparative Sociology* 14(1973), pp. 89–103; Joffre Dumazedier, *Toward a Society of Leisure* (New York: Free Press, 1967), pp. 123–138. The best book-length studies are Dean MacCannell, *The Tourist,* and Louis Turner and John Ash, *The Golden Hordes: International Tourism and the Pleasure Periphery* (London: Constable, 1975). *The Annals of Tourism Research* and *The Journal of Travel Research* publish sociological and business-oriented articles. For the viewpoint of the American tourist industry see such texts as Robert W. McIntosh, *Tourism: Principles, Practices and Philosophies* (Columbus, Ohio: Grid, Inc., 1972), and Donald E. Lundberg, *The Tourist Business* (Boston: Cahner's Books, 1974).

A subcategory of this field is the sociology of camp life. See Roger N. Clark, John C. Hendee, and Frederick L. Campbell, "Values, Behavior, and Conflict in Modern Camping Culture," *Journal of Leisure Research* (Summer 1971), pp. 143–159; Peter Etzkorn, "Leisure and Camping: The Social Meaning of a Form of Public Recreation," *Sociology and Social Research,* 49(October 1964), pp. 76–89; and Gregory P. Stone and Marvin J. Taves, "Camping in the Wilderness," in *Mass Leisure,* Eric Larrabee and Rolf Meyersohn, eds. (Glencoe: Free Press, 1958), pp. 290–305. For first-hand observations of municipal camp life in the 1920s, see Oscar Lewis, "Free Auto Camp Ground," in Odell Shepard and Robert Hillyer, eds., *Essays of Today (1926–1927)* (New York: Century, 1928); Norman Hayner, "Auto Camps in the Evergreen Playground," *Social Forces* 9(1930): 256–266; Harry B. Ansted, "The Auto-Camp Community," *Journal of Applied Sociology* 9(1924), pp. 136–142. Peter Schmitt, *Back to Nature,* and Earl Pomeroy, *Golden West,* also discuss camping.

In addition to the touring magazines and guides listed in the footnotes, look for information on municipal camps in such city management journals as *American City, American Municipalities, City Manager Magazine,* and such state organs as *Minnesota Municipalities* and *Texas Municipalities.* A more complete list may be found in the Public Affairs Information Service's annual *Bulletin.* In *Reader's Guide* look under "Camps, Tourists" and "Automobile Touring." The most useful engineering guides are C. P. Halligan, "Tourist Camps," Michigan Agricultural College, *Special Bulletin 139,* Rural Landscape Series 2 (East Lansing, 1925), and Roland S. Wallis, "Tourist Camps," *Engineering Extension Service Bulletin,* Iowa State College, Ames, Iowa, 21, no. 36 (Feb. 7, 1923). Rebecca N. Porter probes the camp's social significance in "The New Hospitality," *Scribner's,* June 1921, p. 735.

Limiting Access
Pay Camps, 1923–1928

For an overview of the whole problem of overselling and hobo "undesirables," see "Gasoline Gypsies," *Survey,* May 15, 1925, p. 229; Adeline A. Buffington, "Automobile Migrants," *Proceedings of the National Conference of Social Workers* 52(June 1925), pp. 258–264; Marjorie L. Poole, "Tin Can Tourists Terrifying California," *Literary Digest,* May 16, 1925, pp. 73–76. Frederic F. Van de Water best typifies the middle-class tourist's moralistic reaction in *The Family Flivvers to Frisco,* pp. 100–115. For discussion of migrant workers and the automobile in the 1920s, see "Problem of the Automobile Floater," *Monthly Labor Review* 21(Oct. 1925), pp. 699–701; John J. Hader, "Honk Honk Hobo," *Survey,* August 1, 1928, pp. 20–21. Not until the 1930s did social workers and scholars take a more objective look at migrants. See Marion Hathway, *The Migratory Worker and Family Life* (Chicago: University of Illinois, 1934); Grace E. Kimble, *Social Work with Travelers and Transients* (Chicago: University of Chicago, 1935). Carey McWilliams surveys pre-depression migration in *Ill Fares the Land: Migrants and Migratory Labor in the United States* (Boston: Little, Brown, 1942), pp. 91–185. See also Carter Goodrich et al., *Migration and Economic Opportunity* (Philadelphia: University of Pennsylvania, 1936); C. Warren Thornthwaite, *Internal Migration in the United States* (Philadelphia: University of Pennsylvania, 1934); and Warren S. Thompson, *Research Memorandum on Internal Migration in the Depression* (New York: Social Science Research Council, 1937).

For doubts about the car culture in the 1920s, see Robert S. Lynd and Helen Merrell Lynd, *Middletown* (New York: Harcourt, Brace, & World, 1956); James J. Flink, *The Car Culture*, pp. 140–167; Blaine A. Brownell, "A Symbol of Modernity: Attitudes Towards the Automobile in Southern Cities," *American Quarterly* 24(March 1972), pp. 2–44.

The case for the pay camp is most forcefully made by Bertha Streeter, "Hygiene of the Tourists' Camps," *The Forecast*, June 1927, pp. 370–372; Frances Scarborough, "Texas Tourist Camp Problems and Their Solutions," *Texas Municipalities*, Sept. 1924, p. 107; and Harry N. Burhans, "Standardization of Auto Tourist Camps," *Municipal and Country Engineering*, August 1924, p. 82. As with the chapter on municipal camps, readers should consult the municipal management journals and *Reader's Guide*.

Early Motels
1925–1945

Here investigators must work almost exclusively from industry sources. *Hotel Management* and *Hotel Monthly*—both indexed in the *Industrial Arts Index*—provide the hotel perspective. For early motor camps see *Tourist Trade* (1933–1934), *Highway Host, Tourist Court Journal* (1937–   ), and, after 1949, *American Motel Magazine*. *National Petroleum News* is useful for camps attached to gasoline stations. Clara Keyton's *Tourist Camp Pioneering Experiences* (Chicago: Adams Press, 1960) is an invaluable first-hand account for 1925–1940. Road guides of the American Automobile Association trace cabin developments through detailed listings of selected camps. Indeed, the changing title of these guides documents this rapid evolution: *Official Camping and Campsite Manual* (Washington, D.C.: 1925); *Official AAA Camp Directory* (1928); *Official Directory of Cottage Camps, Courts, and Inns* (1933); *Directory of Motor Courts* (1938).

Although there are many textbooks on motel management, only two cover prewar tourist cabins: Walter B. Wilkinson, *Profits in Tourist Camps* (Lansing, Michigan: Travel Research, 1940), and Harry Barclay Love, *Establishing and Operating a Year-Round Court*, United States Dept. of Commerce, Industrial (Small Business) Series No. 50 (Washington, D.C.: Government Printing Office, 1945). For more recent developments, see *American Motel Magazine's Market Analysis of the Motel Industry* (Chicago: 1952); Geoffrey Baker and Bruno Funaro, *Motels* (New York: Reinhold Publishing Corporation, 1955); C. Vernon Kane, *Motor Courts—From Planning to Profits* (New York: Ahrens, 1954); and Gerald W. Lattin, *Modern Hotel and Motel Management* (San Francisco: W. H. Freeman, 1968). Unfortunately, virtually all postwar literature tends to overlook the importance of prewar experimentation. For economic analysis of recent trends, see Howard E. Morgan, *The Motel Industry in the United States: Small Business in Transition* (Tucson: Bureau of Business and Public Research, University of Arizona, 1964); and Royal Ship and Robert Moore Fisher, *The Postwar Boom in Hotels and Motels* (Washington, D.C.: Federal Reserve System, Staff Economic Studies, 1965).

Popular magazines eagerly charted the rise of cabin camps. The following articles were particularly instructive: "'Bungalette' Camp for Motor Tourists," *Popular Mechanics*, March 1922, pp. 416–417; Frank E. Brimmer, "The 'Nickel-and-Dime' Stores of Nomadic America," *The Magazine of Business*, August 1927, pp. 151–153; "That Bungalow Camp," *Saturday Evening Post*, August 27, 1927, pp. 35–37; Frank E. Brimmer, "Outdoor Hotels," *Woman's Home Companion*, July 1928, p. 42; "Tourist Camps 'Deluxe' in the Southwest," *Forbes*, August 1, 1928, pp. 25–26; Henry Street, "Broad Highways and Modern Inns," *Building Age*, August 1928, pp. 69–71; J. O. Dahl, "Tourists Accommodated— and No Questions Asked," *Hotel Management*, October 1929, pp. 299– 304; John J. McCarthy and Robert Littell, "Three Hundred Thousand Shacks," *Harper's*, July 1933, pp. 180–188; L. H. Robbins, "American Hobnobs at the Tourist Camp," *New York Times Magazine*, August 12, 1934, p. 9; "The Great American Roadside," *Fortune*, September 1934, pp. 53–63; Henry Schmidt, Jr., "Overnight Rest-Cabins Spreading," *Literary Digest*, June 9, 1934, p. 40; E. L. Yordan, "Motor Camps Win New Friends," *New York Times*, July 14, 1935, Sec. X, p. 1; "I'll Answer Your Questions on Tourist Camps," *Hotel Management*, July 1936, pp. 18–19; "America Takes to the Motor Court," *Business Week*, June 15, 1940, pp. 19–40.

There is virtually no archival material. By chance I did run across several boxes dealing with the NRA Code controversy of 1933–34. Located in the National Archives under "Tourist Code and Motor Court Trade," they contain postcards, letters, pamphlets, and NRA internal memoranda—all useful in gauging the state of the tourist camp industry at that time.

Index

Page numbers in italics indicate illustrations.

Chimpanzees

by Rachel Grack

BELLWETHER MEDIA • MINNEAPOLIS, MN

Note to Librarians, Teachers, and Parents:

Blastoff! Readers are carefully developed by literacy experts and combine standards-based content with developmentally appropriate text.

Level 1 provides the most support through repetition of high-frequency words, light text, predictable sentence patterns, and strong visual support.

Level 2 offers early readers a bit more challenge through varied simple sentences, increased text load, and less repetition of high-frequency words.

Level 3 advances early-fluent readers toward fluency through increased text and concept load, less reliance on visuals, longer sentences, and more literary language.

Level 4 builds reading stamina by providing more text per page, increased use of punctuation, greater variation in sentence patterns, and increasingly challenging vocabulary.

Level 5 encourages children to move from "learning to read" to "reading to learn" by providing even more text, varied writing styles, and less familiar topics.

Whichever book is right for your reader, Blastoff! Readers are the perfect books to build confidence and encourage a love of reading that will last a lifetime!

This edition first published in 2019 by Bellwether Media, Inc.

No part of this publication may be reproduced in whole or in part without written permission of the publisher. For information regarding permission, write to Bellwether Media, Inc., Attention: Permissions Department, 6012 Blue Circle Drive, Minnetonka, MN 55343.

Library of Congress Cataloging-in-Publication Data

Names: Koestler-Grack, Rachel A., 1973- author.
Title: Chimpanzees / by Rachel Grack.
Description: Minneapolis, MN : Bellwether Media, Inc., 2019. |
   Series: Blastoff! Readers. Animals of the Rain forest | Audience: Ages 5-8. |
   Audience: K to grade 3. | Includes bibliographical references and index.
Identifiers: LCCN 2018031003 (print) | LCCN 2018037391 (ebook) |
   ISBN 9781681036731 (ebook) | ISBN 9781626179493 (hardcover : alk. paper)
Subjects: LCSH: Chimpanzees--Juvenile literature. | Rain forest animals--Juvenile literature.
Classification: LCC QL737.P94 (ebook) | LCC QL737.P94 K64 2019 (print) | DDC 599.885--dc23
LC record available at https://lccn.loc.gov/2018031003

Editor: Betsy Rathburn   Designer: Jeffrey Kollock

Printed in the United States of America, North Mankato, MN

Table of Contents

Chimpanzees are **primates** that live in West and Central Africa.

Their **tropical** rain forest
biome has many trees.
Time to swing!

Chimpanzee Range

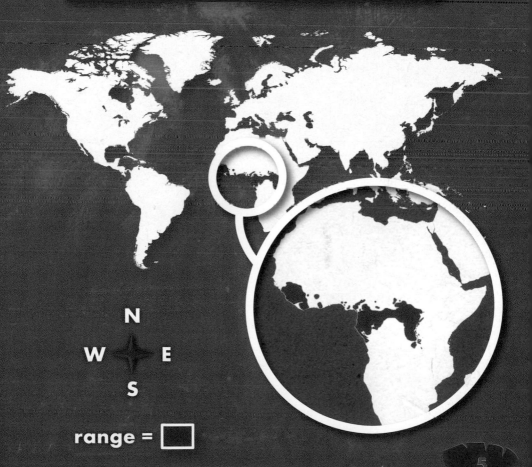

N
W — E
S

range = ☐

5

Chimps are **adapted** to tree travel. **Opposable thumbs** help them grip branches.

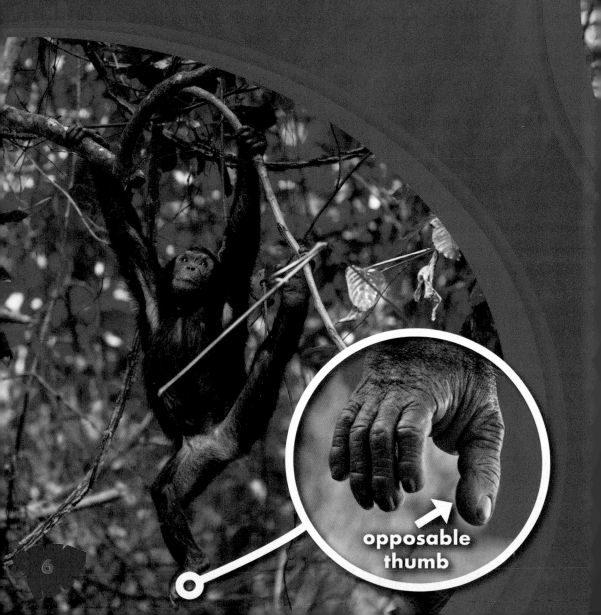

opposable thumb

Their long arms are great for traveling through the forest.

Rain forests are home
to many noisy animals.

Special Adaptations

opposable
thumbs

long arms

big ears

It can be hard to pick out
the voices of other chimps.
Big ears help chimpanzees hear!

9

Tree Houses

Chimp families
live in groups.
They use sounds and
facial expressions
to **communicate**.

Hoots, screams, and
roars are warnings.
Chimps show their
teeth when afraid!

Rain forests grow thick with
plant life. Chimps eat certain
plants to stay healthy.

Some leaves calm
an upset stomach.
Others fight sickness.

13

The rain forest **canopy** gives chimps safe places to sleep.

canopy

nest

They build new nests every night.
They cover woven branches with
soft beds of leaves.

Finding Food

Chimpanzees are not picky eaters. They sometimes hunt small animals.

But their main meals are fruits, plants, and **insects**. Chimps especially love figs!

Chimpanzee Stats

Least Concern	Near Threatened	Vulnerable	Endangered	Critically Endangered	Extinct in the Wild	Extinct

conservation status: endangered

life span: about 40 years

17

Chimpanzees use tools to
find food. They poke sticks
down ant hills to catch bugs.

18

They crack open nuts with stones.

Chimpanzee Diet

figs

kola nuts

army ants

Chimps use tools to drink, too. They dip leaves in rainwater to soak up a drink.

Chimpanzees are smart
rain forest animals!

21

Glossary

adapted—well suited due to changes over a long period of time

biome—a large area with certain plants, animals, and weather

canopy—the uppermost level of the rain forest

communicate—to share thoughts and feelings using sounds, faces, and actions

facial expressions—looks on faces that show feelings such as happiness, sadness, or anger

insects—small animals with six legs and hard outer bodies; an insect's body is divided into three parts.

opposable thumbs—thumbs that can touch the other fingers and toes so that hands and feet can grasp and hold things

primates—animals that use their hands to grasp food and other objects; primates are related to humans.

tropical—related to places that are hot and humid

To Learn More

AT THE LIBRARY

Hansen, Grace. *Jane Goodall: Chimpanzee Expert and Activist*. Minneapolis, Minn.: Abdo Kids, 2015.

Kenan, Tessa. *It's a Chimpanzee!* Minneapolis, Minn.: Lerner Publications, 2017.

Riggs, Kate. *Chimpanzees*. Mankato, Minn.: Creative Education, 2016.

ON THE WEB

FACTSURFER

Factsurfer.com gives you a safe, fun way to find more information.

1. Go to www.factsurfer.com.

2. Enter "chimpanzees" into the search box.

3. Click the "Surf" button and select your book cover to see a list of related web sites.

Index